LBJ AND THE CONSPIRACY TO KILL KENNEDY

A Coalescence of Interests:

A Study of the Deep Politics and Architecture of the Coup D'Etat to Overthrow Kennedy

Other Books by Joseph P. Farrell:

LBJ AND THE CONSPIRACY TO KILL KENNEDY

Joseph P. Farrell

Adventures Unlimited Press

LBJ and the Conspiracy to Kill Kennedy

Copyright 2011
by Joseph P. Farrell

ISBN: 978-1-935487-18-0

Published by:
Adventures Unlimited Press
One Adventure Place
Kempton, Illinois 60946 USA
auphq@frontiernet.net

www.adventuresunlimitedpress.com

Cover by Terry Lamb

10 9 8 7 6 5 4 3

LBJ AND THE CONSPIRACY TO KILL KENNEDY

A Coalescence of Interests:
A Study of the Deep Politics and Architecture of the Coup D'Etat to Overthrow Kennedy

Above all, to my best friend through so many years,
Scott Douglas deHart:
A true master, adept, and poet of deep mysteries, who crossed the Rubicon with me:
Anything I could say, any gratitude I could express, are simply inadequate for you;

You are a true

And to
Tracy S. Fisher:
You are, and will always be, sorely missed;

"I myself think that a sophisticated appraisal of the evidence must force one to the conclusion that there was a plot involving the executive branch of the government to remove Kennedy from office and, by fabricating the evidence..., make his death appear a historical quirk of fate."
David S. Lifton,
Best Evidence, p. 697.

"In any country of the world, except America, this event would have been viewed suspiciously as a bloody 'coup.'"
Craig I. Zirbel,
The Texas Connection, p. 3.

TABLE OF CONTENTS

ACKNOWLEDGEMENTS AND PRELIMINARIES

This was not a book that I originally intended to write, at least, not now. I had long been fascinated with the assassination of President John F. Kennedy ever since witnessing the events as a boy of six. From that moment, I read everything I could on the matter, and after I began writing professionally, I resolved to put my own perspective on the matter to paper someday. As many readers of my books know, I tend to plan out several books in advance of what is actually published, and to do so in such a manner that the books all flow in an orderly sequence, from subject to subject, theme to theme. Hence, my "JFK" book I had not planned to write until approximately two years from now.

But when Adventures Unlimited Press owner and publisher, and personal friend, David Hatcher Childress contacted me this summer to write this book, I agreed. Hence, this book is something of a first for me, for it is a book specifically written at a publisher's request. In his original contact with me, the premise of the book was to be an examination of "the Texas Connection" and the probable role of President Lyndon Johnson in the conspiracy.

However, as there had been books previously written on this subject, I persuaded David to allow me to take a slightly different approach: How could one reconcile LBJ's probable role in the affair, either as a planner, or as a "soldier" for hidden interests, with the wider context of various groups – Cubans, Mafiosi, rogue groups in federal intelligence agencies, Nazis, gun-runners, and so on – that had always been alleged to be involved in the conspiracy? Could this be done?

More importantly, could a putative structure of the conspiracy be uncovered by such a methodology, and could speculative roles within it be assigned to the various groups that other researchers have suggested were involved? Which groups might have been involved with the planning? Which exercised "veto power" over its operational parameters? Which were simply "in the know" and willing to allow the plot to proceed to further their own interests? Who had the power to cover it up?

In the course of a few emails back and forth, I persuaded David to allow me to try this approach, which emphasizes not so much the crime itself, as the research of others, and a new attempt at analysis and synthesis. As always, I owe David Childress a deep debt of gratitude for allowing me to opportunity to write about radical ideas.

I owe another deep debt of gratitude to my friend Dr. Scott D. DeHart, who has been consistently my best friend for almost the last twenty years. During the course of writing this book, it was he to whom I turned for criticism, comments, suggestions, and editorial advice. For your consistent confidence and belief in me, and your encouragement, my friend, my deepest thanks!

And finally, last but not least, many and deep thanks to all my readers over the years, who have followed me on a long and winding trail through a forest of details that, at first, seem unrelated, but that reveal themselves upon deep analysis to be bizarrely related, in the deep politics and deep physics of the past and present.

Joseph P. Farrell
Spearfish, South Dakota
2010

PART ONE:
THE CONSPIRATORS AND THE CRIMES

"To further complicate this maze of business, finance, European money, holdover Nazis, and intelligence agents, various investigators – including some from Life *magazine – found that some of the banking connections from this secret empire reached to Mafia chief Meyer Lansky and his Bahamas gambling operations."*
Jim Marrs,
Crossfire: the Plot that Killed Kennedy, p. 500.

INTRODUCTION:
PERSONAL REMINISCENCES AND A HIGH OVERVIEW

On November 22, 1963, the United States of America became nothing more than a very rich and powerful version of a very corrupt banana republic with nukes, an insane nation under the control of the power-mad and insane. On that day, America lost its innocence as the rich, powerful, and corrupt murdered our president, John Fitzgerald Kennedy. And on that day, I too, at the time a boy of six home sick from school and watching the epic unfold on television, lost my innocence as well when I heard our young president had been murdered in cold blood, in a public square, and watched the drama of that weekend unfold on television, the arrest of Oswald, his subsequent murder on national television by Jack Ruby, the whole doleful state funeral. Those of us alive at the time will always remember it, and remember what our nation was like before it happened. The U.S.A. was innocent prior to that event in a way that is difficult for most people now to grasp.

To be sure, the forces of evil and corruption that surrounded and eventually murdered President Kennedy were there *before* the murder. But in Dealey Plaza in Dallas, they brazenly stepped out into the open, and declared their existence and power in a ritual bloodbath for all to see. Those who were *not* alive when that happened, or not old enough to remember, will never really understand the metaphysical and spiritual change wrought that day, that occurred because of that murder, that was *effected* by it, for it was a ritual of black magic in almost every sense, including human sacrifice.

My sisters were not yet even married, their children not yet born. My maternal and paternal grandparents were still alive, some of my cousins were mere babies at the time. My best friend for almost the last half of my life would be born almost a year later. And by the time I graduated high school as the long and pointless Vietnam War was winding down, I was eighteen years old, he but eleven, and I lived throughout my teenage years with the always present traumatizing thought of being drafted and sent off to a war in a jungle that no one wanted, and no one understood.

Those forces unleashed in Dallas that day affected my life, his life, his children's lives, our sisters' lives, their friends' lives and their friends' childrens' lives, everyone's life, in ways no one can calculate, for in the intricate calculus of human and cultural action, the magical implications set into motion that day are with us still. All of it – the Vietnam War,

1

Watergate, Iran-Contra, the BCCI and Nugan Hand bank scandals, Ruby Ridge, Waco, the Oklahoma City Bombing, 9/11, a presidential "election" and constitutional crisis over hanging chad, another over whether a sitting president is even a U.S. citizen at all - it is all the stuff of a bad opera libretto, the sort of thing one expects in a third world banana republic. All of it has been an endless succession of scandals and corruption coming from within, a sequence of calculated traumas to the American psyche, orchestrated by the same circles of power and corruption that openly declared their existence on November 22, 1963, when they murdered a president who in a bold effort was trying to root them out and destroy their power. And since then, it has been an endless succession of sock-puppet "presidents" who are little more than mouth pieces for the plutocrats and oligarchs who hold them thrall.

I remember, too, as a boy of six, watching the new president, Lyndon Baines Johnson – how apt now his middle name seems! – being sworn into office as the thirty-sixth president of the United States of America on Air Force One at Love Field in Dallas with the wife of the slain president looking on, still wearing her blood-stained dress. The air of gloom hanging in the living room of our house in Sioux Falls, South Dakota was palpable as we watched the ceremony take place. My father said nothing, but merely grunted in disgust. My father was not pleased, that I knew. My mother sat on the sofa, nervously sewing and quietly crying. I looked at the new President, and I remember vividly thinking "I don't like him." Ten years and fifty thousand American casualties in Vietnam later, I knew why. Decades and a raft of books and articles on the assassination later, I know even more why.

A year later when I was but seven, President Johnson's "blue ribbon panel" to investigate the murder, the Warren Commission, published its twenty-six non-indexed volumes, which were quickly excerpted in newspapers around the country. The impression that the excerpt in the local newspaper made on a boy of seven is with me still, for with apologies to the History Channel, the Discovery Channel, to the endless television documentaries attempting to defend its nonsense, to the Rush Limbaughs and Gerald Posners and Arlen Specters and the "expert authorities" and priesthoods who defend its dogmas, the boy of seven decided that the "magic bullet" just did not "work," and the man of fifty-three still thinks that.

The Kennedy Assassination has fascinated, and haunted me, ever since, and I have written about it elsewhere in connection with my other

2

research interests.[1] There I described the assassination as a "coalescence of interests" each with its own motivation for murdering the president. It is with that "coalescence of interests," and with Lyndon Baines Johnson, that this book is principally concerned, for Johnson sits like the spider in the center of a vast web of conspiracy, touching each of the strands in that web, and ultimately, if there was a conspiracy, he and he alone had the power to pull off some of its requirements.

When we speak of a conspiracy with respect to the murder of President Kennedy, however, we must take cognizance of several facts, each of which guides the methodology of this book.

1) If there was a conspiracy to assassinate President Kennedy, then the likelihood is that the motivations of whatever conspirators were involved were *political*. Hence, the motives of those groups advanced by various JFK assassination researchers must be examined, and plausible speculative connections to Johnson must be ascertained;

2) As in any conspiracy, there will be various layers of those involved:

a) there will of course be an inner circle of plotters and planners;

b) there will be a second tier of "people in the know" but not actively involved in its planning and execution, or perhaps providing logistical support behind the scenes. We argue that it is this second layer of "people in the know" that comprises the bulk of the "coalescing interests" that have been advanced by various researchers as having been involved in the assassination; and,

c) there will be a third layer of people unwittingly involved in aspects of the plot but innocent of any real wrong-doing or evil purpose. In terms of this three-fold structure, it is argued that Johnson had to be involved in at least the second level. But as will be seen, a solid *prima facie* case can be made for his active involvement in the planning itself;

3) There are at least *three* conspiracies in terms of the *events* of the assassination, and these too must be born in mind:

a) The conspiracy to commit the murder itself;

b) The conspiracy to deflect attention away from the existence of that conspiracy, and to fix responsibility for the murder on a

---

[1] Q.v. my *SS Brotherhood of the Bell: NASA's Nazis, JFK, and MAJIC-12* (Kempton, Illinois: Adventures Unlimited Press, 2006), p. 455.

scapegoat, or, alternatively, to fix responsibility on only one of its possible active participants, namely, Oswald;

c) The conspiracy to alter the forensic evidence of the President's body and to initiate and perpetuate a cover-up. Again, it is at this level that the *prima facie* case for Johnson's involvement becomes quite strong;

As has been indicated, the basic thesis of this book is that the conspiracy involved a coalescence of interests of various groups that other researchers have proposed were involved in the assassination. Methodologically this implies, to a certain extent, that other assassination researchers' conclusions are essentially correct and that they are not, in the end, mutually exclusive. They form a vast network, a web of relationships and motives. The question is, how are their motives related? How could they have all been coordinated? What was their level of probable involvement, and in what aspect of the conspiracy – the murder itself, the creation of the Oswald-Lone Nut theory, or the alteration of forensic evidence and the perpetuation of a cover-up – were they most likely involved? In short, what was the *structure* of the conspiracy?

When viewed in this way, and when these questions are asked, there is one obvious connection between the various parts of the conspiracy, the motives of its various involved groups and players, and that obvious connection is Lyndon Baines Johnson, thirty-sixth president of the United States of America.

We thus propose to examine the groups other researchers have advanced for having been involved in the murder. We shall then review the crime itself and the persuasive if not overwhelming evidence for tampering with President Kennedy's body for the explicit purpose of molding the cover-up. After this, we shall review the possible *motives* that each group had for murdering President Kennedy, and from this argue to their potential position as planners, or as passive players "in the know". Finally, we shall look at Johnson himself, and his essential role at the center of it all.

Methodologically, this approach imposes a certain template over the analysis. If there were in fact *three* parts to the conspiracy – the part to commit the murder itself, the part to frame Oswald, and the part to control the cover-up that would be required afterward – then this template will impose certain conditions upon the normal technique of investigating suspected individuals and groups, for while a given group of individual might have the means, motive, and opportunity to carry out the first two parts of the conspiracy, they might not do so to be able to

4

carry out the third part, the long-term cover-up that would be inevitably necessary. Our template, in other words, looks like this:

	Means	*Motive*	*Opportunity*
The Murder Itself			
The Framing of Oswald			
The Long-term Cover-up			

As we proceed through this book, we shall gradually fill in the blanks of this template, to derive a putative structure of the conspiracy itself, which will in turn aid in the analysis of the levels at which each alleged group or individual might have been involved, and how they relate with other groups and individuals within the overall structure.

This approach also aids in distinguishing it from the two types of approaches exhibited in assassination research literature hitherto put forward, for that literature, as will be seen in the main text, may be classified into two distinct groups. The first group argues merely that there *was* a conspiracy based upon the well-known inconsistencies within the massive amount of evidence presented in the Warren Commission's twenty-six volumes themselves. This group argues a now well-known case based upon various factors, from the impossibility of Oswald achieving the marksmanship feat he is alleged to have achieved, to the statements and reaction of witnesses present at Dealey Plaza who insist the shots came from the Grassy Knoll, who insist that there were more than three shots, to the observations of the Dallas doctors of the wounds on the president's body, the impossibility of the "Magic Bullet" having traversed two bodies through bones and so on, to emerge in more or less pristine condition on a stretcher at Parkland Hospital. Beyond this, however, this group of research does not attempt any detailed analysis of the structure of the conspiracy itself; it merely argues that there *was* a conspiracy.

The second class of assassination literature does attempt to analyze the structure of the conspiracy, by positing one particular group to the exclusion of others, was more or less the central player in the planning and execution of the crime. This second group thus tends to ignore the three components of the conspiracy – the crime itself, the framing of Oswald, and the ensuing long-term cover-up – by focusing only on the first, or first two, components, and by ignoring the evidence for the wider

5

involvement of other groups, individuals, and interests implied by the third.

Within this class, there is a kind of sub-group that focuses on the *third* component of the conspiracy, the cover-up itself, and rightly draws the conclusion that of all the groups with connections to the assassination, only certain ones were had the means, motive, and opportunity to perpetuate a cover-up. On this basis, these researchers tend to propose a structure that neglects the other players and their possible roles.

As will be seen, however, this approach ignores the potential significance of an often-overlooked class of evidence, and what it might indicate about the structure of the conspiracy: the dead "witnesses," the "people of interest," and most importantly, the ritual and magical aspects of the murder. Close examination of this ritual aspect also reveals significant clues about the groups involved in it, and the roles they played.

*Thus, the question this book attempts to answer is not so much **who** was involved, but **how** they were involved.* Any such analysis as is offered here is, of course, highly speculative, but it seems to me that nearly fifty years after the assassination, that it is high time to begin the process of arguing and advancing various structures for the conspiracy, and drawing the necessary lessons from it.

That being said, it is time, then, to have a look at the various groups that assassination researchers have put forward as having possible connections to it.

6

1
A COALESCENCE OF INTERESTS:
THE GROUPS ALLEGED TO HAVE BEEN INVOLVED WITH
THE ASSASSINATION OF PRESIDENT JOHN F. KENNEDY

*"There is but one way all of this could have been managed, both
before and after this elaborate coup d'état. That is with absolute
control from the highest echelons of the superpower structure of this
country and the world."*
L. Fletcher Prouty[1]

Just about everybody that one can imagine has been put forward as
having had some involvement in the murder of President John
Fitzgerald Kennedy in Dallas, Texas on November 22, 1963. There
is of course, the "Lone Nut" theory centering on Lee Harvey Oswald. But
the list does not stop there. Everyone from Soviets and anti-Soviet
Russian exiles,[2] pro- and anti-Castro Cubans,[3] Mafiosi,[4] rogue CIA and
FBI groups,[5] the Secret Service,[6] arch-conservative Texas oilmen,[7] the
American military,[8] homosexual priests in obscure Old Orthodox
Catholic churches,[9] even obscure NASA and quasi-military agencies,[10]

---

[1] L. Fletcher Prouty, *JFK: The CIA, Vietnam, and the Plot to Assassinate
John F. Kennedy* (New York: Birch Lane Press Book, 1992), p. 316.
[2] Jim Marrs, *Crossfire: the Plot that Killed Kennedy* (New York: Carroll
and Graf Publishers, Inc., 1990), pp. 113-134.
[3] Ibid, pp. 135-155.
[4] Ibid, pp. 156-180.
[5] Ibid, pp. 181-252.
[6] David S. Lifton, *Best Evidence: Disguise and Deception in the
Assassination of John F. Kennedy* (New York: Carroll and Graf Publishers,
1980). Throughout his study of the assassination, Lifton points out that the
Secret Service had possession of the president's body, and was the agency that
discovered the bullet fragments, and the magic bullet, from Oswald's alleged
murder weapon, and is thus implicated in any attempt to fasten the responsibility
for the murder on Oswald, and is also implicated in the attempt to alter the
forensic evidence in the president's body itself.
[7] Marrs, op. cit., Ibid, pp. 253-300.
[8] Ibid, pp. 301-312.
[9] Craig Roberts and John Armstrong, *JFK: The Dead Witnesses* (Tulsa:
Consolidated Press International, 1995), pp. 46-47, concerning David Ferrie. See
also: Jim Garrison, *On the Trail of the Assassins* (New York: Time-Warner,
1988), pp. 127-140.

7

Lyndon Baines Johnson,[11] and last, but not least, Nazis both foreign and domestic,[12] have been put forward as having been involved at some level in the conspiracy to assassinate the president.

But this is not the problem.

The problem is that oddly compelling cases can be made that each was involved. Thus, there is an additional problem: *which* "group" does one select as being the one that planned and committed the crime? Or are they all somehow involved or implicated? And if the latter, how then does one make sense of the whole thing? What possible speculative structure did the conspiracy have, and what level in the conspiracy did they each occupy? Were they active planners? Quiescent bystanders "in-the-know" but willing to allow the plan to proceed out of their own self-interests? Or were they somewhere between the two?

While it may seem strange to propose that *all* or at least *many* of this bizarre list of groups was somehow involved in the conspiracy, there was at least *one* important player in the assassination drama who maintained precisely, and insistently, that the conspiracy was very large, larger than *anyone* could possibly imagine: Jack Ruby, Oswald's murderer.[13] Ruby insisted in his testimony to the Warren Commission that he be taken to Washington, D.C., in order to testify, since he was in fear of his life if he did so in Dallas. The Commission refused. At this juncture, Ruby stated "Well, you won't ever see me again. I tell you that... A whole new form of government is going to take over the country, and I know I won't live

---

[10] The obscure NASA agencies in question are the Defense Industrial Security Command (DISC) allegedly headed by Dr. Wehrner Von Braun. NASA's connection via this agency was first discussed in the so-called Torbitt Document, a typewritten memorandum originally entitled "Nomenclature of an Assassination Cabal." Torbitt, a pseudonym, was a south Texas lawyer familiar with the investigation of New Orleans District Attorney Jim Garrison and some of the Torbitt document is a reflection and summary of some of the odder aspects of Garrison's research. The document is reproduced in its entirety in *NASA, Nazis, and JFK: The Torbitt Document and the JFK Assassination* (Kempton, Illinois: Adventures Unlimited Press, 1996).

[11] Johnson's involvement is the subject of Craig I. Zirbel's *The Texas Connection* (New York: Time-Warner, 1991). This book will become a central component of our case that Johnson was intimately connected to most of the groups alleged to have been involved at some level in the conspiracy, and thus a key member of the actual "planning committee" of the assassination.

[12] Joseph P. Farrell, *The SS Brotherhood of the Bell: NASA's Nazis, JFK, and Majic-12* (Kempton, Illinois: Adventures Unlimited Press, 2006), pp. 56-67.

[13] Craig Roberts and John Armstrong, *JFK: The Dead Witnesses*, p. 44.

8

to see you another time."[14] Just *what* Ruby meant by "a whole new form of government" we shall determine later in our examination of the "dead witnesses," but it is clear that Ruby believed the assassination was very large, and that its motivation was entirely political. It was perforce, if one accepts the statements of Oswald's murderer, *not* the happenstance affair of the Lone Nut murdering the president.

A. The Soviet Connection
1. Oswald and the U-2

As is now well-known, the alleged assassin in the JFK murder — or as he himself put it with more accuracy, the patsy — Lee Harvey Oswald, defected to the Soviet Union in October of 1959,[15] only to return to the United States on June 13, 1962[16] with his wife, Marina, the daughter of a colonel in the GRU, Soviet military intelligence, in tow. Needless to say, getting *into* the Soviet Union in those days was difficult enough. Getting *out* with the daughter of a GRU colonel was even more so. These circumstances have prompted a number of assassination researchers to question the whole scenario of whether or not his initial defection and subsequent "re-defection" back to the USA was part of some covert intelligence operation.

The political atmosphere between the Soviet Union and the United States when Oswald defected was highly charged, and this political atmosphere is crucial to a proper understanding of why some assassination researchers believe — with good reason — that Oswald's defection may have been part of a covert operation.

On the American side, President Dwight D. Eisenhower was faced with a growing monster: America's thermonuclear arsenal and the plans to use it that the Strategic Air Command under U.S. Air Force Generals Curtis Lemay — mastermind of the devastating fire-bombing campaigns against Japan in World War Two — and Thomas Power had drawn up. While the public stance and policy of the United States government was to abjure any first use of nuclear weapons in a military confrontation with the Soviet Union (this was, after all, the era of Eisenhower's "Atoms for Peace" program), the policy of Generals Lemay and Power, and the

---

[14] Marrs, *Crossfire*, p. 429.

[15] For the best study of the paper trail generated among the FBI, CIA, and State Department by Oswald's defection, see John Newman, *Oswald and the CIA* (New York: Carroll and Graf Publishers, 1995).

[16] Ibid, p. 249.

9

planners at the Air Force Strategic Air Command was anything but.[17] LeMay "was convinced a first strike was absolutely essential for victory," and to that end "he planned to launch that strike without the President's go-ahead if he had to."[18] Eisenhower early in his administration had informed the Joint Chiefs of Staff to rein in their plans for nuclear war and impose some sort of mechanisms for control over them.[19] By August of 1960, Eisenhower demanded to see the actual plans for the nuclear bombardment of the Soviet Union, and by November of 1960 — the month of the razor-thin victory of John F. Kennedy over Vice President Richard Nixon — Eisenhower saw the unwieldy plan, called the Single Integrated Operational Plan, or SIOP.[20]

Eisenhower was completely disgusted when he saw the plan, for it called for nothing less than a first strike with 3,267 nuclear warheads,[21] in an aim to annihilate all of Eastern Europe, the Soviet Union, and Communist China in one decisive radioactive blow. And this was just the *beginning.* "SAC planned to follow this apocalyptic spasm with thousands and thousands more bombs, everything we had on hand. Ten nations would be obliterated. Five hundred million people would die."[22] What Eisenhower did *not* know, and what he was never even told, was that the US military planners had planned for a total escalation to all out thermonuclear war any time American and Warsaw Pact soldiers exchanged combat. President Eisenhower realized that "he had lost control over the power of the nuclear arsenal,"[23] and while he did not warn the nation directly of the threat to its security that this posed, he did make his celebrated "military-industrial complex" speech to the American people on January 17, 1961:[24]

> Our military organization today bears little relation to that known by any of my predecessors in peacetime, or indeed by the fighting men of World War II or Korea. Until the latest of our world conflicts, the

---

[17] Tim Weiner, *Blank Check: The Pentagon's Black Budget* (New York: Time-Warner, 1991), p. 35.

[18] Ibid.

[19] Ibid., p. 36.

[20] Ibid., pp. 36-37.

[21] Ibid., p. 37.

[22] Ibid.

[23] Ibid.

[24] While this author was only four years old at the time, he vividly remembers that speech, because it interrupted his favorite TV program!

United States had no armaments industry. American makers of plowshares could, with time and as required, make swords as well.

But now... we have been compelled to create a permanent armaments industry of vast proportions. Added to this, three and a half million men and women are directly engaged in the defense establishment. We annually spend on military security more than the net income of all United States corporations.

This conjunction of an immense military establishment and a large arms industry is new in the American experience. The total influence — economic, political, even spiritual — is felt in every city, every statehouse, every office of the federal government...

In the councils of government, we must guard against the acquisition of unwarranted influence, whether sought or unsought, by the military-industrial complex. The potential for the disastrous rise of misplaced power exists and will persist.

We must never let the weight of this combination endanger our liberties or democratic processes. We should take nothing for granted.[25]

Clearly, the former supreme commander of Allied forces in Europe during World War Two was worried about *something* threatening "our liberties and democratic processes," and, if one is to read his speech in the context of the military's plans to turn the Soviet Union, Communist China, and Eastern Europe into a glowing cinder at the first provocation, he clearly understood the threat as emanating from within the circles of military and corporate power within the United States itself.

In short, he was warning Americans about the possibility of a rogue element within the federal government that had become a hidden government and policy-making body in its own right. We shall see later in this chapter how Eisenhower's remarks might also be construed as containing an even deeper warning, about something lurking at an even deeper and possibly international level.

In any case, it is in this highly charged atmosphere of Eisenhower's attempts during his administration to reign in military planning that a summit was planned between him and Soviet Premier Nikita Khrushchev in Paris in May of 1960. But the summit was not to be, for on May 1, 1960, the day of the Soviet Union's celebrated military May Day parades in Red Square, American pilot Francis Gary Powers' high altitude U-2 spy plane was shot down over Sverdlovsk in the Soviet Union.

Here it is *Khrushchev's* reaction that is crucial, a reaction that has been little noticed, and its potential significance not even guessed-at by

---

[25] President Dwight D. Eisenhower, Farewell Address to the Nation, January 17, 1961, cited in Tim Weiner, *Blank Check*, pp. 37-38.

most assassination researchers, for Khrushchev was himself engaged in a struggle within his own government between hold-over Stalinist "hard liners" and his own attempts to "liberalize" the Communist government of Russia.[26] It is this fact that makes Khrushchev's reaction so significant, for *he knew how to recognize the signs and footprints of such rogue elements working against the publicly stated policies of a government.* Here is the way assassination researcher Jim Marrs puts Khrushchev's reaction to the Russian downing of Powers' U-2:

> Khrushchev was furious, *yet he tried to give Eisenhower latitude* in disclaiming any knowledge of the incident. He stated that the U-2 flight *may have been the work of "American aggressive circles" trying to "torpedo the Paris summit, or, at any rate, prevent an agreement for which the world is waiting."*
>
> After days of half-truths and evasions, Eisenhower finally admitted that the spy plane was acting on his orders and took responsibility for the fiasco, just as John Kennedy would take responsibility for the Bay of Pigs invasion a year later.[27]

While it is certainly true that the CIA's U-2 spy plane reconnaissance of the Soviet Union was known to Eisenhower personally, it does not diminish the significance of what Khrushchev was really saying, nor the possible reasons why he said it, *for he was saying almost exactly the same thing as Eisenhower said in his farewell speech: there was a rogue element within the American government establishing and executing its own policies, a rogue element that did **not** want any peace between the two superpowers, but rather, wanted an escalation of tensions.*

For his own part, and due to the political pressures on him, Khrushchev of course had to back out of the summit. But why, in doing so, was he pointing the finger at "American aggressive circles" and not at Eisenhower himself? Was this merely propaganda posturing on his part, or did Khrushchev know something?

One of the things he *may* have known, though it is highly unlikely, is that the White House, as part of its preparations for the Paris summit, "had directed all aerial surveillance," in other words, all U-2 flights, "of

---

[26] Of course, all this is relative. Khrushchev was no innocent, being appointed as a commissar to the Ukraine by Stalin himself, in which capacity he oversaw the campaign to collectivize Soviet agriculture, a campaign which led to the deportation and deaths of thousands if not millions.

[27] Jim Marrs, *Crossfire: The Plot That Killed Kennedy*, p. 114, emphasis added.

Communist territory to cease until further notice..."[28] But that was not all.

Yet, on May 1, 1960, a U-2 spy plane flown by Francis Gary Powers left Pakistan on a straight-line overflight (sic) of the Soviet Union en route to Bodo, Norway, contrary to the Eisenhower orders.
...
   The same man who was in charge of the Cuban exile program..., Richard Bissell, deputy director of plans for the CIA, was the man who ran the U-2 program and who, ostensibly, sent the Powers flight over the Soviet Union on May 1, 1960.[29]

In other words, the mere *existence* of Powers' flight *and its downing* indicates the existence of a covert policy established by elements within U.S. intelligence in defiance of President Eisenhower himself. While there is *no* evidence to suggest that Khrushchev knew about Eisenhower's order, his words suggest that he *might* have known.

The other thing that Premier Khrushchev *probably* knew was the defection of Lee Harvey Oswald to the Soviet Union, some six months *prior* to the shooting down of Powers' U-2. A review of the facts is in order to see why Khrushchev may not simply have been mouthing propaganda, but stating his considered and informed opinion.

That informed opinion may have been shaped by the evidence that Oswald's "defection" to the Soviet Union may not have been genuine, but made in the interest of a deeply covert agenda being run by someone within American intelligence. While stationed at Atsugi Air Force base in Japan when he was a Marine, Oswald, according to his commanding officer, worked in the radar center, and would have had by the nature of the case to possess at the minimum a "Secret" clearance.[30] But Atsugi airbase was more than an ordinary airbase, for that is where some of the top secret CIA U-2 reconnaissance flights over the Soviet Union and Communist China originated. In fact, it is now known that Oswald and some of his Marine buddies actually stood *guard* over the hangar housing the top secret aircraft:[31] "The U-2 program was TOP SECRET and more, but it was no secret to the marines in Oswald's unit. They saw the planes, they tracked them, and they even communicated with them.

---

[28] L.Fletcher Prouty, *JFK: The CIA, Veitnam, and the Plot to Assassinate John F. Kennedy*, p. 124.
[29] Ibid., p. 125.
[30] John Newman, *Oswald and the CIA*, p. 26.
[31] Ibid., p. 28.

That is, until Oswald defected to the Soviet Union..."[32] Oswald's defection was therefore no ordinary defection.

In fact, it was downright *extraordinary*, for when Oswald walked into the American embassy in Moscow to surrender his passport and announce his intention to defect, he went further. Just how *much* further is revealed by the cable from the Moscow embassy to the State Department in Washington, D.C.:

> Oswald offered the information that he had been a radar operator in the Marine Corps and that he had voluntarily stated to unnamed Soviet officials that as a Soviet citizen he would make known to them such information concerning the Marine Corps and his specialty as he possessed. He intimated that he might know something of special interest.[33]

Indeed he did, for as a radar operator at Atsugi, he was tracking and *guarding* America's then most advanced spy plane and its flights over Russia. John Newman comments on the oddity of Oswald's behavior at the embassy as follows:

> Part of what made Oswald's stated intent to reveal state secrets so remarkable is that it had not been solicited.... Peculiar indeed — to walk into an American Embassy anywhere in the world, let alone Moscow at the height of the Cold War, and to announce, in the presence of American consular officials, one's intent to commit a deliberate act of espionage is an extraordinary act.[34]

But this was not all.

When conducting a search for Oswald's CIA files, Newman discovered a "black hole" in the CIA that was "consuming every scrap of paper on Oswald in the days immediately following his defection, a black hole that kept the Oswald files away from the spot we would expect them to go — the Soviet Russia division."[35] Ultimately, that sensitivity is due to Oswald's knowledge of the U-2 program, the normal altitudes at which it flew over the Soviet Union, the radio frequencies

---

[32] Ibid., p. 30.
[33] FSD-234, p. 2, cited in Newman, *Oswald and the CIA*, pp. 5-6.
[34] John Newman, *Oswald and the CIA*, p. 13.
[35] Ibid., p. 27.

used, and so on, all of which were some of the most highly classified matters in the U.S.A.[36]

As Newman himself observes, the pilot of the downed U-2, Francis Gary Powers himself, believed that Oswald's defection gave the Soviets the altitude at which the U-2 flew, and the frequencies and timing of flights over the Soviet Union, for Oswald's radar specialty was precisely to work with altitude ranging radar.[37] All of this strongly argues in Newman's opinion — and this author concurs — that Oswald's CIA files went into the bowels of James Jesus Angleton's counter-intelligence operations.[38] This would be the *logical* place for them to go, given the sensitivity of Oswald's knowledge of the CIA's reconnaissance over-flights of the Soviet Union.

2. Oswald, The FBI, and the CIA: Hoover's Concern of a Second Oswald

By the summer of 1960, there is yet another indicator that a deeply covert agenda was being played out by Oswald's defection to the Soviet Union, for FBI director J. Edgar Hoover addressed a letter to the Office of Security of the State Department, warning of the possibility that there might be a *second* Oswald using Oswald's identity and birth certificate.[39] This, it should be noted, is the first mention of a second Oswald.

3. Francis Powers' Statement concerning Sabotage of his U-2 Flight

There is a final, and very significant, clue that Oswald's defection, the downing of Francis Gary Powers' U-2 on May 1, 1960, and the resulting sabotage of the Eisenhower-Khrushchev summit may have been the result of a deeply covert and rogue operation, and that is a statement Powers made himself. Jim Marrs, who wrote the single most important and encyclopedic study of the assassination, *Crossfire: the Plot That Killed Kennedy*, notes that

> In 1977, Powers told a radio audience that he believed his U-2 *had been brought down by a bomb placed on board.* Shortly after making this statement, he was killed when his helicopter, used to report news for a Los Angeles television station, ran out of gas and crashed.[40]

---

[36] Ibid., pp. 35, 37-38.
[37] Ibid., p. 43.
[38] Ibid., p. 37.
[39] Jim Marrs, *Crossfire,* p. 123.
[40] Jim Marrs, *Crossfire,* p. 115, emphasis added.

15

What has all this to do with Oswald? There are, says Marrs, two further "tantalizing clues." One was a letter Oswald wrote to his brother, describing Powers as "a nice bright American-type fellow *when I saw him in Moscow.*"[41] The other is, that "of Oswald's three May Days spent in Russia, the only one unaccounted for is May 1, 1960 — the day the U-2 was captured."[42] Powers, as will be discovered later, is but one of many key figures surrounding the Kennedy assassination who die under questionable circumstances, and in numbers far too high, to be a mere statistical fluke.

But how does one reconcile these two things, Powers' statements that Oswarld's surrendering of radar and U-2 flight information to the Soviet Union may have had something to do with the downing of his U-2 on the one hand, and his statement that he believed his aircraft to have been deliberately sabotaged by a bomb on board? The reconciliation is, in fact, rather easy if one bears in mind once again Khrushchev's statements pointing the finger to rogue groups in America, for if the Soviets failed to shoot down his aircraft on their own, then the on-board bomb would do the trick. In fact, if Powers' U-2 *did* carry a bomb and was sabotaged, then the Russians would have quickly been able to determine this by an examination of the wreckage of Powers' U-2, and Khrushchev would most likely have been informed of this fact.

U-2 Pilot Francis Gary Powers

---

[41] Ibid., emphasis added.
[42] Ibid.

16

The CIA's Top Secret High Altitude U-2 Spy Plane

Retired U.S. Air Force colonel Fletcher Prouty, who was a top Pentagon liaison man with the CIA's covert operations, noted several additional anomalies about Powers' U-2 flight.

> This was not the normal U-2 flight. Much was made of the fact that the pilot had with him a vial (needle) of poison; so that rather than expose his native land to charges of willful violation of the air space and sovereignty of the Soviet Union, he could silence himself in death. The code of the spy. Yet little was made of the antithetical fact that the pilot also had a parachute which would save his life. Much was made of the fact, afterwards, that this was a "civilian" aircraft and that it was flown by a "civilian" pilot. Yet this pilot had been permitted to carry with him on this flight his military identification card, complete with name and picture, along with a pocketful of other identifying cards, all of which easily placed him at military installations, in military instrument flight schools, and on military facilities just days before the flight. He was hardly a deniable spy.[43]

This was not the only set of anomalies.

These violations of normal security procedures raise significant questions about the whole purpose and motivation of Powers' flight.

> How did it happen that they broke with policy procedures for that special flight by letting him take off loaded with incriminating evidence

---

[43] L. Fletcher Prouty, *The Secret Team: The CIA and Its Allies in Control of the United States and the World* (New York: Skyhorse Publishing, 2008), p. 447.

that proved he was a U.S. spy pilot? Who was it who wanted this special U-2 flight on May 1, 1960; two weeks before the summit conference, to fail and then to become so glaring an admission of guilt when it did fail that it would inevitably doom the summit conference along with it? The incidence of these things, too many things, give weight to the thought that this flight was intended to be something rather special.

Nothing was said that all clandestine operations personnel, and especially the select coterie of U-2 pilots, were required to submit to a complete inspection before takeoff, which included the removal of all clothes and other personal effects and the issue of sanitized, non-identifiable clothing and equipment sufficient only for the flight. Neither pilot nor plane were sanitized on this flight as was required on other flights.[44]

U-2 was possibly sabotaged

Indeed, the questions do not really stop even there, for Powers, as an experienced U-2 pilot, would have been more than familiar with the normal sanitization process, and would have been very unlikely to have taken such identification with him, *unless ordered to do so*. Thus, it is also highly likely that he knew even before he took off that his mission was likely *meant to be unsuccessful*.

In fact, there *is* an indication that Powers knew, before he ever took off from Pakistan, that his mission was designed to be a deliberate failure, and that is disclosed by another anomaly about the flight:

When the plane went down, its signals faded and it was lost from tracking radar. The engine had stopped, and Powers was gliding the plane down from its extreme altitude, which was so high that the air's oxygen content was insufficient to support combustion. The normal combustion of the jet engine at that altitude had to be assisted by the infusion of a trace of raw hydrogen from a small liquid hydrogen cryogenic storage bottle. If by some chance the engine either coughed itself out, or if something happened to this slight hydrogen supply and the engine flamed out, it could not be restarted at that altitude. The pilot would have had no recourse other than to let down and see if he could restart the engine at some lower altitude. The evidence that the engine would not restart even at thirty thousand feet indicates that the trouble was most likely hydrogen deficiency and not a normal fuel flameout. Had it been a simple flameout and had there been plenty of hydrogen, the engine should have restarted, as others had in similar circumstances.

---

[44] L. Fletcher Prouty, *The Secret Team*, p. 448.

When the plane did not restart, Powers was forced to let it continue to spiral toward the earth, and then at a safer altitude either bail out (a high altitude bailout is dangerous and violent) or continue on down to the ground.[45]

Thus, it was far simpler to sabotage Powers' U-2 flight, not with a bomb on board the plane, but with a hydrogen tank only partly full. Knowing the rate of fuel consumption of a U-2, the saboteurs could in fact calculate roughly where in the Soviet Union the U-2 came down; they could *control* it. In any case, Powers' behavior in gliding the plane downward gives lie to his later statements that he suspected a bomb had been put aboard the flight. As a U-2 pilot of experience, he knew exactly how to sabotage his own flight, and given that he was carrying identification in complete violation of normal procedure, it seems clear that he knew his flight was *meant* to fail.

The story gets even more interesting once the U-2 had crashed, for Allen Dulles then suggested that the Administrator of NASA, T. Keith Glennan, "release *a prepared cover story*"[46] to the effect that the U-2 was nothing but a "high altitude weather research aircraft" that had accidentally violated Soviet airspace.[47] When Powers crashed, Khrushchev very deliberately only announced the crash of an aircraft and the pilot, without releasing any further details. NASA's cover story came out, and then Khrushchev pounced. He produced Powers, announced his name, and produced the aircraft itself. Pictures of it, shown all over Soviet television and during Powers' show trial, were even more interesting, for they

Interesting.

showed an aircraft that was relatively undamaged, when one considers that the Russian story was that it was hit by a rocket in the air and then crashed into the ground.... The elaborate pictures of the plane, which the Soviets released at the trial, show neither bullet damage nor rocket fragment damage...[48]

---

[45] L. Fletcher Prouty, *The Secret Team*, p. 450.
[46] Ibid, p. 451.
[47] Ibid. The involvement of NASA in these dark machinations may point to deeper connections between the CIA and the space agency, and to possible motivations for NASA's involvement at some level within the architecture of the conspiracy, as will be seen in a later chapter.
[48] Ibid, p. 450.

19

All this places Khrushchev's statement to Eisenhower that there may have been a rogue element within certain American circles into an even more interesting context, for by showing pictures to the world of a plane showing no damage from bullets or rockets, Khrushchev was backing up his statement with clear evidence that told his American counterpart that the Russians *knew* that the flight had been sabotaged, and Eisenhower, a career soldier, would not have needed analysts to tell him that.

These considerations lead Colonel Prouty to ask the "special question," and that is, "Who sent him out in the first place?" His answer is illuminating: "...only high level officials...could have launched that flight."[49] Officials like Richard Bissell, in charge of CIA covert ops, including the U-2 flights, or even CIA Director Allen Dulles. It is significant in this regard that after the Bay of Pigs invasion fiasco, that it was these two men, along with General Charles Cabell, that Kennedy fired.

Who ordered the flight?

4. Yuri Nosenko

There is another prime consideration in evaluating Oswald's "defection" and its probable role in the assassination, and that is the defection — if one may call it that — of Soviet KGB officer Yuri Nosenko to the CIA, on January 20, 1964, just a mere two months after the assassination. As a part of a Soviet disarmament delegation to Geneva, Nosenko made a telephone call, and offered to defect to the United States.

> The defection of Yuri Nosenko set in motion a chain of events that would lead to bitter divisions between the CIA and FBI as well as within the CIA itself.
>
> Once he was in American hands, CIA officials were shocked to learn that Nosenko claimed to have been the KGB official who had personally handled the case of Lee Harvey Oswald during his stay in Russia. Nosenko said — based on two mental examinations made of Oswald — the KGB found the would-be defector not very bright and even "mentally unstable." And that the KGB had never debriefed Oswald about his military background nor ever considered recruiting him as an agent.[50]

---

[49] Ibid., p. 449.
[50] Jim Marrs, *Crossfire*, p. 130.

But the Soviet Union's whole handling of Oswald belies Nosenko's testimony, for as is now well-known, Oswald was given a spacious apartment — by any standards in the Soviet Union for the day, much less for an American defector who was "mentally unstable" - and if it had never debriefed him about his possible knowledge of radar secrets, if Oswald's secrets were never even examined by the KGB, one would have thought a one room apartment in Moscow would have sufficed for the international drifter. The Soviet Union's treatment of Oswald belies Nosenko's allegations.

For these types of reasons, many in the CIA were extremely suspicious of Nosenko. James Jesus Angleton, head of the CIA's counter-intelligence division, as well as the CIA's counter-intelligence faction itself, "still believes that Nosenko's defection was contrived by the KGB for two purposes: to allay suspicions that the Soviets had anything to do with the JFK assassination, and to cover for Soviet 'moles,' or agents deep within U.S. intelligence."[51] Indeed, given Premier Khrushchev's own warnings about rogue elements within American intelligence, it is very likely that Nosenko is telling at least a *partial* truth, namely, that while Oswald was likely *debriefed* by the KGB concerning his radar secrets — making it likely his defection had something to do with the downing of Powers' U-2 — it is *unlikely* that the KGB ever recruited him as an agent, but rather, as the facts indicate, paid him off with a spacious apartment and good job in Minsk.

5. Conclusions: Oswald and a Rogue Operation

So what do we have that argues that Oswald was part of a deeply covert, rogue operation? There are four important points strongly arguing for this:

1) Francis Gary Powers, the U-2 pilot shot down and captured in the Soviet Union, and subsequently released in a "spy-swap" exchange, stated his beliefs that:
   a) Oswald's defection had something to do with his flight being shot down; and,
   b) he suspected his flight was also sabotaged by a bomb on board his aircraft;
   From these two facts one may reasonably conclude that Oswald's defection *was* part of a deliberate and rogue covert operation

---

[51] Ibid., p. 131.

whose intended and successful effect was to sabotage the impending summit between Eisenhower and Khrushchev. A close examination of these two points will show why, for in the case of the first point, it is clear that flight and radar data supplied by Oswald would have been instrumental in helping the Soviets down Powers' U-2, but, as a back-up fail-safe plan, sabotage would have insured the plane's demise. *Someone*, in other words, was going to a great deal of trouble to insure that Powers was shot down, and that the summit was cancelled. *Someone* wanted the tensions between the Western and Soviet blocs to continue to escalate. Bissell is already implicated, but who else would have wanted this, and why?

2) The absence of standard CIA files and the resulting "black hole" is a strong indicator that Oswald became a subject of extreme concern to CIA counter-intelligence. Nosenko's defection to the CIA further establishes this claim, for he alleged that he was the KGB officer handling Oswald's case directly, and it is known that Angleton took a direct and lasting interest in the Nosenko affair. The important point here is that if Oswald became a concern to CIA counter-intelligence, then this dramatically increases the likelihood that his "defection" to the Soviet Union did *not* represent a genuine CIA operation or policy at all, but rather, the covert operation of some rogue group within it, or within other government intelligence agencies. This conclusion is further established by the next point:

3) FBI Director J. Edgar Hoover informed the State Department that the FBI had reason to believe that while Oswald was living in Russia, someone else appeared to have taken over his identity in *this* country by using his birth certificate; and last but by no means least,

4) There is Premier Khrushchev's statement that it was his opinion that the whole downing of Powers' U-2 was an operation of aggressive circles in the American government, i.e., a rogue operation. This was neither an idle, nor unconsidered, statement for the leader of the Soviet Union to have made during the height of the Cold War and for all of the reasons previously surveyed, for it may have been the considered conclusion and opinion of his own intelligence analysts. Khrushchev's statement indicates the clear concern of the Soviet leader that someone wanted to drive and escalate tensions between the two super-powers.

There is one final point that must be noted. Given Oswald's activities, both before and after the Soviet "defection," his strange ability always to end up in the center of the storm, one must conclude that Oswald was likely actively aware of his participation, at some level, in covert operations.

Based on these considerations (and others to follow later), we rule out any Soviet involvement in the assassination plot to kill President Kennedy, but by the same token, we do not rule out a Soviet *connection* via Lee Harvey Oswald, and whatever covert interests his defection to the Soviet Union may have represented.

B. Cubans: Pro- and Anti-Castro
1. The 54-12 Committee, the Bay of Pigs, and the Cuban Missile Crisis

After the assassination, many conspiracy theorists put forward Fidel Castro's regime as one possible culprit in the murder. But we may easily dispense with this idea by citing the words of Castro himself, given in a 1977 CBS interview with Mill Moyers:

> It would have been absolute insanity by Cuba... It would have been a provocation. Needless to say, it would have been to run the risk that our country would have been destroyed by the United States. Nobody who's not insane could have thought about (killing Kennedy...).[52]

Indeed, Castro is right, for American intelligence agencies would have quickly run down any sort of involvement by the Castro regime, the American media would have been whipped into a feeding frenzy, and retaliation would have been instant, swift, and overwhelming. A further factor weighs heavily against any such Castro involvement, and that is President Kennedy's secret agreement with Premier Khrushchev that America would not invade Cuba in return for the removal of the Soviet nuclear missiles from the island, the very missiles that provoked the Cuban Missile Crisis. Castro would not have endangered this agreement, nor would his Soviet masters, who kept him on a very short leash, have allowed him to do so.

However, the same *cannot* be said of the involvement of the anti-Castro Cuban community in the United States. Here there are clear and palpable motives, and significant indications, that it was involved in the

---

[52] Jim Marrs, *Crossfire,* p. 154.

23

conspiracy, indications of a level of involvement to be speculated upon later in this book.

In order to comprehend the possible role of the anti-Castro Cuban movement in the conspiracy to murder President Kennedy, one must have an adequate appreciation of those *motivations* for involvement, and this can only be had by an examination of the role of the Bay of Pigs invasion and of Kennedy's handling of the Cuban Missile Crisis in *forming* those motivations. The plans for a CIA-backed invasion of Cuba by anti-Castro Cubans themselves began early in 1960, during the final months of the Eisenhower Administration.[53] As a part of this plan, the CIA also incorporated the idea of assassinating the Cuban leader himself in a coordinated action along with the invasion, a plan which gradually encompassed the idea of getting the American mafia to carry out the assassination.[54]

> President Dwight Eisenhower knew none of this. All he knew was that on March 17, 1960, at the urging of a top-secret committee for covert operations — known as the 5412 Committee because it was authorized by National Security Council Directive 5412.2 — he had authorized a CIA plan entitled "A Program of Covert Action Against the Castro Regime." This plan offered a four-point program — 1) the creation of a Cuban government in exile, 2) a "powerful" propaganda offensive, 3) the creation of a "covert intelligence and action organization" inside Cuba, and 4) "a paramilitary force outside Cuba for future guerilla action."[55]

The head of this 54-12 committee was none other than Eisenhower's vice-president, Richard M. Nixon.[56] Allen Dulles, then Director of the CIA, and later a member of Lyndon Johnson's Warren Commission, was unaware of many of the details of this planning himself, as he had turned over much of the operational planning to - guess who? - deputy director Richard M. Bissell, Jr.[57]

When presidential candidate Kennedy was first briefed by Dulles on the plan on July 23, 1960, the plan did not yet include a full scale paramilitary invasion with air support, but only air drops and guerilla

---

[53] Jim Marrs, *Crossfire*, p. 138.
[54] Ibid., p. 139.
[55] Ibid.
[56] Ibid.
[57] Ibid., p. 138.

infiltration.[58] Another briefing that was "long on vague generalities and short on details" was given to president-elect Kennedy by CIA director Dulles and deputy director Bissell shortly after the November 1960 election.[59]

The results are now well-known, for on April 16, 1961, a small force of obsolete World War Two B-26 medium bombers took off from a CIA airfield in Nicaragua and bombed Castro's small air force. This was followed on Monday April 17, 1961, with the full-scale landing of a Cuban anti-Castro paramilitary brigade with American naval logistical support.[60] The plan called for a second air strike to catch Castro's air force on the ground, but with international outcry against the invasion mounting, Kennedy, on the advice of his secretary of state Dean Rusk, ordered a halt to any further airstrikes, thus depriving the Cuban brigade on the beaches of any air support.[61] As the invasion fell apart under Castro's air attacks and artillery bombardments, Kennedy authorized the American navy ships to evacuate the brigade, but its commanders refused, continuing to believe in the pledges of support that they had been given, and requesting ammunition, naval gunfire support, and the air support that "never came."[62] Needless to say, the brigade was decimated by Castro's forces.

The result of this disaster sent shockwaves through the American military and intelligence communities, and through the anti-Castro Cuban community within the United States:

> As news of the debacle spread, everybody concerned was furious.
>
> Kennedy believed he had been led down a primrose path by optimistic CIA officials.[63] He felt betrayed. The CIA planners felt betrayed in that the actual invasion had been scaled down on Kennedy's orders. The military felt betrayed because they had not been allowed to help in the planning of the invasion. And the Cuban exiles felt betrayed most of all because they had been led to believe they had the full support of the U.S. government.
>
> ...
>
> Infuriated by this disastrous defeat, Kennedy nevertheless took the burden of blame. He told reporters: "There's an old saying that victory

---

[58] Ibid, p. 139.
[59] Ibid, p. 140.
[60] Ibid.
[61] Ibid, p. 141.
[62] Ibid.
[63] Namely, Allen Dulles, CIA director, and Richard Bissell, deputy CIA director.

has a hundred fathers and defeat is an orphan. What mattered was only one fact: I am the responsible officer of government."

No one — especially in the CIA, the military, organized crime, or in the Cuban exile community — was to forget this acceptance of responsibility.[64]

The Kennedy Administration then made matters much worse by fanning the flames of resentment ever further.

The "flames" that it fanned were, in this case, the potential of thermonuclear flames of the Cuban Missile Crisis. Again, I remember this event well, even though only a boy of five at the time. But the air of tension around the dinner table with my parents and my youngest sister was so tense night after night that October of 1962, as we all nervously watched Walter Cronkite, that one could cut it with a knife. There were nervous questions from my mom and sister to my father whether the Soviets would atom bomb Sioux Falls if it came to war. Doubtless similar conversations were had at dinner tables all across the country as the crisis unfolded.

The crisis began on October 22, 1962, when President Kennedy appeared on all three national television networks, and announced to the nation and to the world that American reconnaissance aircraft — the U-2 again — had photographed the construction of offensive nuclear missile launching areas in Cuba, along with the missiles themselves.[65] These intermediate range nuclear missiles were capable of striking the entire eastern United States east of the Mississippi river, and do so with almost no warning or notice.

Kennedy not only had to play very careful diplomacy with Khrushchev, and to do so in the era before there was a White House-Kremlin direct hotline, but he also had to play a careful game of diplomacy within his own government with the military, most of whom were urging the President strike the bases hard, knowing full well that it would result in World War Three. Kennedy stood his military advisors down, and ordered a blockade of Cuba to turn back the approaching Soviet freighters bearing more missiles bound for Cuba. The tension was so extreme that smoke poured from the chimneys at the Soviet Embassy in Washington, D.C.; the Russians were burning their secret papers in preparation for war.

---

[64] Jim Marrs, *Crossfire*, p. 141.
[65] Ibid, pp. 142-143.

As Soviet ships carrying missiles approached the U.S. naval blockade of Cuba, the world watched and trembled. Nuclear holocaust seemed imminent. Then the Soviets blinked. Their freighters turned back and everyone breathed a (sigh) of relief. Only much later did the American people learn that Kennedy had accepted a proposal from Khrushchev that included a pledge not to invade or support any invasion of Cuba.[66]

Part of that deal included the establishment of direct hotlines between the White House and the Kremlin, to avoid similar incidents in the future by allowing direct diplomacy and communication between the Soviet and American leaders. As we shall also see in a subsequent chapter, there were even deeper deals — *much* deeper deals - afoot between Kennedy and Khrushchev to end the tensions of the Cold War, deals that may have cost Kennedy his life, and Khrushchev his premiership.
    In any case, the problem created by the Cuban Missile Crisis was that Kennedy's skillful diplomacy

earned him further rebuke by military and CIA officers who believed the presence of missiles justified a United States invasion of Cuba and the elimination of the Castro regime.
    These suspicions only made the military and intelligence officers, along with their Cuban protégés, more convinced that Kennedy was "soft on Communism."[67]

Thus the two events — the Bay of Pigs invasion and the Cuban Missile Crisis — combined to give the CIA, the military, and the anti-Castro Cuban exile community potent motivations to see an end to the Kennedy Administration.
    However, in addition to potential motivations, there are significant indicators of actual involvement in the assassination by the anti-Castro Cuban community.

2. Oswald and the Anti-Castro Cubans

As premier assassination researcher Jim Marrs aptly stated the case, it was at an old office building in the French Quarter of New Orleans, 544 Camp Street, "that the paths of Lee Harvey Oswald, the FBI, the

---

[66] Jim Marrs, *Crossfire,* p. 143.
[67] Ibid.

27

CIA, anti-Castro Cubans, and organized crime figures all crossed."[68] The building still stands, and was actually shown in Hollywood filmmaker Oliver Stone's controversial movie, *JFK*, for the building became a central focus of New Orleans District Attorney Jim Garrison's attempt to independently investigate the assassination and prosecute anyone connected to it within his jurisdiction, an effort that eventually led to the famous trial of well-known New Orleans businessman and closet homosexual Clay Shaw in 1967.

It was this building that housed the offices of the CIA-created Cuban Revolutionary Council.[69] One of its members was Carlos Prio Socarras who was, according to the Warren Commission itself, involved in gun-running operations to Cuba with none other than ...Jack Ruby.[70]
But that's not all.

The building at 544 Camp Street stood at the corner of Camp and Lafayette streets. Thus, offices in the same building could have two entirely different addresses.[71] Though the Cuban Revolutionary Council had vacated its offices by the time Oswald arrived in New Orleans, the building did house the offices of former FBI special agent turned "private detective" Guy Bannister, whose office had the address of 531 Lafayette Street. From this building with its two addresses — 544 Camp Street and 531 Lafayette Street — the connections spin out in a bizarre and almost mind-boggling fashion.

For one thing, Guy Bannister was at one time the FBI agent in charge of the Butte, Montana FBI field office in 1947, and was thus intimately involved in the FBI's covert investigation of UFOs, beginning with the famous Kenneth Arnold sighting in June of 1947, the Maury Island UFO affair, and of course, the Roswell Incident in July of 1947. According to "occult politics" researcher Peter Levenda,

> A look at recently declassified FBI files for that period in 1947 show a number of telexes from Bannister, some with his initials "WGB," all pertaining to UFO phenomena, as well as other FBI documents with the designation "Security Matter — X" or simply "SM-X," the origin —

---

[68] Jim Marrs, *Crossfire*, p. 147.
[69] Ibid.
[70] Ibid.
[71] Another fact pointed out in the Oliver Stone movie and in district attorney Jim Garrison's book, *On the Trail of the Assassins.*

the author supposes — of the "X Files," which, at least in 1947, *did* exist at the FBI and was concerned with UFOs...[72]

As Levenda also notes, one of the participants in the infamous Maury Island UFO affair of 1947, Fred Crisman, became, along with Bannister, a subject of interest to the Garrison investigation of President Kennedy's murder, for he was a close associate of Clay Shaw, the man Garrison eventually indicted and brought to trial for his alleged involvement in the assassination.[73] This is not the only odd connection to space matters in the Kennedy assassination, but more of that later...

Former FBI Special Agent and New Orleans Private Detective Guy Bannister

---

[72] Peter Levenda, *Sinister Forces: A Grimoire of American Political Witchcraft: Book One: The Nine* (Walterville, Oregon: TrineDay, 2005), pp. 173-174.
[73] Ibid., pp. 174-175.

On top of all of this, the building at Camp and Lafayette streets was conveniently close to the New Orleans offices both of the FBI and of the CIA, and also conveniently near the Crescent City Garage "where Oswald was seen in the company of FBI agents and it was just around the corner from the William B. Riley Coffee Co., Oswald's employer."[74] Bear the name of Oswald's New Orleans employer — the William B. Riley Coffee Company — in mind, for we will be encountering it again in conjunction with some other amazing connections.

One anti-Castro revolutionary, Silvia Odio, and her sister Annie, stated that in September of 1963, she and her sister were visited at their home in Dallas by three men, two of them Latins, one an "Anglo" who was introduced to her as "Leon Oswald." She was later informed that "Leon Oswald" was an ex-Marine and an expert marksman who would be valuable to the anti-Castro cause.[75] When the assassination of the president occurred, Oswald's face was, of course, plastered on every television screen and newspaper front page in the country. "Both sisters were shocked and frightened to see photographs of Lee Harvey Oswald since, then and now, they both believe him to be the same man who was introduced to them as 'Leon Oswald.'"[76]

But that wasn't the *only* problem. Once the FBI found out about the Odio-Oswald visit, it naturally investigated the matter and prepared a report for the Warren Commission, but it had not completed the investigation by the time that the Commission had published its report.[77] The sighting was inconvenient because the Commission had already concluded that Oswald was on his way to Mexico City for his famous appearance at the Russian and Cuban embassies there, and thus could not have been in Dallas visiting the Odios! Jim Marrs draws the obvious implication: there were *two* Oswalds:

> The Odio story caused great problems with the Warren Commission Report. If Oswald was in Dallas, he couldn't have been traveling by bus to Mexico at the same time. And, if the Oswald in Odio's apartment was not the real Oswald, then it is clear that someone was impersonating him with an eye toward implicating Oswald in the

---

[74] Jim Marrs, *Crossfire*, p. 148.
[75] Ibid., pp. 150-151.
[76] Jim Marrs, *Crossfire*, p. 152.
[77] Ibid.

assassination. Small wonder the Commission decided to let the matter rest.[78]

This is not the only instance where there are one too many Oswalds on the stage, as we shall see.

There is, for example, the possibility that Oswald's strange and contradictory behavior in New Orleans might be the result of *two* Oswalds, for as is well-known, Oswald became involved with the Fair Play for Cuba Committee, a *pro*-Castro organization, handing out its leaflets, leaflets that were stamped with the address of — you guessed it — 544 Camp Street, the building shared with the offices of arch-conservative anti-Communist private detective Guy Bannister, while at the same time, Oswald is seen in the company of FBI agents at the Crescent City Garage, and later by the Odios in Dallas in the company of *anti*-Castro Cubans! Oswald, in other words, "while maintaining a posture as a pro-Castro Marxist, nevertheless was in continuous contact with several anti-Castro elements."[79]

Consequently, when the Kennedy Administration angered the CIA, the military, and the anti-Castro Cubans with its decisions during the Bay of Pigs fiasco, and later with the Cuban Missile Crisis, one need look no further than to the building at Camp and Lafayette streets, to Oswald's activities in that building and its environs, and within those communities to see the deep connections, and the deep involvement, of all three and, through the proximity to Bannister, perhaps of the FBI as well. The question now is, *who had the **most** experience in running such exile communities and to organize them as a covert paramilitary force?* The answer is disturbing, but before we look at that answer, we must look at *another* group, also with deep New Orleans and Cuba connections, whose ire the Kennedy administration managed to earn.

C. The Mafia
1. World War II, the OSS, and Lucky Luciano

The deep connection between organized crime — the Mafia or Cosa Nostra — and American intelligence agencies goes back to World War Two, and to the fact that under Benito Mussolini's Fascist regime in Italy, the crime syndicates of Sicily were virtually shut down, being driven into hiding by Mussolini's secret police as he made good on his promise to

---

[78] Ibid, p. 152.
[79] Ibid, p. 155.

end organized crime. When Italy entered the war as an Axis power, American military officers contacted Lucky Luciano, celebrated crime lord in New York, to assist the war effort by reviving the Sicily base of the syndicate. This Luciano was only too happy to do, and he coordinated these activities from his jail cell while serving a prison sentence.[80]

By the time American and British troops invaded Sicily in 1943, local Mafiosi assisted the Allied troops by disclosing German positions and routes through German minefields.[81] As a reward for his "services rendered" during the war even though he was in prison, Luciano was pardoned, returned to Sicily, where he reorganized the Mafia as an international drug syndicate.[82] Thus began what many believe to be the historical basis for the deep connections between intelligence agencies and the international narcotics trade.[83]

2. Giancana and Marcello

The relationship continued, as we have seen, well after the war, as the Mafia's contacts within Castro's Cuba were considered by the CIA as a means of assassinating the Cuban leader as a component of the Bay of Pigs invasion, and it is disclosed by an effort of President Kennedy's justice department, under the direction of his younger brother, Attorney General Robert Kennedy, to prosecute mob boss Sam Giancana. Robert Kennedy soon discovered that Giancana had powerful allies, namely, the CIA, which was trying to intercede on Giancana's behalf. Investigating further, the Attorney General discovered the reason: The CIA and Mafia were in league in a scheme to assassinate Castro, and Giancana was crucial to the plot.[84] Once again, by leaning on a well-known mobster, the Kennedy Administration had managed to earn the ire of two powerful groups, this time, of the CIA and the Mafia.

To make matters very much worse, Attorney General Robert Kennedy, on his personal orders, had New Orleans mobster Carlos Marcello unceremoniously deported to Guatemala in the spring of 1961

---

[80] Jim Marrs, *Crossfire*, pp. 161-163.

[81] Ibid, p. 163.

[82] Ibid.

[83] The relationship is not as difficult to understand as might initially be perceived, for drug money provides a potentially rich and lucrative source of off-the-books funding for "black projects," covert operations, and "secret research."

[84] Jim Marrs, *Crossfire*, p. 142.

32

when he showed up to the office of the Immigration and Naturalization Service in New Orleans for his quarterly report as an alien.[85] Eventually Marcello made his way back into the United States, where a meeting was held at Marcello's estate outside of New Orleans in September of 1962. According to Edward Becker who witnessed the meeting and later testified to the House Select Committee on Assassinations, Marcello compared the President and his brother, the Attorney General, as the head and tail of a dog, "cut off the head and the dog will die, tail and all. The analogy was clear — with John Kennedy out of the way, Bobby Kennedy and his war on crime would come to an end."[86] Marcello, according to Becker, "even had a plan. Marcello said he would use a 'nut' for the job, someone who could be manipulated so that the killing could not be traced back to him."[87]

It is with Marcello, therefore, that we have the first clear indicators of Mafia involvement in, and planning for, the assassination. Moreover, it is through Marcello that a number of other connections to the assassination may be traced.

> The House Select Committee on Assassinations determined that there were many connections between Marcello and the JFK assassination — Marcello's associate in Dallas, Joe Civello, was close with Jack Ruby; a Marcello employee, David Ferrie, was first Lee Harvey Oswald's Civil Air Patrol leader and said to have been in contact with Oswald during the summer of 1963; and Oswald's uncle, Charles "Dutz" Murret, was acquainted with Marcello's personal driver as well as other associates of Marcello.[88]

David Ferrie was, of course, one of the principal focuses of New Orleans District Attorney Jim Garrison's investigation of the assassination, and we will encounter him again, and through him, even more bizarre connections.

3. Lansky and Batista, Trafficante and Castro

The Cuban dictator overthrown by Fidel Castro's revolution in 1959, Fulgencio Batista, had run the country since 1952 when he seized power in a bloodless military coup, after being ousted in an election in 1944.

---

[85] Ibid, p. 165.
[86] Ibid.
[87] Ibid.
[88] Jim Marrs, *Crossfire,* pp. 165-166.

The person financing this coup d'état was allegedly none other than mobster Meyer Lansky. With Batista in power, casino licensing concessions were obtained for the mob, which soon was building and opening casino after casino in the island nation. Cuba became, along with Las Vegas, a gambling capital, with a booming economy.[89] Lansky was not the only mobster involved in the mob's Cuban gambling operations, for the undisputed Mafia master of Cuban gambling was Santos Trafficante, Jr. Trafficante held this position since Lansky, a Jew, could not be "considered an official member of the Mafia-dominated American crime syndicate."[90] When Fidel Castro entered Havana on New Year's Day, 1959, Batista and Lansky fled, and Lansky's brother, along with Trafficante, were jailed by Castro,[91] who by 1960 had shut down all Mafia gambling operations in Cuba, costing the mob millions of dollars in lost revenue, and giving them a reason to become involved in CIA plots to overthrow the regime.

The jailing of mobsters by Castro was particularly ironic in Trafficante's case, for the Mafia had decided, in an effort to come out on top regardless of whether Batista or Castro emerged victorious in the struggle, to supply arms to both parties. Handling the Mafia's gun running to Castro was Trafficante's associate Norman Rothman, who actually managed one of Trafficante's casinos in Havana.[92]

4. Hoover, Johnson and the Mob: Some Brief Preliminaries

Squatting like the proverbial political toad in the middle of all of this mob activity was Lyndon Baines Johnson, Senate Majority leader in 1959, vice-presidential candidate in 1960, and Vice-President in 1961.

Johnson, throughout these "career moves," was a very close friend of FBI director J. Edgar Hoover, and both men had their own peculiar ties to the Mafia. Assassination researcher David E. Scheim, notes that Hoover, while

ignoring the Mob in his official capacity... was less exclusive in his personal relationships. He often stayed for free at the Las Vegas hotels of construction tycoon Del E. Webb, whose holdings were permeated with organized crime entanglements. Hoover and Webb also met frequently on vacations in Del Mar, California. During Hoover's annual

---

[89] Ibid, p. 168.
[90] Ibid.
[91] Ibid, p. 169.
[92] Jim Marrs, *Crossfire*, p. 391.

trips to that city's luxurious Del Charro Motel, his bill was paid by its owner, Clint Murchison, Jr.[93]

Murchison was a Texas oil tycoon, with deep connections to the Teamsters Union boss, Jimmy Hoffa. He was also a major financial contributor to Lyndon Johnson, and was involved with Johnson's aide, Bobby Baker, another figure with connections to organized crime.[94] More will be said on the Bobby Baker affair in due course, but for now, our attention must remain focused on Hoover.

Hoover's connections and associations with the Mafia went much deeper, however, for he was known to take frequent trips to Manhattan where he would meet with New York City crime boss Frank Costello in Central Park.[95] Notes Scheim: "The impropriety was glaring - the FBI chief meeting the top Mafia chieftan, impeding efforts to fight the Mob, and resisting a proper investigation of the Mob's suggested assassination of a president."[96]

The observation is not without some merit, for on November 29, 1963, a scant week after President Kennedy's murder, Hoover and the new president, Johnson, discussed the necessity of forestalling any independent Congressional or Texas state investigations, and convincing the public of the FBI's case that Oswald was the lone assassin. That same day, Johnson issued an executive order creating his "blue ribbon" panel, the Warren Commission, to investigate the assassination.[97] In other words, after only a week of investigation by the FBI, the conclusion that Oswald acted alone was already drawn months before the Commission issued its report to the same effect, and ignoring the evidence in its own twenty-six non-indexed volumes that clearly indicated a deeper conspiracy was at work! With that foregone conclusion, no investigation of the Mafia, and therefore, of Hoover's and Johnson's potential involvement in or foreknowledge of the assassination would proceed.

Indeed, Johnson himself was no stranger to corruption and organized crime contacts, for it is a well-known fact that he received $500,000 in payoffs from Marcello associate Jack Halfen, a ring leader of a Houston,

---

[93] David E. Scheim, *Contract on America: The Mafia Murder of President John F. Kennedy* (New York: Zebra Books, Kensington Publishing Group, 1988), p. 244.
[94] Ibid.
[95] Ibid, p. 245.
[96] David E. Scheim, *Contract on America*, p. 245.
[97] Ibid, p. 246.

Texas bookmaking ring.[98] While this is not yet the place to discuss in detail the scandal surrounding Lyndon Johnson's aide Bobby Baker and its own deep connections to organized crime, it should be noted that Johnson's close associate, the lawyer Abe Fortas, who initially represented Baker, was replaced by Edward Bennett Williams, a lawyer with long experience representing such clients as Frank Costello, Teamster boss Jimmy Hoffa, and Chicago mob chief Sam Giancana.[99] And Fortas? He became, at Johnson's insistence, a coordinator between the FBI, the Justice Department, and the Texas Attorney General's office during the Warren Commission's investigation![100] Fortas was subsequently nominated to be a Supreme Court justice by Johnson, and then withdrawn when public scrutiny again brought Johnson's whole relationship to Bobby Baker and organized crime again into the spotlight.

D. The CIA, FBI, ONI, NASA and the Secret Service: Oswald Again
1. Oswald, the CIA, ONI, and FBI

Once again, the alleged assassin in the Kennedy murder is central figure connecting the possible, if not probable, involvement of numerous government agencies at some level in the assassination. Veteran conspiracy and assassination researcher Jim Marrs outlines the solid case that he was indeed such an operative. The question is, *was* Oswald in fact a spy, a covert agent?

> After reviewing all available evidence, the answer to the above question seems to be a resounding "yes."
> The following is a quick look at some of the evidence pointing to Oswald's involvement with spy work:
>
> - His childhood — a bright loner who read a wide range of books and was drawn to unpopular ideas, attracted by spy stories (The TV show "I Led Three lives" and Ian Fleming's James Bond novels were among his favorites) — perfectly fits the profile of persons most desired for intelligence work.
> - Oswald's Marine career is checkered with inconsistencies and unexplained events that suggest secret intelligence training.
> - His assignment to Atsugi base in Japan, which housed a large CIA facility.

---

[98] Ibid, p. 247.
[99] Ibid, p. 250.
[100] Ibid, p. 251.

- Oswald's incredible ability with the Russian language. Several Russians, including his wife, said he spoke like a native, yet this high-school dropout reportedly taught himself Russian from books.
- The fact that several persons — including a former CIA paymaster, Oswald's Marine roommate, and fellow Marine Gerry Patrick Hemming — have suggested that Oswald worked for U.S. intelligence.
- The manner in which Oswald traveled so easily in and out of Russia as well as the unaccounted-for funds he used suggests intelligence guidance.
- The ability of this American "defector" to leave the Soviet Union with his Russian-born wife at a time when most Russians were being denied exit permits.
- The ease with which this would-be defector obtained passports both in 1959 and 1963.
- The fact that Oswald wrote a lengthy report on his activities in Russia and, later, made a detailed report to the FBI concerning his Fair Play for Cuba activities in New Orleans.
- Oswald's notebook contained the word "microdots," a common spy technique of photographically reducing information to a small dot.
- Oswald's nonbinding "defection" to Russia fit perfectly the profile of an Office of Naval Intelligence program to infiltrate American servicemen into the Soviet Union during the late 1950s.
- One of Oswald's closest contacts, George DeMohrenschildt, was himself an intelligence operative, first for the Nazis and later for the CIA.[101]

For the moment we must forego comment on the crucial figure of Oswald's Dallas associate George DeMohrenschildt, to point out the obvious connections of Oswald to the FBI and the CIA, and the possible connection to the ONI. In the case of the FBI the connection is particularly striking, since Oswald's ostensible pro-Marxist Cuban activities in the Fair Play for Cuba Committee in New Orleans were the subject of a written FBI report, making it highly likely that he was some sort of covert informant for Hoover's agency.

There are other indications that Oswald's connection to the FBI and ONI was more than merely casual. For example, the *circumstances* surrounding his activities for the Fair Play for Cuba Committee are more than odd, to say the least. Arrested and jailed for the minor infraction of disturbing the peace while distributing leaflets for the Committee, Oswald immediately requested to see an FBI agent! The meeting

---

[101] Jim Marrs, *Crossfire,* pp. 189-190.

occurred on August 10, 1963, the day after his arrest, a Saturday. This, notes Jim Marrs, hardly seems the time "for a quick FBI response to the request of a police prisoner jailed for a minor infraction. Yet Special Agent John Quigley soon arrived at the New Orleans police station and met with Oswald for an hour and a half."[102]

The peculiarities between Oswald and the FBI only grow more acute when one examines his contacts in Dallas. In fact, once Oswald arrives in Dallas, the activities and connections between him and the FBI become downright *bizarre*. During the Warren Commission investigations, for example, many Dallas FBI agents swore that Oswald had never been any sort of FBI informant. Yet, Special Agent James Hosty, assigned to the FBI's Dallas field office, and who was given the task to monitor the Oswalds, had his name, address, telephone number, car license number in Oswald's own personal notebook. This fact was omitted, perhaps conveniently, in an FBI report to the Warren Commission. Hoover explained this away in testimony before the Commission by stating that it was not unusual for agents to leave their contact information with people they had been assigned to investigate.[103] Hosty at first confirmed, then later denied, that the FBI knew Oswald while the latter was in Dallas, a strange statement to make, since chief of the FBI field office in Dallas demanded that the Dallas police allow agent Hosty to question Oswald while he was in their custody![104] Oswald himself, approximately two weeks prior to the assassination for which he would be blamed, walked into the Dallas FBI field office and told the receptionist he wanted to see agent Hosty. When informed that he was not available, Oswald wrote a note for the receptionist to give to him. Hosty in turn later mentioned that he had been ordered not to mention this note from Oswald, the man he first, then later denied, knowing.[105]

Add to all this yet another incredibly ironic fact, for on January 22, 1964, the attorney general for the state of Texas, Waggoner Carr, contacted the Warren Commission to inform them that Oswald had been on the FBI's payroll as informant number S-179 for a salary of $200 per month. According to Carr, the *source* of this information was none other than former FBI agent and Dallas District Attorney Henry Wade, the very man who, had Oswald lived to go to trial, would have tried him, and who was seen on television sets all over the nation, after the

---

[102] Ibid, pp. 226-227.
[103] Ibid, p. 231.
[104] Jim Marrs, *Crossfire,* p. 233.
[105] Ibid.

apprehension of Oswald by the Dallas police, announcing that he was certain of Oswald's guilt![106] Quips Marrs, "If Oswald was working for the FBI, it could explain many things."[107]

As noted previously in Jim Marr's review of the reasons to suspect that Oswald was a covert operative, there was a program by the Office of Naval Intelligence (ONI) to try to infiltrate American military personnel into the Eastern Bloc as agents. While no definitive documentary proof of this has ever been forthcoming, oddly enough, the FBI *did* receive files on Oswald from the ONI.[108]

The fact that both Oswald, and New Orleans private detective and former FBI agent Guy Bannister, both worked out of the offices of the building at Camp and Lafayette streets in New Orleans is also significant. But is there any more direct evidence that the two men actually knew each other?

There is, and it comes from Bannister himself.

Bannister, who conveniently died of a heart attack in 1964 before he could be questioned about his contact with Oswald, definitely knew Oswald, for the latter was seen by some of Bannister's employees handing out the Fair Play for Cuba leaflets. The employees brought it to Bannister's attention. According to his secretary Delphine Roberts, Bannister "simply laughed, and... told his secretary... 'Don't worry about him... He's with us. He's associated with the office.'"[109]

[handwritten note: Bennister conveniently dies of a heart attack!]

---

[106] Marrs, *Crossfire,* p. 231.
[107] Ibid, p. 232.
[108] Ibid, p. 225.
[109] Ibid, p. 237.

HANDS OFF CUBA!

Join the Fair Play for Cuba Committee

NEW ORLEANS CHARTER
MEMBER BRANCH

Free Literature, Lectures

LOCATION:

L. H. OSWALD

EVERYONE WELCOME!

*The Fair Play for Cuba Committee Leaflets Oswald handed out in New Orleans. Note the rubber stamp of Oswald's name and the **absence** of a location for the group*

Oswald handing out Fair Play for Cuba Committee leaflets in New Orleans

2. The FBI, the Secret Service, Hoover, and Johnson

Jim Marrs aptly observes that anyone with an interest in the conspiracy surrounding President Kennedy's assassination "Must take a long hard look at the FBI and the Secret Service. The former — as we now know — monopolized the investigation of the tragedy while the latter failed to prevent it."[110] Indeed, as we shall see the Secret Service plays a crucial role, if not in the conspiracy to plan and execute the murder itself, then at the least in the conspiracy to cover-up what had actually happened. As we shall see in the coming chapters, the Secret Service initially had control over the most crucial pieces of evidence, including the President's body.

As for the FBI, there are direct links between the two men who had the most hatred for the Kennedys: J. Edgar Hoover[111] and Lyndon Baines Johnson. The two were neighbors in Washington, D.C., and often dined privately together.[112] This relationship itself is a deep clue into the nature of the roles played by each man, and the agencies they controlled, for Hoover could manipulate the post-assassination investigation, which he completely controlled, via the FBI, and Johnson, as the new President, had the power to control the military and to create the Commission that would act as the mouthpiece for Hoover's investigation![113] It is equally plausible that Hoover via his vast network of agents, including the strong indications that Oswald had *some* sort of operative status with the FBI, "caused it to happen simply by not preventing it."[114]

3. The CIA and "Murder Incorporated"

But what about Oswald and the CIA? Was there any connection between him and the agency, beyond the already discussed connection of Oswald to the CIA's top Secret U-2 base at Atsugi airbase in Japan where he served in the Marine Corps? During the time of the Warren Commission hearings, the senior CIA official Richard Helms stated that the CIA had never had nor contemplated *any* relationship with

---

[110] Ibid., p. 211.
[111] Ibid., pp. 221-22.
[112] Ibid., p. 223.
[113] Ibid., p. 251.
[114] Ibid., p. 240.

41

Oswald.[115] Yet, in 1976 a CIA document was declassified. According to Jim Marrs, "this document, written by an unidentified CIA officer three days after Kennedy's assassination, states 'we showed intelligence interest' in Oswald and 'discussed... the laying on of interviews.'"[116] But this is by no means all that finally emerged from the bowels of the agency. In 1977 after several Freedom of Information Act requests by various assassination researchers, a crucial document — a "201 File" on Oswald — was finally released by the agency. In effect, a 201 file is a *personnel* file, indicating that someone is "on the payroll."

The CIA, of course, has explained away the existence of this file as simply indicating that the agency had some sort of intelligence or counter-intelligence interest in Oswald, in clear contradiction to Helms' earlier statements to the Warren Commission.[117] But the former executive assistant to the CIA's deputy director, Victor Marchetti, left no doubt on the matter: "'Basically, if Oswald had a '201 ' file, he was an agent.'"[118] In the light of all the previous discussion concerning Oswald's "defection" to the Soviet Union and his subsequent "re-defection" to the U.S.A., there seems little reason *not* to conclude that Oswald was a deeply covert operative at least for the CIA, if not also an informant for the FBI.

a. Ruby's Bizarre Behavior: A Speculation

There is yet another bizarre aspect of the assassination that points to possible CIA involvement in its actual execution, and that is Jack Ruby's very *odd* behavior during his murder of Oswald on national television, and then immediately *after* it. As is well known, the CIA had several mind-control black projects underway during the 1950s and early 1960s under various code names, the most famous being MKULTRA. While the goals of these programs were many and varied, at least one of them was to create the perfect "Manchurian Candidate," a programmable assassin who could be ordered to carry out executions, and to exhibit such bizarre behavior that he could be written off as a "lone nut."[119]

---

[115] Jim Marrs, *Crossfire*, p. 191.
[116] Ibid.
[117] Ibid, p. 192.
[118] Ibid. For a thorough discussion of Oswald's "201" file, see John Newman, *Oswald and the CIA*, pp. 47-52, 168-198.
[119] For a further discussion of such mind control techniques and technologies and their implications for historical interpretation, see my *Genes,*

42

In this case, attention must be focused on Jack Ruby's behavior both during and immediately after his murder of Lee Harvey Oswald on Sunday, November 24, 1963 on national television. The scene is unforgettable to all who have seen it, and I, again, will never forget it. Oswald is ushered into the basement of the Dallas police garage by Dallas police detectives. They stand to either side of him, but there are no policemen in front of him.

A car horn can be heard honking in the background, as if to give a signal.

Jack Ruby steps forward and says loudly, "Oswald!"

He then sticks his pistol in Oswald's chest, and pulls the trigger as Dallas police detective Leavelle looks on in anger and shock. A loud report is heard, followed instantly by a moan from Oswald.

Jack Ruby murdering Oswald on national television. Ruby is the man in the hat and dark suit and fedora, right of center in the picture. Ruby's pistol is visible in his right hand

---

Giants, Monsters and Men (Port Townsend, Washington: Feral House, 2011), ch. 3.

A Coalescence of Interests

At this juncture, Ruby's behavior is straight out of the celebrated movie about programmed assassins, *The Manchurian Candidate:*

> Oswald was pushed to the floor by Leavelle while (officer) Graves grabbed Ruby. Graves told researcher Edward Oxford:
> "By the time Ruby got that shot off, why I had him down. His hand was still flexing. I was saying to him, 'Turn it loose! Turn it loose!' I pried his finger off the trigger. He was still trying to work it. Empty the gun into Oswald, I expect, if he could."[120]

At that point, Ruby was taken from the basement to the very cell Oswald had just vacated. Once there, "Ruby asked his captors: 'What happened?' From that point on Ruby displayed an odd inability to recall the Oswald shooting with any clarity."[121]

But that is not the only strange behavior. It got much worse. Don Archer, one of the Dallas police detectives that placed Ruby in jail noted even more strangeness from Ruby immediately after the murder. Speaking on British television in 1988, Archer stated:

> His behavior to begin with was very hyper. He was sweating profusely. I could see his heart beating. We had stripped him down for security purposes. He asked me for one of my cigarettes. I gave him a cigarette. Finally after about two hours had elapsed... the head of the Secret Service came up and I conferred with him and he told me that Oswald... had died. This should have shocked (Ruby) because it would mean the death penalty. I returned and said, "Jack, it looks like it's going to be the electric chair for you." Instead of being shocked, he became calm, he quit sweating, his heart slowed down. I asked him if he wanted a cigarette and he advised me he didn't smoke. I was just astonished at this complete difference of behavior from what I had expected. I would say his life had depended on him getting Oswald.[122]

Ruby's behavior is that of a man either under duress and orders to carry out a specific assignment — the elimination of Oswald — or possibly that of a man who had been somehow programmed to carry out the murder.

[120] Jim Marrs, *Crossfire*, p. 422.
[121] Ibid, p. 423.
[122] Jim Marrs, *Crossfire*, pp. 423-424.

44

Lest this possibility seem unlikely, let it be recalled that Ruby was intimately involved in the Mafia gun running operations to Cuba, and that means, in turn, was somehow connected to the CIA.[123]

b. The French Connection and Permindex

There is yet another CIA-Mafia connection to the assassination, a connection with its own deeper, murkier significance. In 1979 the House Select Committee on Assassinations came to the conclusion that at least one gunman had indeed fired on the President from somewhere on the Grassy Knoll, and hence, the Committee concluded — contra the Warren Report — that a conspiracy existed to murder the President. The Committee concluded that a second possible gunman was also involved, and settled on what at first glance may seem an unlikely possibility.

The possibility was suggested by a CIA document numbered 632-796, released in 1977, prior to the Select Committee hearings.[124] It is dated April 1, 1964 and has the handwritten title at the top, "Jean Soutre's Expulsion from the U.S."[125] No more than half a page long, the document states the following:

> 8. Jean SOUTRE aka Michel Roux aka Michael Mertz — On March 5, (1964) the FBI advised that the French had (withheld) the Legal Attache in Paris and also the (withheld) had queried the Bureau in New York City concerning subject, stating that he had been expelled from the U.S. at Fort Worth or Dallas 18 hours after the assassination. He was in Fort Worth on the morning of 22 November and in Dallas in the afternoon. The French believe that he was expelled to either Mexico or Canada. In January he received mail from a dentist named Alderson... *Subject is believed to be identical with a Captain who is a deserter from the French Army and an activist in the OAS...* The French are concerned because of DeGaulle's planned visit to Mexico. They would like to know the reason for his expulsion from the U.S. and his destination. Bureau files are negative and they are checking in Texas and with the (Immigration and Naturalization Service)...[126]

---

[123] See Peter Dale Scott's thorough review of Ruby's deep connections both to the Mafia and as a government informer in *Deep Politics and the Death of JFK* (Berkeley: University of California Press, 1993), pp. 127-208.

[124] Ibid, p. 202.

[125] Jim Marrs, *Crossfire,* p. 203.

[126] Ibid, emphasis added.

When the dentist Alderson was contacted by the FBI, he informed them that Soutre was a member of the right wing para-military French underground movement in Algiers, the OAS.[127] Additionally, Soutre's alias, Michael Mertz, appears again in connection with the OAS, or L'Organisation de l'Armee Secrete, the right-wing French resistance determined to kill President DeGaulle and maintain French control over Algeria, only this time Mertz is said to have been an operative who infiltrated the group, assisting in breaking up several bomb plots against DeGaulle.[128] Thus there is an ambiguity concerning Soutre/Mertz. On the one hand, he was either a French military deserter whose membership or connections with the OAS were genuine, or he was an operative assigned to infiltrate the group.

It is, however, the OAS *itself* that interests us here, for this organization had shadowy ties not only with the corporation said to be the very "Murder Incorporated" that was a front for the CIA and various post-war Fascist and Nazi groups, but also is alleged to have *direct* ties with those groups. We will encounter that corporation — Permindex — subsequently when we explore the most bizarre group connected with the assassination. For now, there is yet *another* bizarre connection of a Federal agency to Oswald.

4. Coffee Cups and Space Capsules:
The Reilly Coffee Company and NASA

Adrian Thomas Alba, the owner of the Crescent City Garage where Oswald was seen speaking to FBI agents, stated that he met Oswald shortly after the latter had lost his job at the Riley Coffee Company in New Orleans allegedly for "malingering." Oswald seemed unperturbed, and, according to Alba, stated he soon expected to be working at the NASA plant near New Orleans. Oswald reportedly stated "I have found my pot of gold at the end of the rainbow."[129] If the idea of coffee company employees subsequently finding work with the space agency sounds implausible, think again, for

> ...oddly enough, five Reilly Coffee employees, all of whom were in contact with Oswald, did join the NASA facility shortly after Oswald's departure. Former New Orleans district attorney Jim Garrison came

---

[127] Ibid, pp. 203-204.
[128] Ibid, p. 204.
[129] Jim Marrs, *Crossfire*, p. 230.

across these intriguing employment shifts during his ill-fated JFK assassination probe. Oswald left the coffee company on July 19, 1963, just a few weeks before he began his public show of handing out "Fair Play for Cuba Committee) material. According to Garrison, Alfred Claude, the man who hired Oswald at Reilly, went to work for Chrysler Aerospace Division located at NASA's New Orleans facility. Emmett Barbee, Oswald's immediate superior at Reilly, followed Claude to the NASA center in a few days. And within weeks they were joined by John D. Branyon and Dante Marachini, both of whom worked with Oswald. Branyon and Marachini also began aerospace careers at the New Orleans NASA center. Marachini, who had gone to work for Reilly the same day as Oswald, also was a friend of CIA-Mafia agent David Ferrie.

To compound the oddities, Garrison found that two of Ferrie's friends also went to work for the NASA center about this same time. James Lewallen, a friend of Ferrie who lived in the same apartment house as Marachini, went to work for Boeing, located in the NASA complex. Melvin Coffee, who had accompanied Ferrie on his strange Texas odyssey the night of the assassination, was hired by NASA at Cape Kennedy.[130]

Clearly there is some deep connection between the Reilly Coffee Company, its employees, Oswald, and NASA, connections that will be more fully explored in chapter three.

New Orleans District Attorney Jim Garrison

---

[130] Ibid., p. 230.

A Coalescence of Interests

E. Big Oil
1. Murchison, Hunt, De Mohrenschild, and The Gehlen Organization

Big oil also has its connections to the assassination. We have already had occasion to refer to Lyndon Johnson's connection to Texas oil magnate Clint Murchinson. Oswald, for example, addressed a note to H.L. Hunt, another Texas oil tycoon, dated November 8, 1963.[131] The note read, rather ambiguously, but suggestively, as follows:

Dear Mr. Hunt:

I would like information concerning my position.

I am asking only for information.

I am suggesting that we discuss the matter fully before any steps are taken by me or anyone else.

Lee Harvey Oswald[132]

Just what "position" Oswald would be talking about, or what steps would be taken by him or anyone else is a mystery, but the language is chillingly suggestive within the total context of everything else known about Oswald, including the fact that he had to be murdered in order to insure his silence. As for Hunt, he was, of course, a very close friend of Lyndon Johnson and one of his largest financial contributors.

Hunt clearly had more than a passing interest in the assassination, for Hunt was also a close friend of FBI director J. Edgar Hoover, and employed several former bureau agents in his corporate empire.[133] Hunt also went to the trouble of quickly procuring his own personal copy of the famous Abraham Zapruder film of the assassination shortly after the event. Doubtless he was able to do this as he frequented the same gambling clubs as Erwin Schwartz, Zapruder's business partner, and a

---

[131] Craig I. Zirbel, *The Texas Connection* (New York: Time-Warner, 1991), p. 198.
[132] Ibid, p. 199.
[133] Harrison Edward Livingstone, *Killing Kennedy and the Hoax of the Century* (New York: Carroll and Graf, 1995), p. 116.

48

man with his own known associations to mob boss Carlos Marcello, and Jack Ruby![134]

Hunt's behavior in purchasing a private copy of the Zapruder film was not the only unusual behavior he displayed after the assassination. Hunt was a close friend and financial backer of the right-wing General Edwin A. Walker, another Texan. With Hunt's backing Walker ran for Governor of Texas in 1962 but was defeated by John Connally. Walker had deep connections to the John Birch Society, the Minutemen, and other extremist right wing organizations of the period, and after his defeat was involved in formulating plans "for a preventive strike."[135] Whatever the object of that preventive strike might have been, we do know that H.L. Hunt's son, Nelson Bunker Hunt, was the one responsible for taking out the full page anti-Kennedy advertisement in the *Dallas Morning News* on November 22, 1963, which began with the headline

---

[134] Harrison Edward Livingstone, *Killing Kennedy*, p. 123.

[135] James Hepburn, *Farewell America: The Plot to Kill JFK* (Roseville, CA: Penmarin Books, 2002), p. 242. This book is a reprint and translation of the 1968 French examination of the deep politics *l'affaire Farewell*, a book that many strongly suspect emanated from within the Russian KGB or from French intelligence (q.v. pp. 6-7). It is known that the book did find its way to President DeGaulle's desk. As William Turner states it in his Introduction to the reprint:

"The immense breadth of knowledge contained in the manuscript dictated that Hepburn, whoever he was, was the beneficiary of a network of sources. Although borrowing liberally from published critics of the Warren Report, the manuscript displayed tremendous scope in the ...interlinkage between the large American corporate and banking interests and the ever-growing U.S. intelligence apparatus, and the international petroleum cartels. Brought alive by sinister portraits of CIA spymaster Allen Dulles, the cantankerous Dallas oilman H.L. Hunt, Roy Cohn and a bevy of military brass and Mafia chieftans, it advanced the theory that JFK was killed by an ad hoc amalgam of powerful interests, public and private, which had nightmares about a Kennedy dynasty that might extend through a Teddy presidency. The amalgam was called The Committee. It sponsored and carried out the assassination of JFK at both the supervisory level and the 'gun' level." (p. 7).

The book is thus the first to advance the thesis later argued in more detail by Peter Dale Scott in *Deep Politics and the Death of JFK*, and that I argued previous in my book *The SS Brotherhood of the Bell*. This present book attempts to argue to a putative structure of the deep politics of the conspiracy itself.

"Wanted for Treason," and displaying a profile picture of the President.[136]

The strange behavior of H.L. Hunt does not stop there, for at 12:23 PM on November 22, 1963,

> from his office on the 7th floor of the Mercantile Building, Haroldson Lafayette Hunt watched John Kennedy ride towards Dealey Plaza, where fate awaited him at 12:30. A few minutes later, escorted by six men in two cars, Hunt left the center of Dallas without even stopping by his house.
>
> At that very moment; General Walker was in a plane between New Orleans and Shreveport. He joined Mr. Hunt in one of his secret hideaways across the Mexican border. There they remained for a month, protected by personal guards, under the impassive eyes of the FBI. It was not until Christmas that Hunt, Walker and their party returned to Dallas.[137]

Walker's presence at Hunt's Mexico hideaway increases the likelihood of some involvement on Hunt's part, for it was precisely General Walker that Marina Oswald accused her husband, Lee Harvey, of attempting to assassinate prior to the murder of Kennedy. Given the Oswalds' heavy handling by George DeMorhenschildt, and his own deep connections to the Hunts and Murchisons and the Texas oil community, it would seem that yet another legend was carefully created to implicate Oswald — albeit on the flimsiest of evidence — in the assassination.

One has only to look at President Kennedy's policies regarding "big oil" to discover the potential motivations for such oil men to involve themselves with a conspiracy to murder the president. President Kennedy's assault on the privilege of big oil began with the Kennedy Act which was passed into law on October 16, 1962. This law "removed the distinction between repatriated profits and profits reinvested abroad."[138] This effectively prevented big oil companies from escaping taxation by hiding assets in foreign subsidiaries. Kennedy also proposed to abolish the oil depletion allowance, which allowed oil companies to claim "up to 27.5 percent of as tax exempt."[139] Jim Marrs states that this effectively meant that oil companies stood to "lose nearly $300 million *a year* if the

---

[136] Peter Dale Scott, *Deep Politics and the Death of JFK,* p. 214.
[137] James Hepdurn, *Farewell America*, pp. 243-244.
[138] Jim Marrs, *Crossfire*, p. 277.
[139] Ibid.

depletion allowance was diminished."[140] Hunt was also associated with Oswald's "handler" in Dallas, the shadowy George DeMohrenschildt, himself a member of the closely-knit Dallas oil geology community. Again, we shall defer further commentary on DeMohrenschildt until a later chapter, for he, like Lyndon Johnson, is one of the few people with a known direct connection to the assassination's principals, who had his foot in virtually every shadowy intelligence agency possible.

It was Hunt and his sons, Nelson Bunker and Lamar, that ran their own private intelligence and foreign policy group with its own deep and murky, and very disturbing, connections. According to Peter Dale Scott:

> In the 1960s this group's self-named "Foreign Intelligence Digest" network incorporated some of Kennedy's most outspoken ideological opponents in the United States: men like Frank Capell (the first to break the explosive story of the Kennedy-Marlyn Monroe affair) and Billy James Hargis, the "Christian Crusade" ally of General Edwin Walker's army indoctrination program in West Germany. *German neo-Nazis and Abwehr veterans[141] rounded out this group,* along with a Cuban exile, Jose Ignacio Rasco, whose group (the MDC, or Christian Democratic Movement), funded the Cuban exile guerilla training camp on Lake Pontchartrain in Louisiana....
>
> One avowedly racist member of this network was Austin J. App, chairman of the Federation of American Citizens of German Descent. According to a British book, *the West German intelligence network, the BND,[142] may have funded App's federation, to the tune of $280,000 in 1964.* If so, The Hunt-Willoughby connection can be called transnational, in that it melded assets, and probably funds, from overseas to supplement the Hunt Family's assets.[143]

In other words, the intelligence connections that formed part of the Hunts' network consisted not of rogue elements within the American

---

[140] Ibid, emphasis added.

[141] Abwehr: German military intelligence and counter-intelligence during World War Two, until July of 1944 under the command of the enigmatic Admiral Wilhelm Canaris, later executed for his involvement in the July 1944 bomb plot against Hitler.

[142] BND: *Bundesnachrichtendienst,* or "Federal Security Service," the official name for General Reinhard Gehlen's old military intelligence network during World War Two. Once West Germany became a sovereign nation, this essentially unreconstructed Nazi military intelligence organization became the nucleus of West German intelligence.

[143] Peter Dale Scott, *Deep Politics and the Death of JFK,* p. 213, emphasis added.

CIA, but the ultimate in rogue intelligence organizations, the West German BND, the organizational continuation of Nazi General Reinhard Gehlen's military intelligence group for the Eastern Front during World War Two, *Fremde Heere Ost* (Foreign Armies East).

But this isn't the least of the downright weird associations of the Hunts, Willoughby, and their "Foreign Intelligence Digest" group with post-war Nazis. In my book *Roswell and the Reich*, I noted that many of the Nazi scientists brought to New Mexico to work on America's post-war missile program maintained mysterious contacts with overseas sources, received money in private mail drops, and often stole across the border into Mexico where it appeared that they maintained contact with some Nazi-controlled organization in Latin America.[144] Thus, it is entirely possible that Hunt's Mexican hideaway formed part of a much larger network of private and foreign intelligence interests in Mexico.

Shortly after the assassination, one member of this network of private and German intelligence, Frank Capell, was active in disseminating the idea that the murder was the work of Communists. Such a line well in keeping with the Gehlen Organization's own early attempts to exacerbate East-West tensions by over-estimating Soviet military capabilities and intentions.

But this was not the only shadowy connection to Nazis and deeper agendas.

According to Peter Dale Scott once again,

> Capell was not acting alone: "phase one" stories linking Oswald and Ruby to Communists were circulated by Willoughby's associate *Philip J. Corso,* a veteran of army intelligence who had retired by 1963 to work for the segregationist Senator Strom Thurmond, and Cuban exile Salvador Diaz Verson, a former chief of Cuban military intelligence.
>
> ...In 1963-64 Corso and Willoughby were part of a secret right-wing group, the "Shickshinny Knights of Malta" (so called after their headquarters in Shickshinny, Pennsylvania, to distinguish them from the more famous Roman Catholic Sovereign Military Order of Malta based in Rome). The group provided a home to dissident retired military officers dissatisfied with the CIA's internationalism, many of them... veterans of the old Hunt-MacArthur-Pawley coalition in the early 1950s...
>
> Corso built on this anti-CIA paranoia by telling his friend and fellow Senate staffer James Sourwine, who made sure it was relayed to the

---

[144] See my *Roswell and The Reich: The Nazi Connection* (Adventures Unlimited Press, 2010), pp. 350-358.

FBI, that Oswald was tied to a Communist ring inside the CIA, and was doubling as an informant for the FBI.[145]

This is, of course, the same Lt. Col. Philip J. Corso who wrote the famous — or depending on one's lights, infamous — book about the alleged Roswell UFO crash in 1947, *The Day After Roswell*, and it is this same Lt. Col. Corso who was involved in aspects of Operation Paperclip, bringing Nazi scientists to this country after the war. Additionally, as I pointed out in *Roswell and The Reich*, Corso oddly though suggestively repeatedly points the finger toward Nazi Germany as the origin for the technologies allegedly recovered at Roswell.[146]

By implication, then, one can throw not only Nazis into the groups involved in the assassination, but one can add yet another possible bizarre deep political reason for the assassination: space, and the advanced technologies represented by UFOs.

F. The Military

With the military, there is a clear and unambiguous case to be made for deep involvement in the conspiracy. Normally, Texas military intelligence units would have been used to augment Presidential security during any trips to that state. But according to Colonel Fletcher Prouty, the 112th Military Intelligence Group at Fort Sam Houston, the 4th Army's headquarters, was ordered to "stand down," over the unit commander's strong objections. Such an order, notes Prouty, would have had to have come from a very high level in the Pentagon.[147]

What was the military's motivation? As has been seen, Kennedy earned the ire of the military for his taking of responsibility in the Bay of Pigs invasion, and in his handling of the Cuban Missile Crisis. But there was, possibly, another motivation, for there is clear evidence that Kennedy was planning to scale back, and then withdraw, American involvement in Vietnam. This, of course, made him "soft on Communism." As Jim Marrs aptly observes, "Viewed from the broadest perspective, it now seems possible to state that the opening shots of the full-scare war in Vietnam were in Dallas, Texas."[148]

---

[145] Peter Dale Scott, *Deep Politics and the Death of JFK*, pp. 214-215.
[146] Q.v. the discussion in *Roswell and The Reich*, pp. 231-249.
[147] Fletcher Prouty, *The Secret Team*, p. .
[148] Jim Marrs, *Crossfire*, p. 311.

The military, in other words, had ample motivation to be involved in a conspiracy to murder the President, and, given the "stand down" order to the 112th Military Intelligence Group - an order that makes *no* sense other than in the context of diminishing presidential security as much as possible to allow the operation to proceed — it clearly was involved.

G. The "Banksters"

In May of 1961, only a few months into the Kennedy Administration, a small paperback book by author Stan Opotowsky was published called *The Kennedy Government.* The book consists of eighteen short chapters, most of which are devoted to brief biographies of the men selected by President Kennedy for his cabinet. There, on page sixty-seven in chapter seven, one may read the following ominous words about Kennedy and his Secretary of the Treasury, C. Douglas Dillon:

> The men who are watching Kennedy and Dillon most warily during this administration are the defenders of the Federal Reserve Bank. They fear that the bank's powers to set interest rates will be usurped by the administration so the rates can be juggled for political reasons. Both Kennedy and Dillon *deny any such ambitions.*
>
> There are some in Washington who say that the lean, dour, balding man whom Kennedy selected as Treasury Secretary will deny such ideas when they seem unpopular and then return to them at a more propitious time.[149]

The quiet rumblings from the Kennedy Administration heard by the private international bankers who owned the powerful Federal Reserve Bank exploded like a financial hydrogen bomb in May of 1961 when President Kennedy signed Executive Order 11,110 on June 4, 1963, just five months before the assassination.

Once again, veteran assassination researcher Jim Marrs is worth citing extensively to see just how directly Kennedy took aim at the power of these bankers and their privileged fiefdom of financial power:

> Kennedy apparently reasoned that by returning to the Constitution, which states that only Congress shall coin and regulate money, the soaring national debt could be reduced by not paying interest to the

---

[149] Stan Opotowsky, *The Kennedy Government* (New York: E.P. Dutton-Popular Giants, 1961), p. 67, emphasis added.

54

bankers of the Federal Reserve System, whom print paper money then loan it to the government at interest.

He moved in this area on June 4, 1963, by signing Executive Order 11,110 which called for the issuance of $4,292,893,815 in United States Notes through the U.S. Treasury rather than the traditional Federal Reserve System. That same day, Kennedy signed a bill changing the backing of one- and two-dollar bills from silver to gold, adding strength to the weakened U.S. currency.

Kennedy's comptroller of the currency, James J. Saxon, had been at odds with the powerful Federal Reserve Board for some time, encouraging broader investment and lending powers for banks that were not part of the Federal Reserve System. Saxon also had decided that non-Reserve banks could underwrite state and local general obligation bonds, again weakening the dominant Federal Reserve banks.[150]

What Kennedy's Executive Order effectively did, in other words, was to rob the Federal Reserve and its stockholders of the very thing that gave them their power: their money monopoly over the issuance of the facsimile of money or monetized debt. Some of these United States notes actually made it into circulation (the author remembers spending some of them as a boy), but quickly disappeared as the bankers followed a millennia-old tradition when states attempted to reclaim their sovereign power to issue money debt-free: the bankers simply removed the notes from circulation when they entered their banks, and destroyed them.[151]

These interests thus had more than enough motivation to eliminate Kennedy, and thus, just for good measure, they probably gave the green light to the assassination plot as well, thereby sending a clear message to any of his successors.

And this brings us to the final group, the most bizarre of them all...

H. The Post-War Nazi International

Just about the *last* people one would expect to have any sort of involvement in the Kennedy Assassination are the Nazis. Yet, here as elsewhere, the more one digs, the more surreal the connections become. While we will reserve the review of the more fantastic connections for a

---

[150] Jim Marrs, *Crossfire*, p. 275.

[151] Ibid. For the ancientness of this tactic of dealing with "recalcitrant governments," see my *Babylon's Banksters: The Alchemy of Deep Physics, High Finance, and Ancient Religion* (Port Townsend, Washington: Feral House, 2010), pp. 202-204.

later chapter, there are a number of connections that must be mentioned here. We have already noted the strange connections between the Hunt family's private network and West German intelligence, but a little more historical background to these connections is necessary.

Entry to these connections may be gained by going back to the closing days of World War Two, and to a secret deal negotiated by the then head of the Zurich branch of the OSS, Allen Dulles — later director of the CIA and fired by Kennedy for his part in the Bay of Pigs invasion — and Nazi general Reinhard Gehlen. The practicalities of the deal were also negotiated by American General Edwin L. Sibert.

General Gehlen was the head of the Wehrmacht's *Fremde Heere Ost,* or "Foreign Armies East," that is, he was the head of all of Nazi Germany's considerable military intelligence organization in the Soviet Union and the Eastern Front. His organization is reputed to have had over 4,000 agents operating behind Soviet lines during the war. That organization he planned to turn over, intact, to the Americans *after* the war.

General Gehlen subsequently recalled the terms of this deal in his memoirs:

> I remember the terms of the agreement well:
>
> 1. A clandestine German intelligence organization was to be set up, using the existing potential to continue information gathering in the East just as we had been doing before. The basis for this was our common interest in a defense against communism.
> 2. This German organization was to work not "for" or "under" the Americans, but "jointly with the Americans."
> 3. The organization would operate exclusively under German leadership, which would receive its directives and assignments from the Americans until a new government was established in Germany.
> 4. The organization was to be financed by the Americans with funds which were *not* to be part of the occupation costs, and in return the organization would supply all its intelligence reports to the Americans.
> 5. As soon as a sovereign German government was established, that government should decide whether the organization should continue to function or not, but that until such time the care and control (later referred to as "the trusteeship") of the organization should remain in American hands.

6. Should the organization at any time find itself in a position where American and German interests diverged, it was accepted that the organization would consider the interests of Germany first.[152]

As I noted in *The SS Brotherhood of the Bell,*

> (One) whole department of the American Federal government — indeed, one of its most *sensitive* departments — was being run by agents of the Third Reich in a classic Trojan Horse operation! With the thousands of agents in Gehlen's "Organization," and its extensive network of "émigré exile" groups and fronts, historian Carl Oglseby noted that the Gehlenorg "substantially pre-empted the CIA's civilian character before it was ever born... Thus, whatever the CIA was from the standpoint of law, it remained from the standpoint of *practical intelligence collection a front for a house of Nazi spies.*"[153]

Thus, when President Kennedy attempted to smash the CIA into a thousand pieces in the wake of the Bay of Pigs invasion, one of the fiefdoms of power that his action directly threatened was this deep postwar Nazi Trojan horse operation within and parallel to American intelligence.

Therefore if there *was* a rogue element within American intelligence — and we have seen there *was*, since U-2 flights continued over the Soviet Union in the days prior to the Eisenhower-Khrushchev Paris summit, in spite of President Eisenhower's order that they be suspended — then the Nazi connection must not be ignored, for they, along with their hawkish American counterparts in the Agency, had the most to gain from an increase in tensions between the Soviet Union and the United States.

Indeed, it was Gehlen's organization that performed the first close post-war analysis of Soviet military capabilities and intentions in 1948, at the behest of the CIA. Gehlen's organization vastly and deliberately overestimated those capabilities and intentions and thus the analysis contributed in no small part to the rise of Cold War tensions, and the expansion of American defense spending during the Truman administration to meet *a threat that was largely a creation of Nazis.*

---

[152] General Reinhard Gehlen, *The Service: The Memoirs of General Reinhard Gehlen,* trans. from the German by David Irving (New York: Times Mirror, 1972), p. 122.
[153] Joseph P. Farrell, *The SS Brotherhood of the Bell* (Kempton, Illinois: Adventures Unlimited Press, 2006), p. 77, emphasis added.

This is not yet the place to examine the other deep connections of Nazism with the assassination. Suffice it for the moment to note that the post-war underground Nazi movement had ample reasons, along with its host agency, the CIA, to participate in the conspiracy. Those reasons, as we shall eventually see, run even deeper into the fabric of American society and Eisenhower's "military-industrial complex."

I. Preliminary Conclusions and Methodological Observations

So at this end of this high overview, what do we have?

A return to the template of the introduction will exhibit in summary form what this chapter has shown: that *all* of the groups had sufficient motivation to commit the crime, that all of them were certainly capable of having, or acquiring the means, to commit it, and that all of them, theoretically at least, had the opportunity to do so.

It is when we turn to the *second* level, the framing of Oswald, that the circle narrows, for while all groups certainly would have had the motive to frame him, only those with some sort of *deep* intelligence connections could have framed him in the manner he was and over the prolonged period of his evident intelligence handling.

	Means	*Motive*	*Opportunity*
The Murder Itself	Anti-Castro Cubans The Mafia FBI (Hoover) CIA Big Oil The Military Bankers (Federal Reserve) Nazis	Anti-Castro Cubans The Mafia FBI (Hoover) CIA Big Oil The Military Bankers (Federal Reserve) Nazis	Anti-Castro Cubans The Mafia FBI (Hoover) CIA Big Oil The Military Bankers (Federal Reserve) Nazis
The Framing of Oswald	FBI (Hoover) CIA The Military Nazis	FBI (Hoover) CIA The Military Nazis	FBI (Hoover) CIA The Military Nazis
The Long-term Cover-up			

Note that it is at the more difficult level of the framing of Oswald that the number of potential groups directly and actively involved diminishes considerably, for only a wide-spread intelligence network could conduct Oswald's "defection" to the Soviet Union, facilitate his re-entry into the United States, introduce him into the anti- and pro-Castro Cuban circles, and, as has been seen, there was persistent FBI contact with Oswald. While it may seem implausible to place the Nazis in this list, it should be recalled that General Gehlen's organization had a high number of agents behind the Iron Curtain in Eastern Europe and Russia. and that it was, for all intents and purposes, the on-the-ground human intelligence presence within the Soviet Union that the American CIA ultimately relied upon. Thus, the Gehlenorg forms the most likely basis for continued contact with Oswald while the latter was in the Soviet Union. Since this organization was effectively the operational Soviet desk of the CIA until it was turned over to the West German government in 1956, and since it maintained close liaison with the CIA after that point, it is safe to say that *it is the probable point of contact between Oswald and the CIA if indeed any contact was maintained between the two while Oswald was in Russia.* This would explain not only Oswald's fluency with Russian, but also apparently with German.

There are two facts that now must be mentioned in this regard. It is known that when Oswald was arrested, the FBI found in his address book the names and address of the leader of the American Nazi Party, George Lincoln Rockwell.[154] Additionally, Oswald's Marine buddy, Nelson Delgado, stated for the Warren Commission that he not only heard Oswald speaking Russian, but German as well.[155] As will be seen, there are even deeper connections between Oswald, the FBI, the CIA, and the post-war Nazis via his handler in Dallas, George DeMohrenschildt.

As can be seen from this review and the table, if one constructs a theory of the conspiracy, *all* of the groups surveyed have ample motivations for the assassination, for each was directly threatened by the policies of the Kennedy Administration, and each stood to gain from a coup d'état that would remove it. *Methodologically, therefore, this would imply that, rather than focus on one particular group as having planned and executed the assassination, one should proceed from the assumption that they were all involved at some level, and attempt on the basis of a careful examination of the murder and the ensuing cover-up, to ascertain what functions each of these groups might have fulfilled within the conspiracy, and what level of involvement they occupied in it.* It is at the

---

[154] Sybil Leek and Bert R. Sugar, *The Assassination Chain* (New York: Corwin Books, 1976, p. 171.

[155] Lincoln Lawrence and Kenn Thomas, *Mind Control, Oswald, and JFK: Were We Controlled?* (Kempton, Illinois: Adventures Unlimited Press, 1997), p. 71.

second level that the circle of active players grows narrower. One key to this puzzle lies in the immediate aftermath of the murder, with what happened to the forensic *evidence* in the ensuing cover-up, and who controlled that evidence and what they did with it. That evidence was crucial to framing Oswald. To that we now turn.

2
THE "TWO'S" AND THE "TOO'S":
DISTURBING DATASETS, DOPPELGÄNGERS, DUPLICATES AND DISCREPANCIES

"I unearthed a dramatic schism between the Dallas and Bethesda descriptions of President Kennedy's fatal wound."
David S. Lifton[1]

W e know that there was a conspiracy to assassinate President Kennedy quite simply because of what happened to the primary piece of forensic evidence that testified to it: his body. There are two sets of wounds, the "Dallas" set, observed by the doctors who attempted to save the life of the all-but-dead President at Parkland Hospital, and the set observed by navy doctors during the autopsy at the national naval hospital in Bethesda, Maryland. We also know that there was a conspiracy because there seem to be one too many Oswalds, one too many rifles that he allegedly used to do the deed, and too many, or too few, bullets. We know, too, because the rifle by which Oswald allegedly committed the crime could never have done the deed in the time that the Commission said it was done, nor with the accuracy by which Oswald allegedly did it.[2]

One discerns a pattern even in stating the case in this fashion, namely, that the conspirators, in the aftermath of the actual crime, had to move quickly to alter the forensic evidence, because they had also determined to make Oswald the patsy long before the crime occurred. Of all of the forensic evidence that had to be altered — the rifle(s), the bullets, the president's body, and the unwanted Zapruder film of the whole event — it is the body itself that is the most important, and it is here that one begins to see the emergence of the *roles* that some of the groups (surveyed in the previous chapter) played in the conspiracy. *It is, in short, the alterations done to the president's body that begins to show*

---

[1] David S. Lifton: *Best Evidence: Disguise and Deception in the Assassination of John F. Kennedy* (New York: Carroll and Graf Publishers, 1988), p. 309.
[2] For the best, and earliest, review of the problems posed by Oswald's alleged marksmanship, and the Warren Commission's failed attempts to reproduce it, see Harold Weisberg, *Whitewash: The Report on the Warren Report*, pp. 64-75.

the structural outlines of the conspiracy itself. The case that alterations were in fact made on the body is the case put forward, after years of research of the matter, by David S. Lifton.

A. *Two Caskets, Two (or was that Three?) Ambulances, One Body: The Case of David S. Lifton*

The central piece of evidence in deciphering the crime of President Kennedy's murder is his body, for by careful examination of its wounds, the entry points and exit points of any projectiles could be determined, and hence, the direction from which the shots were fired could also be determined. Since the designated patsy, Oswald, had already been situated in his job at the Texas School Book Depository, it was necessary that all entrance wounds on the body had to come from behind the president. There could be no evidence of shots from the front; if there was, this would indicate more than one shooter, and therefore, a conspiracy.

It was this basic scenario that first drew assassination researcher, David S. Lifton, into the Kennedy assassination mystery, for like many Americans, when he first saw the famous film of Abraham Zapruder of the assassination, the final, fatal "kill" shot clearly showed the president's head literally exploding and being propelled *backward*, rather than *forward*, he drew the only possible conclusion based on the simple physics of the murder: the president had been hit by a fatal shot from the front, not behind, as the Warren Report maintained.

Lifton quickly discovered, however, that the one piece of forensic evidence that convinced the Warren Commission that the fatal shots had come from behind the president on that fateful date was the autopsy report submitted by the doctors at the Bethesda naval hospital, who described frontal *exit* wounds, and not frontal *entrance* wounds. There was a clear contradiction between two different data sets: the Zapruder film, and the autopsy report. The "eye" of Zapruder's camera told one thing, the eyes of the doctors in Bethesda told quite another. Lifton drew a somewhat novel conclusion: *at some place, and at some time, between the commission of the crime itself in Dallas, and the autopsy later that Friday night in Bethesda, the body of the president had been altered.*

Lifton decided that the only way to determine "when" and "where" was to examine the whole description of the president's body in Dallas and Bethesda, to review the details of its transmission from Texas to Maryland, in order to determine the circumstances under which it might have been altered, and who possessed the body at the time of its possible alteration. Thus began a long and ghoulish journey into the structure of the conspiracy.

Doing so, he immediately noticed a wide divergence between the two:

> The Dallas doctors described the large hole in the President's head as being located at the right rear, in the "occipital-parietal area." The Bethesda autopsy report noted: "a large irregular defect (hole)... involving chiefly the parietal bone but extending somewhat into the temporal and occipital regions." Both groups of doctors agreed that the large hole was the exit for a missile. Some Dallas doctors provided graphic descriptions of this wound: Dr. Robert McClelland testified:
>
> "As I took the position at the head of the table... I was in such a position that I could very closely examine the head wound, and I noted that the right posterior portion of the skull had been extremely blasted. It had been shattered, apparently, by the force of the shot.... This sprung open the bones... in such a way that you could actually look down into the skull cavity itself and see that probably a third or so, at least, of the brain tissue, posterior cerebral tissue and some of the cerebellar tissue had been blasted out."
>
> This hole was first seen by Secret Service Agent Clinton Hill, after he climbed aboard the Presidential limousine just after the fatal shot struck. A large piece of skull had been blasted away. Hill described the damage:
>
> "The right rear bottom of his head was missing. It was lying in the rear seat of the car. His brain was exposed."
>
> In addition to this large wound of exit, the Bethesda doctors reported that beneath it was a small hole, a bullet entrance wound, approximately a half inch by a quarter inch in size, located "approximately 2.5 cm (1 inch) laterally to the right and slightly above the external occipital protruberence. (sic)"
>
> *None of the Dallas doctors observed such a wound.* Yet it was crucial — the basis for the most fundamental conclusion of the Warren Commission: that the fatal shot struck from behind.[3]

In fact, one will note that the Dallas doctors' description is that of an exit wound to the right rear of the president's head, indicating not a shot from behind (thereby ruling out Oswald in the School Book Depository), but from the front. Additionally, it should be noted that the testimony of the Dallas doctors "was generated immediately. There was no opportunity to tailor it to fit some preconceived notion or strategy."[4]

---

[3] David S. Lifton, *Best Evidence*, p. 39, emphasis added.
[4] Ibid, p. 41.

bullet to the neck! (handwritten margin note)

There was another discrepancy. In Dallas, the doctors working on the President in an emergency room of Parkland Hospital noticed a small puncture wound at the base of the front of the President's neck. They all assumed it was an entrance wound. Desperately trying to save the President, they performed a tracheotomy using the wound, and inserted a breathing tube. The incision, and the wound itself, left clean lines. But by the time the body had reached Bethesda naval hospital, that wound had now become a long, saw-toothed tear, rather than the clean incision of a tracheotomy.[5] Deeper comparisons between the Dallas and Bethesda doctors reveals even more differences, differences that could almost be described as two wholly conflicting datasets.

One major conflict between the two datasets concerns not only the size but the positioning of the major head wound to the President. At Bethesda, navy doctor Commander Boswell described a rectangular shaped wound directly on the back center of the head and extending to the top, approximately 3.9 by 6.7 inches. But the Dallas doctors described a wound to the *right* rear of the head of approximately 2 ½ inches in diameter.[6] Secret Service Agent William Greer, who was present at the Bethesda autopsy, stated that the President's head looked "like a harboiled egg, with the top sliced off."[7] None of the Dallas doctors described this feature of the mortal head wound. Secret Service Agent Clinton Hill, who had scrambled onto the back of the limousine moments after the fatal shot struck the President, stated in his Warren Commission testimony in 1964: "the *right rear* of his head was missing. it was lying in the rear of the car. His brain was exposed."[8] There is no mention in Dallas of the top of the President's skull being missing.[9]

Finally, one of the Bethesda autopsy doctors, Commander Hume, described a skull hole devoid of any scalp or bone. But at Dallas, Dr. McClelland described the right rear wound as having bone protruding through the scalp, as if blasted through it, along with a large flap of scalp.[10]

---

[5] David S. Lifton, *Best Evidence*, pp. 274-275.
[6] Ibid, pp. 310-311.
[7] Ibid, p. 310.
[8] Ibid, p. 312, emphasis added.
[9] See Lifton's discussion on p. 320.
[10] Ibid, p. 321.

1. The Dallas Doctors' Descriptions of the President's Wounds

There is absolutely no doubt, no hesitation, no basis to maintain anything else other than that the Dallas doctors described entry wounds on the president that indicated shots being fired from the front of the president, just as there is absolutely no doubt, no hesitation, and no basis to maintain anything else than that they described exit wounds on the back of his skull.

That said, there are slight differences of description among the various doctors at Parkland Hospital. There are essentially three slightly different patterns of wounds described by the Dallas doctors. The neurosurgeon who prepared the clinical summary of the President and who officially pronounced Kennedy dead maintained that the Parkland physicians saw only two wounds, the small one at the front of the throat and the large wound at the right rear of the president's head. Lifton notes that at that time none of the Dallas doctors had, of course, seen the Zapruder film and had deduced that the wounds were an entrance and exit wound from the same bullet, rather than two separate wounds caused by two separate projectiles.[11] That led Lifton to ask:

> If they were correct in their opinion that a bullet exited from the right rear of the head, but wrong in associating that trajectory with the throat wound, then there must have been another entrance wound somewhere on the head. But where?
> The answer seemed to be either the right or left temple.[12]

This led to the second pattern of wounds described by the doctors, and by other witnesses.

For example, Secret Service agent Sam Kinney described seeing the president stuck by a missile on the right side of the head. Agent George Hickey maintains that he heard two shots and saw that the right side of the president's head was struck.[13] Civilian William Eugene Newman, standing on the right side of the limousine with his wife and two small children at the base of the Grassy Knoll, gave an interview for Dallas station WFAA an hour after the murder, and stated that "a gunshot from apparently behind us hit the President in the side of the temple."[14]

---

[11] Ibid, p. 41.
[12] Ibid, p. 43.
[13] David S. Lifton, *Best Evidence*, p. 43.
[14] Ibid.

Marilyn Sitzman, who was standing next to Abraham Zapruder as he was filming the event atop the pedestal on top of the Grassy Knoll, stated that she had seen the President struck between the ear and eye on his right side.[15]

The skeletal debris also formed a component of eyewitness testimony. For example:

> Motorcycle officers B.J. Martin and B.M. Hargis, riding to the *left rear* of the President, both testified they were splattered with debris from the impact of the fatal shot.... Hargis told reporters on November 22 the fatal shot struck "the right side of the head." He told the Commission: "I was splattered with blood and brain, and kind of bloody water."[16]

Texas Highway Patrolman Hurchel Jacks was particularly inconvenient to the conspirators and to the Warren Commission, for he

> provides the only recorded observation in the twenty-six volumes of a right temporal wound by someone who observed the President's body at Parkland Memorial Hospital. Jacks described what he saw when he sprinted to Kennedy's side:
> "...one of the Secret Service agents said he had been hit, put your coat over him. One of the agents removed his suit coat and spread it over the President's body from his chest up. Before the President's body was covered it appeared that the bullet had struck him *above the right ear or near the temple.*"[17]

Hurchel Jacks was so inconvenient to the cover-story that the Warren Commission did not even bother calling him to take his testimony.

Worse yet, the UPI wire service transmitted a story at approximately 1:47 Central Standard Time. The story stated:

> President Kennedy was shot in the right temple. "It was a simple matter of a bullet right through the head," said Dr. George Burkley, White House Medical Officer. Within minutes, NBC anchorman Chet Huntley repeated the statement to a national television audience.[18]

---

[15] Ibid, p. 44.
[16] Ibid, emphasis Lifton's.
[17] Ibid, emphasis Lifton's.
[18] David S. Lifton, *Best Evidence*, p. 45.

[handwritten: Warren Commission joke!]

Once again, the Warren Commission not only failed to ascertain the source of the UPI wire (reporter Merriman Smith, who had arrived mere seconds after the President) nor did it call the White House Medical Officer, Dr. Burkley.[19]

There is a third, and final, pattern of wounds recorded in Dallas, this time by Dr. Robert McClelland. McClelland was the Assistant Professor of Surgery at Southwestern Medical school and was affiliated with Parkland Hospital. He was one of the physicians attending President Kennedy. McClelland is alone and unique, for when he concluded his handwritten report at 4:45 on the Friday afternoon of the assassination, he stated that "The cause of death was due to a massive head and brain injury from a gunshot wound of the left temple." Lifton notes that "Dr. McClelland was the only Dallas doctor to record the existence of a left temple wound in a report dated November 22."[20] *[handwritten: Shot from the front!]*

In spite of all these differences, there is one consistent pattern to the statements of the Dallas doctors at Parkland Hospital and the eye-witnesses closest to the presidential limousine: they "all indicated a shot from the front" had been the fatal shot, not a shot from behind.[21]

Summing all this up, Lifton states the four major areas of conflict between Dallas and Bethesda in the descriptions of the President's head wounds as follows:

> With regard to the "large" wound, the conflict between Dallas and Bethesda consisted of these four elements:
> 1. *Size.* At Dallas, the hole was described as 2 ¾ inches across; the Bethesda autopsy said it was 5 1/8 inches across, and a diagram gave a largest dimension of 17cm (6.7 inches);
> 2. *Location.* The Dallas wound was described by most of the doctors as "occipital" or "occipitoparietal."The Bethesda doctors said the hole was "chiefly parietal" but extended "somewhat" into the occipital region;
> 3. *Scalp.* The Bethesda wound was entirely uncovered. Humes said it was devoid of scalp. At Dallas, the bones sprung outward, protruding up through the scalp;
> 4. *Brain tissue visible.* At Dallas, the cerebellum "protruded through" the wound. At Bethesda, the "major portion" of the right hemisphere of the cerebrum was "clearly visible."[22]

---

[19] Ibid.
[20] David S. Lifton, *Best Evidence*, p. 45.
[21] Ibid, p. 47.
[22] Ibid, p. 327.

This left only three logical possibilities:

1) The doctors in Dallas were correct, and the doctors in Bethesda were either wrong in their observations, or misrepresented what they saw;
2) The doctors in Bethesda were correct, and the doctors in Dallas were incorrect in their observations; or,

3) Both groups of doctors were correct and accurately recorded their observations.[23]

Lifton, following sound methodology, assumes that both sets of physicians have no reason to lie, and that both are competent observers. This leads to the inevitable conclusion that "Their descriptions conflicted because the size and location of the wound had been altered during the time interval that separated the two groups of observations."[24] And *that* meant that someone had already tampered with the evidence of the biggest political crime in American history; the evidence itself had now become corrupted. It had become *politicized.*

2. The Bethesda Autopsy (or Was that Autopsies?)

But was the Bethesda autopsy indeed an accurate reflection of the navy pathologists' observations?

With that question, the plot gets murkier, and the circle of conspirators involved in its planning and cover-up narrows considerably. As early as December 18, 1963, rumors were already floating in the major media — this time in articles in the *Washington Post* and the *New York Times* — that there had been a change in the initial autopsy report and the version finally submitted to the Warren Commission.[25]

Lifton uncovered evidence of precisely that. An FBI report dated December 9, 1963 stated that "Medical examination of the President's body revealed that one of the bullets had entered just below his shoulder to the right of the spinal column at an angle of 45 to 60 degrees downward, that there was *no point of exit, and that the bullet was not in the body.*"[26] In other words, there was no transit of the bullet which was needed to exit the President, and strike Governor Connally, the "magic

---

[23] David S. Lifton, *Best Evidence*, p. 327.
[24] Ibid.
[25] Ibid, p. 80.
[26] Ibid, p. 83, Lifton's emphasis.

bullet" needed to pin the whole responsibility for the assassination on the designated patsy, Oswald. A little over a month later, on January 14, 1964, another FBI report restated the non-transit nature of the shoulder wound: "Medical examination of the President's body had revealed that the bullet which entered his back had penetrated to *a distance of less than a finger length.*"[27]

Indeed, the lead navy doctor on the autopsy team, Commander Humes himself stated "Attempts to probe in the vicinity of this wound were unsuccessful without fear of making a false passage.... We were... unable to take probes and have them satisfactorily fall through any definite path..."[28] That lead Lifton to the radical conclusion that there had been "an earlier, different version of the Bethesda autopsy" than the one submitted to the Warren Commission, which *did* assert a transit of the bullet, back to front.[29] Intriguingly, by the time the FBI had submitted its final Summary Report to the Commission, the non-transiting nature of the wound had been changed to a transiting wound.[30]

There is strong evidence that some sort of pressure *was* put on Commander Humes and the other navy pathologists at Bethesda to change their initial observational notes. In order to see why this is so, one must examine carefully the sequence of events during the weekend of November 22-25, 1963, up to Commander Humes' testimony to the Warren Commission and his submission of the final autopsy report to it on March 16, 1964.

After the autopsy at Bethesda on the evening of the assassination, Friday November 22, 1963, the two FBI agents assigned by Hoover to be present and to record and report their observations. This report, now well-known to assassination researchers as the Sibert-O'Niell report after the two FBI agents, James Sibert and Francis O'Niell, who were present during the Navy autopsy, was written that evening under the title "Autopsy of Body of President John Fitzgerald Kennedy."[31] In *that* report, the FBI agents clearly state that when Dr. Humes attempted to probe the back wound with his finger, the wound did not transit. Humes could touch the end of the wound with his fingertip.[32]

---

[27] Ibid, Lifton's emphasis.
[28] David S. Lifton, *Best Evidence*, p. 82.
[29] Ibid, p. 84.
[30] Ibid, p. 87.
[31] Ibid, p. 102.
[32] Ibid.

But by Sunday, November 24, 1963, when the Navy submits its report to Admiral Burkley at the White House, this non-transiting wound has become a transiting wound. The FBI then submits its Summary Report to the Warren Commission on December 9, 1963, and its Supplemental Report on January 13, 1964. In both these reports, guided by the Sibert-O'Niell report, the wound is non-transiting. But the Navy's transiting wound autopsy report is the report that makes its way from Admiral Burkley at the White House, to the Secret Service, thence to the Warren Commission.[33]

In other words, *sometime between Friday evening, November 22, 1963, and Sunday morning, November 24, 1963, the Navy had changed its finding of a non-transiting wound to a transiting wound.* In this light, it is worth noting what Commander Humes stated in his testimony to the Warren Commission: "In the privacy of my own home, early on the morning of Sunday, November 24th, I made a draft of the report which I later revised, and of which this represents the revision. That draft I personally burned in the fireplace of my recreation room."[34] And what of the photographs and x-rays inevitably taken during any autopsy?

Secret Service agent Robert Kellerman, who had been riding in the front passenger seat of the presidential limousine on the day of the assassination, stated that he took these to Robert Bouck "of the Protective Research Section of the U.S. Secret Service."[35] There the trail went cold...at least, in the days of the Warren Commission it did. Not being in possession of any x-rays or photographs, the Commission then allowed the dubious precedent — one that would never have been allowed in a court of law — of letting Humes and the Navy doctors to present their testimony using artists' drawings and charts.

One may be permitted to speculate on the possible chain of events that led to the Commander Humes burning his original draft on Sunday morning. The Sibert-O'Niell report was transmitted to FBI headquarters. That report indicated a non-transiting wound, but what was needed was a transiting wound, since the designated patsy had been deliberately placed in the Texas School Book Depository *behind* the President and the kill-zone on Elm Street. What was also needed was a completely shattered

---

[33] David S. Lifton, *Best Evidence*, pp. 152-154. See especially the flow chart on p. 154.

[34] Ibid, p. 157.

[35] Ibid, p. 136.

skull, obscuring the exit wound at the right rear of the head seen by the Dallas doctors.

It takes little imagination to see that Hoover may have transmitted the contents of the Sibert-O'Niell report to his good friend, now the President of the United States, Lyndon Johnson. Johnson, as commander-in-chief, could then have ordered Admiral Burkley to order Commander Humes to change the report to reflect a *transiting* wound, and thus keep the focus on Oswald, rather than on a second gunman, and therefore, on a conspiracy. We shall see later in this chapter, and in the next, that there is clear evidence that such tremendous pressure *was* exerted on the Navy doctors. But as we shall also discover, they managed to slip careful phrases into their final report that made it past the conspirators.

Given the discrepancies between the Dallas and Bethesda descriptions of the wounds, and given the probable exertion of pressure from above on Commander Humes to alter his original draft of the autopsy report, what had happened? Lifton turned once again to the report of FBI agents Sibert and O'Niell. Here it is best to let him recount the horrible realization that gradually dawned on him in his own words:

> I came to page three of the report. The coffin was about to be opened. The autopsy was about to begin. Sibert and O'Niell described the scene.
>
> "The President's body was removed from the casket in which it had been transported and was placed on the autopsy table, at which time the complete body *was wrapped in a sheet and the head area contained an additional wrapping which was saturated with blood.*"
>
> The agents continued: "Following the removal of the wrapping, it was ascertained that the President's clothing had been removed and it was also apparent that a tracheotomy had been performed..." My heart started to pound as I read what came next.
>
> "...it was also apparent that a tracheotomy had been performed **as well as surgery of the head area, namely, in the top of the skull.**"
>
> (...)
>
> I knew exactly what this meant — **this** was the missing piece of the puzzle.
>
> The Dallas doctors had operated only on the throat. No one had touched the President's head — certainly not with a surgical instrument. Yet those words, if true, *meant that some time after the President was pronounced dead in Dallas, but before the coffin arrived in the Bethesda autopsy room, somebody had performed "surgery" on President Kennedy's corpse.*

71

I was exhilarated, terrified. I wanted to vomit.[36]

And if that was what happened, then it is also possible that evidence of more than one assassin in the form of bullets or bullet fragments, were also removed at that time.[37]

This discovery now permits us to see that the circle of groups actively involved in the planning and cover-up of the conspiracy has considerably narrowed. Lifton puts it this way:

Lifton.

> If it were true that surgery had been performed before the autopsy, *then government officials had to be involved, because the President's body was always in official custody.* From the moment of death at Parkland Memorial Hospital until the time of autopsy at Bethesda, the body (and the coffin containing the body) was accompanied by Secret Service agents. No outsider could have access to the body. A deranged individual, taking advantage of a target of opportunity, could take a shot at the president and possibly put a bullet in his body, but only the highest authority could secretly take one out.
>
> ... It was the model of a ghoulish conspiracy.
>
> (...)
>
> ...I had glimpsed the possibility of treason.[38]

3 part. Conspiracy!

At the minimum, Lifton concludes that at least some within the Secret Service had to be involved as active participants in the conspiracy.[39]

Consequently, what had to be brought together in Dallas was a complex conspiracy of a tripartite structure, a structure that required (1) getting the actual assassins into position, (2) getting the patsy into position and planting the incriminating evidence at "the crime scene" in the School Book Depository, and (3) suppressing or falsifying evidence — the body — that testified to the existence of the first two components.[40]

There was another consideration for the conspirators to take into consideration, and that was the President's brother, U.S. Attorney General Robert Kennedy, head of the Justice Department and FBI director J. Edgar Hoover's boss. Robert Kennedy's presence in that position would have made it likely that the Kennedy family would have

---

[36] David S. Lifton, *Best Evidence*, pp. 171-172, boldface emphasis Lifton's, italicized emphasis mine.

[37] Ibid, p. 175.

[38] David S. Lifton, *Best Evidence*, p. 180, emphasis added.

[39] Ibid, p. 370.

[40] Ibid, p. 372.

insisted any Federal autopsy be done at the naval facility, since the President had, of course, been in the U.S. Navy during World War Two. Any alterations that would have been needed would therefore have had to be factored into the plot, and provision made to alter the body prior to its arrival at Bethesda.

3. Two Caskets

Is there any corroborative evidence that Lifton's reconstruction of the sequence of the alteration of the autopsy report is true? Is there any corroborative evidence that the President's body had been altered at some place and time between its departure from Dallas Air Force One with the new President, Lyndon Johnson, and its arrival at Bethesda Naval Hospital in Maryland?

There is.

When the President's body was taken from Parkland Hospital to Love Field in Dallas to be put aboard Air Force One, it was in a bronze casket donated by a local funeral company for the purpose. The casket was in pristine condition. Yet, on its arrival at Bethesda Naval Hospital in Maryland that evening, the casket, according to members of the military guard assigned to guard it, had sustained damage, including the damage to one of its corners. Some of the handles were missing.[41]

Additionally, there were two *separate* entrances of the casket into the Bethesda morgue, at different times.[42] To confound matters even further, Dennis David, who was posted to Bethesda hospital on the day of the autopsy, informed Lifton that there were in fact *two* caskets, an empty one, a decoy, and one that contained the President's body.[43] David also stated that he had seen the President's body arrive in a *plain* shipping casket, and not the elaborate formal bronze casket that he had left Parkland Hospital in.[44]

As if that were not enough, two of the medical technicians, Paul K. O'Connor and James Jenkins, tasked with preparing the body for the autopsy, informed Lifton that when *they* removed the body from the casket, it was in a *body* bag and *not*, as Sibert and O'Niell's FBI report stated, wrapped in a sheet. "Nobody had put Kennedy in a body bag in Dallas, at least not while Jacqueline Kennedy was in the room. He had

---

[41] David S. Lifton, *Best Evidence*, pp. 400, 411.
[42] Ibid, pp. 484-485.
[43] Ibid, pp. 572-573.
[44] Ibiid, pp. 579-580, 596

been wrapped in sheets, and put in an expensive bronze coffin. A piece of plastic was used to line the coffin."[45] Thus, there *had* to have been hands on the President's body at *some* place and time between its departure from Parkland Hospital and its arrival in Bethesda. O'Connor also stated that the President's body arrived in the plain shipping casket, and not the formal bronze one.[46]

4. Two, (or Was That Three?) Ambulances

We now have two caskets and one body, and differences between Dallas and Bethesda in how the body was wrapped inside whichever casket it was in. In Dallas, it is in sheets and the formal bronze casket is lined with plastic. In Bethesda, it is in a body bag, inside a shipping casket. As if to make this "two casket monte" game even more confusing, there is clear evidence that at least two, and possibly three, ambulances were involved in transporting the President's body from Andrews Air Force base outside of Washington, D.C., to Bethesda.

The mystery began to unravel for Lifton when he plotted the specific times for the arrival of the ambulance with the body from Andrews Air Force Base, and the times noted that the body was received and the autopsy begun. According to the Secret Service reports, the ambulance arrived at the front of the Bethesda hospital at 6:55 EST. The Siber-O'Niell FBI report then states that the body was received for autopsy at 7:35. At 8:00, according to Sibert and O'Niell, the autopsy begins after x-rays and photographs. And according to Sibert and O'Niell once again, and Commander Humes' testimony to the Warren Commission, the first incision is made at 8:15. This left a certain amount of time unaccounted for. Depending on when the autopsy actually began, it left between forty and sixty-five minutes.[47]

But according to statements of members of the military guard assigned to accompany the president's body, the ambulance was expected to arrive at the front entrance of the naval hospital. When the ambulance did not arrive at the expected time, the guard rushed to the rear entrance of the hospital to check there.[48]

The confusion, however, seems to have been caused by a deliberate deception, a deception made ostensibly for reasons of security. One of

---

[45] Ibid, p. 595.
[46] David S. Lifton, *Best Evidence*, pp. 598-599.
[47] Ibid, p. 391.
[48] Ibid, p. 399.

the members of the military guard, James Leroy Felder, was interviewed by Lifton. Felder adamantly maintained that there were two ambulances, with two caskets, and that the one that eventually arrived at the front of the hospital was a decoy, containing an empty casket.[49] Another ambulance arrived at the *rear* of the hospital, containing the shipping casket and the President's body. When the ambulance in the front of the hospital left to bring the casket to the back of the hospital's rear entrance to the morgue, some of the military guard chased it, and reported that the ambulance drove fast, as if trying to lose its military escort.

Lifton was able to establish that in fact two ambulances had met Air Force One, carrying the new President, Mrs. Johnson, and his staff, Mrs. Kennedy, and the rest of Kennedy's staff. Interviewing an army lieutenant, Richard A. Lipsey, a former aide to General Wehle, Lifton discovered that the plan to use two ambulances apparently was formulated at Andrews Airbase. According to Lipsey, an empty ambulance carrying Mrs. Kennedy was in the front of the motorcade, while another ambulance actually carrying President Kennedy's body was further back. It was, he said, a security concern, since the ambulance with Mrs. Kennedy was intended to draw the crowds to the front of the hospital while the ambulance with the body in the casket went to the rear entrance and the morgue.[50] When asked by Lifton whose plan it was to have a "decoy ambulance," Lipsey replied that "I think that came from the White House."[51]

The two-ambulance plan, in other words, came from no less than Lyndon Johnson! Lifton quips, "by this sleight of hand, the ambulance containing the Dallas casket had been able to escape the casket team's custody, and through the artifice of a 'decoy,' a deception had been disguised as a security measure."[52] It is important to note that we now have at least one documented case where the official chain of possession of evidence has been broken.[53]

---

[49] Perhaps this was the formal bronze casket that left Parkland hospital in Dallas, originally containing the President's body. Another member of the military guard, Hubert Clark, corroborated Felder's story that there was a decoy ambulance. See Lifton, *Best Evidence,* pp. 409, 411. Clark was also the member of the guard that stated he saw damage to the casket.

[50] Ibid.

[51] Lifton, op. cit., p. 419.

[52] Ibid, p. 405.

[53] Q.v. Lifton's comments on p. 398.

5. The Possible Place and Time of the Alterations

As noted previously, Lifton was able to track down and interview Dennis David, who was posted to the Bethesda hospital. David also informed Lifton that one of the autopsy doctors, Commander Boswell, told him that the ambulance carrying Mrs. Kennedy and the formal bronze Dallas casket that arrived at the front of the hospital, was empty, and that the ambulance carrying the shipping casket arrived at the hospital *before* that carrying the empty casket and Mrs. Kennedy.[54]

If this was true, then the implications were enormous, for it meant that the President's body had been secretly removed from the bronze Dallas casket earlier in the day, at some time before Air Force One took off from Dallas.[55] That left only two remaining possibilities: (1) either the body had been removed from the bronze casket while still at Parkland Hospital, and that Mrs. Kennedy had escorted an empty casket back to Air Force One, or (2) "that President Kennedy's body was removed from the Dallas casket during the events surrounding the swearing in of Lyndon Johnson."[56] There was in fact a brief period on board Air Force One when the body was left unattended.[57] Lifton postulates that the body was removed from the Dallas casket at this time, placed in a body bag, and stowed in the baggage compartment or the forward galley of Air Force One.[58]

Only one question remained: "If the body was hidden aboard *Air Force One*, how did it get to Bethesda, and where could it have been altered?"[59]

Citing transcripts of radio communications between Air Force One and Walter Reed Army hospital that were taped by the U.S. Army Signal corps — transcripts ironically found in 1975 at the LBJ presidential library! — Lifton established that a helicopter had taken off shortly after Air Force One landed at Andrews Air Force base and that in all likelihood, as Mrs. Kennedy was deplaning on a ramp on one side of Air Force One with an empty casket with full television coverage, the body was taken off the plane in a body bag on the other side of the plane and

---

[54] David S. lifton, *Best Evidence*, pp. 575, 577.
[55] Ibid, p. 582.
[56] Ibid, p. 588.
[57] Ibid, pp. 678-680.
[58] Ibid, p. 680.
[59] Ibid.

flown to Walter Reed Army Hospital, where the alterations were done prior to being transported to Bethesda.[60]

In all of these machinations, the finger has pointed to collusion between the FBI, the Secret service, and to pressure applied to the Navy pathologists conducting an autopsy on a body whose evidentiary value had already been quite deliberately mutilated. The finger points beyond the FBI and the Secret Service to the man who now held the power to apply that pressure, and to order events according to his desires. The finger points to Lyndon Baines Johnson.

6. Harrison Livingstone's Position

To all this elaborate sleight of hand involving two caskets, two, or three, ambulances, and ever-shifting autopsy reports, long-time assassination researcher Harrison Livingstone says "nonsense": "The body was not stolen or altered. This theory has done more to retard the solution of the JFK case than any other hoax."[61] No such elaborate conspiracy need to have been launched involving the body; one had only to falsify, to fake, the photographic and x-ray evidence of the autopsy, not the body itself.[62]

Livingstone observes that one need not go into elaborate schemes regarding the alteration of the body, for when the autopsy photographs and x-rays *were* finally released — long after the Warren Commission's work was done — they did not show the wounds where the Navy doctors described them to be in 1963.[63] Commanders Humes and Boswell, he notes, "repeatedly made strong statements saying that *their personal observations and testimony should govern what and where the wounds were, not the photographs.* There is a massive difference between what they saw, recorded, and say versus what the photographs seem to show."[64] This, notes Livingstone, is a "prima facie case for the forgery of the photographs,"[65] the very photographs, it will be recalled, that were turned over to the Secret Service at the White House!

---

[60] Ibid, pp. 681-688.

[61] Harrison Edward Livingstone, *Killing Kennedy and the Hoax of the Century* (New York: Carroll and Graf, 1995), p. 26.

[62] For Livingstone's highly technical case that the x-rays were falsified, see Livingstone, *Killing Kennedy*, pp. 79-114.

[63] Ibid, p. 24.

[64] Ibid, Livingstone's emphasis.

[65] Ibid, p. 51.

It was not necessary, therefore, to posit surgical alterations to the President's body to remove evidence of extra bullets from too many shooters; it was only necessary to forge the photographs and x-rays. And indeed, Livingstone observes that there may *not* have been bullets to remove in any case, since the back and throat wounds he received could have been from "frozen pellets shot from close range along the street's curb that froze Kennedy in place so that the riflemen could not miss."[66] The photographs and x-rays were falsified quite simply to cover-up the evidence of such frontal shots.[67] Livingstone also believes, however, that whoever falsified the photographs and x-rays did so under pressure, and that the job was done so intentionally poorly that the forgery was intended to eventually be discovered.[68]

But the clearest case of a falsification made under duress, a falsification intended to be eventually discovered, comes from the autopsy report of the Navy doctors to the Warren Commission itself; they "compounded their lies to make the whole thing appear preposterous *to those who truly think it through.*"[69] It will be recalled that Commander Humes burned the first draft of his report under circumstances strongly suggestive that he was under pressure to do so. Livingstone cites a crucial paragraph in their final autopsy report:

> The key paragraph in the autopsy report comes near the end; it describes the path of the bullet that hit Kennedy in the back "and made its exit through the anterior surface of the neck. As far as can be ascertained, *this missile struck no bony structures in its path through the body.*"... In the space of two sentences, the doctors essentially tell us the lie they are being forced to say and then in the next sentence tell us it has to be a lie *because no bullet can pass through that way without striking bone. They were telling us it was magic.*[70]

Indeed, they were telling us more than that; they were also telling us that the "Magic Bullet" which was supposed to have done all this was itself magic; it was a bit of *planted evidence.*

---

[66] Livingstone, *Killing Kennedy*, p. 94.
[67] Ibid, p. 99.
[68] Ibid, p. 336. Again, Livingstone's case for the forgery of the x-rays is quite convincing, but highly elaborate and technical.
[69] Ibid, p. 341, emphasis added.
[70] Ibid, p. 342, emphasis added.

7. The Nature of the Case

All of this, says Livingstone, means that any scenario favoring the idea that "the Mafia did it" is simply "an unsupportable thesis in view of the overall evidence of a faked case, and preplanning at a high level, not necessarily of government agencies. Higher than that."[71]

But we may apply Livingstone's logic not only to his own scenario of falsified and forged x-rays and photographs, but to Lifton's scenario of decoy caskets, ambulances, and surgical alterations of the President's body, nor need we presume that the two scenarios are in opposition and mutually exclusive. A paranoia that would alter and falsify photographic and x-ray evidence is a paranoia that would surgically alter the President's body, and vice versa.

Either way, the falsification and suppression of evidence in either scenario indicates that the circle of the highest level of involvement in the planning and execution of the crime *and the cover-up* could not have included the anti-Castro Cubans, the Mafia, or even the bankers, since these groups would not have had the intelligence capabilities to set-up Oswald as a patsy, *and* to possess the forensic evidence itself, *and* to falsify that evidence, whether that of the body, or that of the photographs and x-rays. This requires access to the technological facilities to do so.

We are thus able to narrow the highest levels of the conspiracy down to those that meet the following criteria:

1) They must possess direct and immediate access to intelligence networks;

2) They must possess direct access to the radiological, photographic, and surgical technologies and techniques to allow the falsification of the pathological, radiological, and photographic evidence, and as such must possess direct access to the forensic evidence;

3) They must possess access to medical personnel that would be able to perform surgical alteration, either under duress, or because such personnel lack normal human scruples that would prevent them from doing so.

Viewed in this way, we have now narrowed the highest level of involvement and planning *of the crime* down to those interests represented — in order of likely involvement, by:

---

[71] Ibid, p. 360.

1) Rogue elements within the Federal agencies mentioned in chapter one, i.e., to the FBI, CIA, ONI, Secret Service, and NASA;
2) The military.

This is not to say that the other groups are not involved in some way — even in *major* ways — in the conspiracy or even in the planning of the crime, or in vetoing certain aspects of planning along the way. It is merely to say that the central core, the "planning committee" as it were, *must* represent not only ties to all those groups with an interest and motivation to eliminate President Kennedy, but it must represent strong ties and influence to those two elements above. Only those two elements have the means, motives, and opportunity to carry out the *cover-up* of the conspiracy.

B. The Two(or is that Three?) Faces of Oswald
1. The Mexico City Oswald

Thus far we have covered the means, motives, and opportunities of those groups that could have committed the crime itself, in chapter one, and the means, motives, and opportunities of those groups that could have conceived and executed the post-assassination falsification of evidence in the cover-up in the previous sections of this chapter. If the examination of the means, motives, and opportunity in the case of the crime itself exposes those groups likely to be involved at the peripheral levels of the conspiracy, and the examination of the means, motives, and opportunity in the case of the cover-up exposes the very narrow circle of interests and groups at the core of its planning and execution, then it is with the *positioning of Oswald at the scene of the crime itself along with the evidence to incriminate him* that exposes the subtleties of its structure, and the hidden "deep" players and "deep politics" of those groups possessing veto power over the details of the plot, as they represent the high stakes involved.

That Oswald was a "deeply handled" individual with profound and covert ties to various intelligence agencies has been demonstrated. One need only look at how deeply obfuscated the "Oswald trail" really is in order to ascertain the subtle levels and layers of the conspiracy. We have already noted in chapter one how the FBI was concerned that someone was using Oswald's birth certificate as identity while Oswald himself was in Russia.

But the pattern apparently continued after Oswald's return to the United States. For example, while one Lee Harvey Oswald was in New Orleans, maintaining ties with both the pro- and anti-Castro communities, and handing out pro-Castro leaflets while making reports on his activities to the FBI, being vouched-for by Guy Bannister, and boasting he would soon have a job at NASA, *another* "Lee Oswald" was in Mexico City on October 1, 1963, visiting the Soviet Embassy, according to a CIA teletype to the FBI, the Department of State, and the Department of the Navy. The cable stated that the Mexico City Oswald was "approximately 35 years old, with an athletic build, about six feet tall, with a receding hairline."[72]

The CIA explained to the Warren Commission that on the day of Oswald's alleged visits to the Soviet Embassy, a Saturday, the camera surveillance of the embassy was turned off, and that on the day of his alleged visit to the Cuban embassy, the camera surveillance system "just happened to break down."[73]

But *on the very day of the assassination*, the CIA sent photos to the FBI of it had taken outside of the Soviet Embassy of a man it claimed was Oswald.[74] And *this* is the man the Agency said was claiming to be Oswald:

The Mexico City Oswald. This picture was Commission Exhibit 237

---

[72] Jim Marrs, *Crossfire*, p, 193.
[73] Ibid, p. 195.
[74] Ibid.

Obviously, this man bears no resemblance whatsoever to the "real" Oswald, but he does bear a strong resemblance to the "35 year old man with a receding hairline and athletic build" that the CIA had cabled the FBI, State Department, and Department of the Navy about earlier. Clearly, *someone* was impersonating Oswald, and to a purpose.

Moreover, the fact that we know the CIA *was* keeping a close eye on Oswald — recall only his 201 file mentioned in chapter one — means that it is *highly* unlikely that the CIA did not know what he looked like. This raises the distinct possibility that some *other* group was behind the appearance of the Mexico City Oswald.

2. Jack White and The Russian vs. Marine Corps Oswalds

Further evidence of more than one Oswald was uncovered by Texas assassination researcher Jack White. White discovered when he brought the facial features of Oswald's Marine photograph, the left side of his face in the photo composite below, into alignment with a photo of the right side of his face supposedly taken in Russia, that the two pictures showed entirely different men, even though the resemblance was otherwise quite strong, for the left ear on the Marine Oswald is much lower than the right ear. Additionally, there is a slight difference of the hairline and cheek bone structure on each man.

Jack White's two faces of Oswald

Oswald 6'1" vs 5'9" (handwritten)

Finally, Jim Marrs notes that Oswald's Marine Corps records describe his height as 6'1", whereas by the time of Oswald's autopsy report, he has shrunk *four inches* to a height of 5'9"![75]

When these facts are added to all the previously noted anomalies in Oswald's behavior and associations, it is abundantly clear that some group with deep intelligence resources went to a great deal of trouble:

1) to find a near double of Oswald, and either send the real or the double Oswald to Russia during a specific period, and with specific secrets, that led to the downing of Powers' U-2 and to the exacerbation of Soviet-American tensions;
2) to create a tapestry of alleged Oswald associations with various groups both on the political right and left (recall Oswald's pro- and anti-Castro associations on the one hand, plus the presence within his address book of the address of the leader of the American Nazi Party on the other, and Guy Bannister's statement that Oswald was "with us");
3) to associate Oswald with the FBI upon his return to the United States.

Whether or not Oswald or some Oswald doppelgänger went to Russia in 1959 is really, for our purposes, immaterial, for the ease by which Oswald entered, and then left, the Soviet Union is a strong indicator that he had the help of some intelligence group to get *into* the country, had the help of some group while he *stayed* in the country, and had the help of some group to get *out* of the country. As we shall discover in the next chapter, the fact that Oswald was sent by the Soviets to Minsk, the capital of the Belo-Russian Soviet Socialist Republic, might be a significant indicator of where that help was really coming from, and who was ultimately "handling" Oswald. As will also be seen, that same indicator will also be a clue as to who might ultimately have been responsible for situating Oswald in Dallas at the "scene of the crime."

For now, let it be noted that if all these things betoken an intelligence handling of Oswald, particularly during his Soviet "defection," then the *one* group with the largest and most pervasive on-the-ground human intelligence network inside the Soviet Union and that was most able to accomplish this at that time was "former" Nazi General Reinhard Gehlen's "organization." As we saw in chapter one, Oswald's defection,

---

[75] Jim Marrs, *Crossfire*, photo insert section.

83

Powers' U-2 flight and its subsequent shooting down, were all part of a design to heighten Cold War tensions. Such a political goal was always a component of post-war Nazi activities, for East-West tensions gave Nazism maneuvering room.[76] Given that Powers' U-2 flight was under the direction of CIA deputy director Richard Bissell, and since it flew in direct contravention of President Eisenhower's orders, we posit the involvement of the Nazi International at a deep level of the conspiracy, in league with this rogue element within the CIA, helping to place and handle Oswald in all the right locations, at the right time. As we shall see in chapter four, Oswald may have been handled *directly* by this group in Dallas.

We posit that this group was intimately involved in situating Oswald at the scene of the crime and placing the evidence there that would eventually incriminate him, and we posit that this group may have been intimately involved in coordinating the activities of the various Oswald doubles, who were apparently active even on the day of the assassination itself.

3. The Altgens Photograph: Billy Lovelady or Lee Oswald?

That there *was* such coordination of his doubles is strongly suggested by the apparent continuation of that activity on the very day of the President's assassination itself.

Ike Altgens was an Associated Press reporter standing on to the front and left of the presidential limousine on Elm Street, and snapped one of the most famous photographs of the assassination at the moment the report of the first shot rang out. Like other photographs and films taken that day, the Altgens photograph has proven to be a considerable difficulty, not only for the official Warren Report version of the assassination, but for assassination researchers themselves.

The Altgens photo shows the presidential limousine at approximately the fourth road stripe on Elm, thus making it possible to roughly position Altgens himself, and the angle at which the picture was taken, on an overhead photo of Dealey Plaza. This was done by the late Harold

---

[76] See my *The Nazi International: The Nazis' Postwar Plan to Control Finance, Conflict, Physics and Space* (Kempton, Illinois: Adventures Unlimited Press, 2008), pp. 181-247.

Weisberg,[77] one of the first, most thorough, and most outspoken critics of the Warren Commission and Warren Report.[78]

The Ike Altgens photograph, taken at the moment of the first shot. Note that the Secret Service Agents in the second car are turned around, looking toward the Texas School Book Depository. The entrance to the depository is visible in the photograph, behind the tree behind the Presidential Limousine.

---

[77] d. Feb 21, 2002.
[78] Weisberg was the author of two essential books for any Kennedy assassination research: *Whitewash: The Report on the Warren Report* (New York: Dell Publishing Co., 1965), and *Whitewash II: The FBI-Secret Service Cover-up* (New York: Dell Publishing Co., 1966).

When the entrance to the School Book Depository was blown up, this is what it showed:

The Altgens Photograph: Blowup of man standing in the entrance of the School Book Depository. Note Weisberg's arrow: Is this Billy Lovelady, or Lee Harvey Oswald?

Oswald's mother, when shown this blow-up, remarked that it was her son.

Lovelady's testimony to the Warren Commission only confounded matters. The testimony was taken at 3:50 PM, April 7, 1964 in the office of the U.S. Attorney in Dallas. Warren Commission associate counsel Joseph A. Ball questioned Loveday:

> Mr. BALL: Which one of the buildings do you work in?
> Mr. LOVELADY: At the one at 411 Elm.
> Mr. BALL: On November 22, 1963, where were you working?
> Mr. LOVELADY: At that morning, you mean?
> Mr. BALL: Yes.
> Mr. LOVELADY: I was working on the sixth floor putting — we was putting down that flooring.

Note that Lovelady states explicitly that he not only works at the Texas School Book Depository at 411 Elm Street, but that the very day of the assassination, he had been assigned to work *on the sixth floor*, the very floor Oswald allegedly shot Kennedy from, according to the Warren Commission's reconstruction of the crime. Continuing:

> Mr. BALL: What time did you quit work that day or knock off for lunch that day?
> Mr. LOVELADY: Same time, 12.
> Mr. BALL: A little before 12?
> Mr. LOVELADY: Well, we came down at 10 minutes til to wash up and get ready for it.
> (...)
> Mr. BALL: What did you do after you went down and washed up, what did you do?
> Mr. LOVELADY: Well, I went over and got my lunch and went upstairs and got a coke and come on back down.
> Mr. BALL: Upstairs on what floor?
> Mr. LOVELADY: That's on the second floor; so, I started going to the domino room where I generally went in to set down and eat and nobody was there and I happened to look on the outside and Mr. Shelley was standing outside with Miss Sarah Stanton, I believe her name is, and I said, "Well, I'll go out there and talk with them, *sit down* and eat my lunch out there, *set on the steps*," so I went out there.
> Mr. BALL: *You ate your lunch on the steps?*
> Mr. LOVELADY: Yes, sir.
> Mr. BALL: Who was with you?
> Mr. LOVELADY: Bill Shelley and Sarah Stanton, *and right behind me.*[79]

Now compare Lovelady's testimony with the blow-up of the Altgens photograph. Lovelady testified that he was *sitting* eating his lunch, and that two people — Bill Shelley and Sarah Stanton — were "right behind" him.

---

[79] Warren Commission, Testimony of Billy Nolan Lovelady, April 7, 1964, emphasis added. It should also be noted that Lovelady was one of many witnesses who described hearing the shots as coming from the Grassy Knoll, and not the School Book Depository:
"Mr. BALL: Where was the direction of the sound?
Mr. LOVELADY: Right there around that concrete little deal on that knoll
Mr. BALL: That's where it sounded to you?
Mr. LOVELADY: Yes sir; to my right..."

Yet, in the photograph, the man is *standing*, and there is *no one* behind him. It should also be noted that the Commission's counsel, Joseph Ball, asks Lovelady not what he *saw*, but what he *heard*, since if Lovelady was sitting, his view of the assassination would have been obscured.

The Lovelady matter gets even more complicated, for Harold Weisberg, who first brought the Altgens photograph and its dramatic implications to the public in 1966, discovered yet another discrepancy between the photograph and Lovelady's testimony. Weisberg found a memo from FBI Director J. Edgar Hoover dated February 29, 1964, that stated that Lovelady "at the time of the assassination and shortly before, he was *standing* in the doorway of the front entrance to the (Texas School Book Depository) where he is employed. He stated *he was wearing a red and white striped shirt* and blue jeans."[80] Note that, if Hoover is correct, Lovelady contradicted his testimony to the Warren Commission given later in April.

The FBI took photos of Lovelady in the shirt that he stated he was dressed in that day:

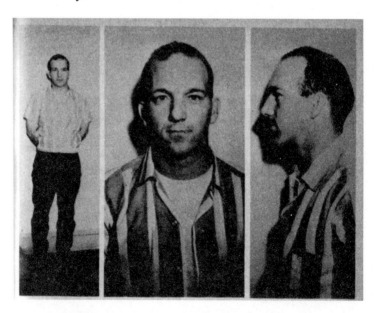

The FBI photos of Lovelady in his striped shirt

---

[80] Harold Weisberg, *Whitewash II: The FBI-Secret Service Cover-up*, photo insert, emphasis added.

There was just one problem, and it is revealed by the arrest photograph of Oswald in the shirt he was wearing when arrested:

Arrest photo of Oswald in the shirt he was dressed in on November 22, 1963

A comparison with the Altgens blowup shows the clear resemblance of the Oswald arrest photograph shirt with the shirt worn by the man in the School Book Depository doorway:

Either way one slices it, there is a problem. If the photo shows *Oswald* in the doorway, then he is not on the sixth floor where the Warren Commission said he was, shooting the President. If, on the other hand, it really does show Lovelady, then how does one account for the discrepancy between the photo which shows him standing, and his testimony, where he said he was sitting? And why is his shirt more like Oswald's, when Lovelady himself said he was wearing a striped shirt?

But beyond this, there is a much larger problem, and that is simply the presence of a close Oswald look-alike at the Book Depository on the day of the assassination itself. In and of itself, this would not be a concern. It is only within the context of the much wider pattern of Oswald doubles that the Lovelady matter assumes more sinister significance. Too many Oswald look-alikes and people using his name repeatedly in places intended to draw attention to him can hardly be accidental. The trail is obfuscated, even at the crime scene itself, on the very day of the assassination.

4. Deputy Sherriff Roger Craig, Oswald, and the Nash Rambler

Adding to the confusion over Oswald in Dallas on that day is the testimony of Deputy Sherriff Roger Craig. Craig, in a written report of November 23, 1963, stated that he had seen Oswald run down the hill from the School Book Depository and get into a Nash Rambler station wagon with another man whom he described as being of dark complexion and possibly Latin. Craig informed captain Will Fritz of the Dallas Police Department. Fritz ignored his report.[81] Craig later repeated his story for New Orleans District Attorney Jim Garrison.[82] If true, then either one is again dealing with two Oswalds, or the Warren Report's story of Oswald leaving by taxi, then doubling back and eventually ending up at the Texas theater where he was arrested, is false.

5. Oswald Tried and Found Guilty in New Zealand Before He is Charged in Dallas

Compounding the appearance of so many Oswalds, there is also the problem of the *timing* of the "Oswald-as-the-assassin" story itself. Here Colonel Fletcher Prouty is a direct witness to the anomaly. Prouty had been ordered by his commanding officer to be the military escort to a

---

[81] Jim Marrs, *Crossfire*, pp. 329-331.
[82] Jim Garrison, *On the Trail of the Assassins*, pp. 109-110.

group traveling to Antarctica, and was on his way back to the U.S.A. through Christchurch, New Zealand, when the assassination occurred. Then, an amazing thing happened that revealed to Colonel Prouty the depth, and planning, that had gone into the murder:

> For those of us who just happened to be in far-off Christchurch, New Zeland, for example, the Kennedy assassination took place at seven-thirty on the morning of Saturday, November 23, 1963.
>
> As soon as possible, the *Christchurch Star* hit the streets with an "Extra" edition. One-quarter of the front page was devoted to a picture of President Kennedy. The remainder of the page was, for the most part, dedicated to the assassination story, from various sources. Who were those sources, and how could so much intimate and detailed information about Oswald have been obtained instantaneously? The answer is that it wasn't obtained "instantaneously." It had to have been prepared before the crime, and like everything else, prepackaged by the secret cabal.
>
> This "instant" news, available so quickly, and completely in far-off New Zealand, is a most important detail of the murder plan. The newspaper ran an "Extra" edition that was on the streets before noon in Christchurch. It ran news items filed by experienced on-the-spot reporters in Dallas, who reported that the president was hit with a "burst" of gunfire. A few lines below, it said, "Three bursts of gunfire, apparently from automatic weapons," were heard.[83]

But the completeness of details in the article about Oswald and his life was not even the real problem. The real problem was the *timing* of the "Extra" edition, and what it portended:

> At the time this edition of the *Star* went to press, *the police of Dallas had just taken a young man into custody and had charged him with the death of a Dallas policeman named J.D. Tippit. They had not accused Oswald of the murder of the President and did not charge him with that crime until early the next morning.* Yet a long article put on the wires by the British United Press and America's Associated Press had been assembled out of nowhere, *even before Oswald had been charged with the crime.* It was pure propaganda. Where did those wire services get it?[84]

---

[83] L. Fletcher Prouty, *JFK: The CIA, Vietnam, and The Plot to Assassinate John F. Kennedy*, p. 306.
[84] Ibid, p. 308.

91

Prouty asks even more searching questions and comes to the inevitable conclusion:

> By what process could the wire services have acquired, collated, evaluated, written, and then transmitted all that material about an unknown young man named Lee Harvey Oswald within the first moments following that tragic and "unexpected" event — even before the police had charged him? How could they have justified the collation of such news until *after* the police had charged him with the crime?
> There can be but one answer: Those in charge of the murder had prepared the patsy and all of that intimate information beforehand.[85]

The Christchurch newspaper "Extra," in other words, points to three — and only three — sources for this possible information, for it points to those with the access to intelligence files on Oswald, and to those with the ability to "handle" both him and his doubles in such a way as to create an incriminating "character background" that would inevitably make him the "patsy" he himself stated he was on American television. The article points clearly to those agencies and groups that *were* in fact keeping files on him.

It points to the FBI, the CIA, and to the other group with a large network of spies in Eastern Europe and Soviet Russia that would be able to maintain surveillance on Oswald and to lend occasional assistance when he needed it. In short, it points to General Gehlen's organization, and therefore, ultimately, to the Nazis.

C. Two (or was that Three?) Rifles and Some Possible Symbolic Messages

A careful look at the alleged rifle, or *rifles*, recovered in the School Book Depository will disclose the deep involvement of one of the groups involved in the assassination, and the symbolic messages it was sending to its American counterparts.

Here again it is Deputy Sherriff Roger Craig who plays an important role, for both he, and Deputies E.L. Boone and Seymour Weitzman stated that the *rifle recovered from the School Book Depository was a 7.65mm German Mauser, **not** the 6.5mm Italian Mannlicher-Carcano that subsequently became the alleged murder weapon.*[86] It is highly

---

[85] L. Fletcher Prouty, *JFK: The CIA, Vietnam, and The Plot to Assassinate John F. Kennedy*, p. 309.
[86] Jim Marrs, *Crossfire*, p. 439.

92

unlikely that three Sherriff's deputies would misidentify such a weapon, nor confuse it with the cheaply made Italian Mannlicher-Carcano, especially as Weitzman was also the owner of a sporting goods store and well-acquainted with firearms of every sort. Even the Dallas police chief at the time, Jesse Curry, admitted that it was entirely possible that a substitution of rifles had occurred, and that the Italian Mannlicher-Carcano in the National Archives was not the weapon originally found in the School Book Depository.[87]

Lt. Carl Day holding the alleged murder weapon, the cheap Italian Mannlicher-Carcano with the misaligned telescopic sight. Note the absence of the ammunition clip

Nitrate Test
No

Another difficult problem was that Oswald failed all nitrate tests; he had not fired *any* weapon on the day of the assassination.[88] Worse yet, when the Mannlicher-Carcano was tested for fingerprints on Saturday, November 23, 1963 in Washington, D.C. by the FBI, even Hoover stated

No finger prints

---

[87] Ibid, p. 440.
[88] Jim Garrison, *On the Trail of the Assassins,* pp. 116, 228. It should be remembered that Oswald was initially arrested and charged with the murder of Officer Tippett with a pistol, and not with the murder of President Kennedy.

"No latent prints of value were developed on Oswald's ...cartridges cases, the unfired cartridge, the clip in the rifle or the inner parts of the rifle."[89]

The FBI then embarked on activity so suspicious that it strongly indicates its culpability and involvement in the second level of the conspiracy, the framing of Oswald, for the Mannlicher-Carcano was flown *back* to Dallas and taken in the company of FBI agents to the funeral home where Oswald had been taken after his murder by Jack Ruby. The purpose of this "visit"? According to FBI agent Richard Harrison, another unnamed FBI agent had wanted to get Oswald's palm print on the rifle for "comparison purposes"![90]

In short, since Oswald had failed the nitrate test which would indicate he had fired a weapon, and since no useable fingerprints were found on the weapon he is alleged to have used, it appears that the FBI wanted to make good and certain that Oswald could be tied to the rifle somehow, even to the extent of planting his palm print on it after the fact!

There is also an obvious symbolism in the two rifles — the incredibly accurate German Mauser, and the incredibly *inaccurate* Italian Mannlicer-Carcano — that were seen by witnesses that day, in that both rifles may symbolize the involvement of that post-war Nazi International in the assassination, *or* may have been intended by someone to misdirect attention to that quarter. If intended as a symbolic message, then perhaps the disappearance of the Mauser and the appearance of the Mannlicher-Carcano was also meant to send a message, that the Nazi element, having been involved with the crime, could literally disappear into the aether like the Mauser itself.[91]

D. Too Many(or was that Too Few?) Bullets

The old adage has it that a picture is worth a thousand words, and in this instance, a few pictures are worth several thousand. This is the now infamous "Magic Bullet," said by the Warren Commission to have passed through a bony area of the President, to have executed an "s" turn

---

[89] Jim Marrs, *Crossfire*, p. 443.

[90] Ibid, p. 444.

[91] Colonel Fletcher Prouty also notes that NBC-TV made a very early report that "the police took possession of 'a British .303 inch rifle...with a telescopic sight.'"(L. Fletcher Prouty, *JFK: The CIA, Vietnam, and the Plot to Assassinate Kennedy*, p. 307). I tend to discount this story because, as far as I have been able to determine, NBC only ran it once. In the case of the German Mauser, it was so identified by the three Dallas policemen who first recovered the rifle from the Book Depository, and none of them were likely to misidentify such a weapon.

in mid-air that would be the envy of any pilot, and then to have struck Governor John Connally in the ribs, smashed into his right wrist, and then to have embedded itself in his left thigh, only to emerge on a stretcher at Parkland Hospital in nearly pristine condition, and with scant evidence — if any — of bone fragments, human tissue, or blood.

The Magic Bullet, Bullet 399 found on a stretcher in Parkland Hospital after the assassination

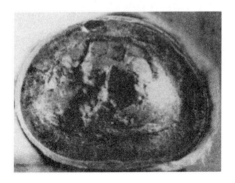

End view of the Magic Bullet

These, however, are the 6.5 bullet fragments actually found in the presidential limousine. Clearly, they have passed through *something.*

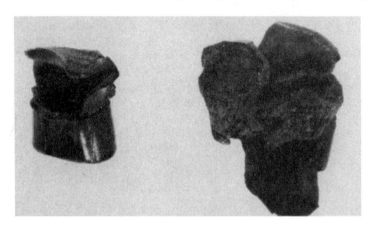

Bullet fragments that were found in the Presidential Limousine, Warren Commission Exhibits 567 and 569

And *this* is a bullet that was intentionally fired through the wrist of a cadaver, in one of the Warren Commission's desperate attempts to "recreate" the circumstances of the crime. Note, this bullet was fired *only* through a wrist, not a bony area of a cadaver, and then through the ribs and wrist of *another* cadaver.

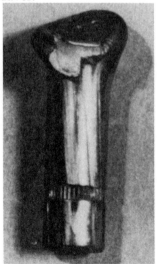

Bullet Number 856, shot through the wrist of a cadaver

This is not the *only* problem with the bullets, and once again it is Deputy Sherriff Roger Craig (and his colleague Luke Mooney) that poses the significant difficulty with his testimony. These two deputies

> have told researchers they saw the three hulls *lying side by side only inches apart under the window, all pointing in the same direction.* Of course, this position would be impossible if the shells had been normally ejected from a rifle. So the evidence of the empty shell casings is suspect.
>
> Just as a matter of speculation, it seems incredible that the assassin in the Depository would go to the trouble of trying to hide the rifle behind boxes on the opposite side of the sixth floor from the southeast window and then leave incriminating shells lying on the floor — unless, of course, the hulls were deliberately left behind to incriminate Oswald.[92]

We have noted already that Lovelady stated in his testimony to the Warren Commission that work was being done that very day on the sixth floor. It would be a simple matter for a two-man team to use this fact to plant the incriminating evidence.

There is still *another* problem with the shell casings used to incriminate Oswald, and it's a whopper:

> Although the Warren Commission published a copy of the Dallas police evidence sheet showing *three* shell cases were taken from the Depository, in later years a copy of that same evidence sheet was found in the Texas Department of Public Safety files which showed only *two* cases were found. This is supported by the FBI receipt for assassination evidence from the Dallas police that indicates only two shell cases arrived in Washington just after the assassination.[93]

So now we have *two* shell cases for *three* shots, one of which includes a magic bullet! So where did the third one go? According to Jim Marrs, Dallas police detective Fritz held on to it "for several days before forwarding it to the FBI."[94] This not only demonstrated a breach in the chain of evidence, it highlighted yet *another* significant problem with the third shell:

---

[92] Jim Marrs, *Crossfire*, p. 438, emphasis added.
[93] Ibid, emphasis added.
[94] Ibid.

This suspicion is compounded by the fact that while the FBI Crime Lab determined that two of the hulls show marks compatible with being loaded in Oswald's rifle, the third showed no such evidence.

In fact, the third hull — designated Commission Exhibit 543 — had a dent on its lip that would have prevented the fitting of a slug. In its present condition, it could not have fired a bullet on that day.[95]

Perhaps this cartridge that couldn't fire a bullet that couldn't be fitted to it was the "Magic Cartridge" that fired "the Magic Bullet."

Let us be very blunt: the Warren Commission's idea that the "Magic Bullet" allegedly passed through bony areas of the President and *then* Governor Connally, smashing one of his ribs, then his wrist, only to embed itself in his left leg, to fall out in *pristine* condition with little to no traces of any human blood or tissue, is a *physics impossibility*. On the other hand, the fact that the bullet clearly *was* fired from the alleged murder weapon means that it had to have been fired in all likelihood into a ballistics tank, in order to obtain the necessary ballistics markings from Oswald's Mannlicher-Carcano.

This means the bullet was most likely a bit of *planted evidence*,[96] but as evidence its value in aid of the single bullet theory is nil, again, for all the above-stated reasons. So why plant such evidence at all? Why would the conspirators draw such attention to themselves by doing so?

The question may be answered by viewing the bullet *in an entirely different way*, namely, that it was not so much a *plant*, as a *message*, from one group involved in the conspiracy, to another. It is meant as a *reminder* and a *threat* from one group to another, that the latter must abide by certain long-term commitments, or else the same thing will happen to them, and the group sending the message will get away cleanly, as cleanly as the bullet "passed through" the President and Governor Connally. Indeed, the idea that the Magic Bullet was a *plant* could only have been done as an "inside job,"[97] and that clearly implies that a signal, a message, may have been sent to the conspirators that would have to cover-up the crime with a ridiculous story, a story that had to include the magic bullet.

The Magic Bullet, in short, was a bit of *theater*, an alchemical meme, a necessary piece to a *psychodrama*, about which we shall have more to say in a subsequent chapter.

---

[95] Jim Marrs, *Crossfire*, p. 438.
[96] David S. Lifton, *Best Evidence*, pp. 92-93.
[97] Ibid, p. 94.

E. Too Many Films, with Too Many, or Too Few, Frames

The final case of something where there is "too much" or "too little" of one thing or another is the famous film taken by Dallas clothier Abraham Zapruder, standing atop the pedestal on the memorial at the Grassy Knoll on the day of the assassination. In this case, there are not only too many, or too few, frames in the film itself, there are also too many *versions* of the film now extant and public, each showing slightly different things, and each showing thereby the hand of redaction and editing.

This film clearly *was* a target of the conspirators and their editors, for in any "authentic" version in which one views it (this author has viewed at least three of the main versions), it clearly shows the President being hit from the right front during the fatal shot, and his head being propelled violently "back and to the left," according to the simple laws of physics.[98] The film thus posed a major problem for the conspirators with their self-evidently prepackaged cover story of Oswald the "Lone Nut" in his perch on the sixth floor of the Depository accomplishing impossible feats of marksmanship and physics with an inaccurate rifle.

But the film and its various versions also poses problems for researchers who have hitherto used it to prove the existence of another shooter, and therefore, of a conspiracy. Harrison Edward Livingstone, one of the best assassination researchers, summarizes the whole problem of the Zapruder film this way: "Keep in mind how many times this nation has been told on television and radio and college lecture audiences that

---

[98] There is, of course, the fanciful Gnostic-neurological nonsense put out by some that this was a *physiological and reflex action* in the President to a fatal shot from *behind*, and the usual "experts" are paraded to say this and reassure us that the body in a reflex action of this sort could *overcome the kinetic energy of a bullet from a rifle striking from behind.* Such comments are nothing less than nonsense, since to prove such an assertion empirically would require taking someone and shooting them in the head from behind until such a neurological response was obtained (doubtless after numerous attempts). Having possibly obtained one such result after numerous attempts and corpses, the exception would then be paraded before us as the rule. For those wanting a visual reminder of the futility and desperation of such "explanations," consider only the numerous films of Nazis executing their victims on the Eastern Front, and provide one example from them of such a "neurological" or "physiological" reaction! Such comments, however, indicate the lengths to which the defenders of the feckless Warren Report will *still* go in order to perpetuate the cover-up.

99

the film was a clock of the assassination."[99] The only trouble is, that films are like wrist watches, everyone's will show a slightly different time and run either slightly faster or slower than real time, and in this case, the problem is compounded by the various *versions* of the Zapruder film that are currently extant, and by another disquieting fact: films can be altered, and in each of the known versions of the film, there are clear indications that this in fact happened.

1. The Other Films, and the Various Zapruder Film Versions

The Zapruder film of the assassination is now well-known around the world for showing a clear, and fatal, head-shot to President Kennedy from the right front, and not from the School Book Depository whence, according to the Warren Commission, it had to come. The problem is, it is erroneous and inaccurate to speak of the Zapruder *film*, for there are in fact several *versions* of it, each showing slightly different things, but each showing the clear and deliberate hand of *editing*. This, really, should not surprise us, for almost every film that we see, from the television news clips to the full length feature or documentary, are edited versions of something else. It is therefore more accurate to speak of the Zapruder *films*, or of the *versions* of it, than simply to say "the Zapruder film."

The questions are: who edited it, who had the *power* to edit it, who had the most to gain from editing it, and why was it done? What do all these versions and edits say about the architecture of the conspiracy?

A look at the versions themselves goes a long way to answering these questions. The problem with the versions begins with Zapruder himself, and his own statements. According to Harrison Edward Livingston, Zapruder maintained that a *copy* of his famous film was flown to Washington D.C. on the very day of the assassination. But this poses a problem right at the outset, for as Livingston observes, "it is completely unreasonable that a *copy* of a film of one of the most major crimes of the century would have been sent for study there, and not the original."[100] Given the likely close cooperation of the Dallas FBI and Secret Service, and given that Zapruder himself indicated that a *copy* of his film was shown to the Dallas FBI and Secret Service in his own

---

[99] Livingstone, *Killing Kennedy and the Hoax of the Century*, p. 153. The phrase "the Hoax of the Century" in the title of Livingstone's book is in fact the chapter title of the chapter dealing with the Zapruder film.

[100] Ibid, p. 117.

100

offices, then we already have "an obvious contradiction in how many copies existed."[101] At the very minimum, on the day of the assassination, we have at least *two* films extant — the one flown to Washington, and the one Zapruder showed the FBI and Secret Service in Dallas — if not *three*, for it will be recalled that oil tycoon H.L. Hunt purchased his own private copy.

In fact, Hunt's "copy" may have been the camera original according to Livingston, the original that spawned the many later versions:

> I had high-level information in Dallas that the original Zapruder film (from Zapruder's camera) was first obtained by H.L. Hunt before *Life* bought what they thought was the original. The FBI, the Secret Service, and the military allowed Hunt to either control the evidence or be used as the front for control of it by those using him. The indication is that Hunt's people obtained it and passed it on to the FBI who sent it to headquarters in Washington shortly after it was developed.[102]

The evidentiary value of the film is thus highly questionable, since Hunt himself is implicated in the plot, as we saw in the previous chapter. The major versions of the Zapruder film are as follows:

1) The *Life* magazine version, which is the most widely known of all the versions and that was the version subpoenaed by New Orleans District Attorney Jim Garrison and shown — for the first time in public — at the trial of Clay Shaw;[103]
2) The Secret Service version which was "loaned to the House Select Committee on Assassinations in 1976";[104] it should also be noted that the Secret Service version includes frames that are *not* present in the *Life* magazine version;[105]
3) The Bill Kurtis version, first aired on the Arts and Entertainment Channel in 1992 during a special called *Who Killed JFK?: On the Trail of the Conspiracies*. In this version the colors are so leached that the film appears like a black and white film. In the Kurtis special, it is stated that this version appeared courtesy of the House Assassinations Committee, but this is highly doubtful

---

[101] Livingston, *Killing Kennedy and the Hoax of the Century*, p. 117.
[102] Ibid, p. 120.
[103] Ibid, p. 125.
[104] Ibid, p. 126.
[105] Ibid.

since the House investigation had concluded long before the
Kurtis special aired;[106]

4) The Dallas FBI field office version, which is now in the National
Archives. This version raises several important questions, as
Livingston is quick to point out:

> One might ask that if the local FBI had to continue to return to see the
> film in Zapruder's office, then how did they obtain this copy? And how,
> if Zapruder did not retain a copy, as was publicly claimed after the sale
> to *Life*, was the FBI able to see a copy in his offices for some time
> after? And... if a copy or the original went to FBI headquarters in
> Washingotn, what happened to that? What happened to H.L. Hunt's
> copy? Why won't the Hunt family discuss this?[107]

The problems these questions raise once again casts a pall of
dubiousness over the film's evidentiary value *if divorced from
the wider context* of eyewitness statements, for not only are there
clearly questions of how many versions there actually are, but
there are clear questions involving the chain of possession and
the authenticity of each version;

5) The version of David S. Lifton, who possesses both a 35mm film
copy as well as one other. This film, according to Livingston, is
"said to be uncommonly clear" and is thus the basis for further
inquiry;[108]

6) Bootleg copies that appeared at the time the *Life* version was
subpoenaed by Garrison. Some of these made their way to
assassination researcher Mark Lane — the lawyer hired by
Oswald's mother to represent him posthumously;[109]

7) The version given to researcher Robert Groden and then aired on
the Geraldo Rivera show on March 6 and 27, 1975. Livingston's
observations about this version are worth citing: "Many have felt
that these men were used to show the film because the original
had been altered and proved the government's case more than it
disproved it. The government's case is protected by a false film
that has *key events removed.*"[110]

---

[106] Livingston, *Killing Kennedy and the Hoax of the Century*, p. 126.
[107] Ibid, p. 127.
[108] Ibid.
[109] Ibid.
[110] Ibid, emphasis added.

Many Zapruder Films!

8) There are indications of a "European" version of the film, in which the infamous "blood-and-brain" halo at the time of the head shot, frame 313, is entirely missing, lending credence to those who believe that this was an effect edited into the film after the fact;[111]

9) Finally, there is the version shown in the 1978 documentary, *In Search of Lee Harvey Oswald*. This version, also in the possession of Robert Groden, appears to be completely unspliced and had all the frames in it, unlike the many other versions, including, and especially, the *Life* magazine version.[112]

What emerges from all this is not only the problem of the chain of possession of the various versions (and these are only the *major* versions), but the fact that the evidentiary value of the film can only rest within the total context of the statements of eyewitnesses, and the other, less famous films of the assassination.

There are three other films of the assassination: the Nix, Muchmore, and Bronson films. Of these, the Bronson film is the least significant, since it was filmed from a position a block away from the actual assassination, and from behind President Kennedy's limousine.[113] The film of Orville Nix, taken across the street from the Grassy Knoll position of Abraham Zapruder, is also in questionable condition, since Nix's daughter maintains that her father "stated that he didn't get the film back from the FBI in the same condition as the one he gave them."[114] The Nix film does, however, show a fragment of the President's skull flying from his head and landing on the trunk of the limousine.

The Muchmore film, also taken from the left side of the limousine across Elm Street from the Grassy Knoll, also has a "halo" frame, but this looks "not even similar to the one we see in the Nix film," and this has led some researchers to conclude it is an edited-in effect.[115]

---

[111] Livingston, *Killing Kennedy and the Hoax of the Century*, p. 127. It should be noted, however, that the "halo" appears both in the Nix and Muchmore films (q.v. pp. 127-128).

[112] Ibid, p. 128.

[113] Ibid, p. 129.

[114] Ibid.

[115] Ibid.

2. Problems in the Zapruder Film

The first, and most obvious, problem with the Zapruder film, in any of its various versions now extant, is the patent and clear contradiction between what it shows, and what the eyewitnesses to the crime reported they saw. Another severe critic of the Zapruder film, James H. Fetzer, Ph.D., observes that the use of the film in and of itself as a means to reconstruct the events of the assassination flies in the face of American jurisprudence and its rules of evidence:

> Whether or not the film remains in government hands surely does not affect the logical properties that distinguish verification from falsification. Moreover, placing such absolute reliance upon a strip of celluloid contradicts the principles of evidence that obtain in cases of this kind. As *McCormick on Evidence,* 3rd edition (1984) observes, "*a photograph (or film) is viewed merely as a graphic portrayal of oral testimony and becomes admissible only when a witness has testified that it is a correct and accurate representation of the relevant facts personally observed by the witness.*" Witnesses take precedence over photographs and films.[116]

As will be seen momentarily, this is the problem, for what the witnesses describe, and what the various versions show, are two different things.

In fact, it is this precise discrepancy that points to an extremely strong case for the editing of the Zapruder film, for as Fetzer notes, "None of the published frames... includes Jean Hill, Mary Moorman, Charles Brehm, Joe Brehm, or Beverly Oliver,"[117] the eyewitnesses to the left of the President's limousine on Elm Street, and the very eyewitnesses interviewed by the FBI and the Warren Commission! How can they be acknowledged to have been present during the assassination, and yet *not* appear in the published frames of the Zapruder film? This can only happen if they have been edited out of the film.

It is because the film, in most of its versions, is admitted to be edited in the form of splices at frames 154-157 and 207-212 (out of 486 frames

---

[116] James H. Fetzer, Ph.D., ed., *The Great Zapruder Film Hoax: Deceit and Decption in the Death of JFK* (Chicago: Catfeet Press, 2003), p. xvii, italics in the original. Fetzer is the McKnight University Professor at the University of Minnesota at Duluth, and the author of many articles on the philosophy of science.

[117] Ibid.

in Robert Groden's "pristine" version)[118] plus the fact that there are inconsistencies between the eyewitness reports and the various versions of the film, that questions have been advanced about the film's authenticity, "even extending to whether Zapruder really took the film that bears his name. And there are good reasons to ask."[119] Fetzer minces no words about the problematical aspects of the film when viewed in the context of other self-evident tampering with the evidence:

> There exists such striking evidence of fraud and fabrication in the death of JFK, not merely in relation to the photographic record but throughout this case — including the fabrication of X-rays, the substitution of a brain for that of JFK, the reshooting of the autopsy photographs, the destruction of the limousine, the substitution of a windshield, the alteration of photographs, planting of a palmprint [sic], and the suppression of evidence — that it is difficult to imagine why anyone would want to defend the position that the film could not have been altered. Given the manipulation of evidence in almost every other respect, it makes more sense to presume that it probably has been faked.[120]

The Limo Slowed & Stopped! [handwritten annotation]

The biggest problem remains the fact that more than fifty-nine witnesses stated "that the limousine either slowed dramatically or came to a complete stop after bullets began to be fired," which was "such an obvious indication of Secret Service complicity that it had to be taken out."[121]

So, beyond the obvious conflicts between the testimonies of numerous eyewitnesses to the slowing and stopped limousine, what are the other problems of the film?

The first is Zapruder himself.

Zapruder's business partner, Erwin Schwartz, had close ties with Dallas Mafiosi, the Campisi brothers, representatives of none other than New Orleans Mafia don Carlos Marcello. Schwartz was a gambling partner with Jack Ruby, often attended the latter's Carousel Club, and additionally, was seen in the same gambling clubs as H.L. Hunt.[122] As has been noted, one of the earliest copies of the film was purchased precisely by H. Hunt, raising the question of whether or not Zapruder

---

[118] James H. Fetzer, *The Great Zapruder Film Hoax*, p. xi.
[119] Ibid, p. ix.
[120] Ibid, p. xv.
[121] Ibid.
[122] Livingston, *Killing Kennedy and the Hoax of the Century*, p. 123.

was planted to film the assassination. After all, "if they could control the autopsy photos and X-rays, getting someone to film the assassination would be a piece of cake."[123]

a. Shenanigans at the Jamieson Lab and the CIA's National Photographic Reconnaissance Center

This hypothesis gains a great deal of credence the closer one looks at the circumstances of the film's handling in the immediate aftermath of the assassination.

The film was taken by Zapruder to the Jamieson Lab in Dallas for quick development, sometime after 6 P.M. on the day of the assassination. Two copies of the film were then given to Secret Service agent Forrest Sorrels of the Dallas Secret Service field office.[124] From there, apparently one copy went to the FBI. This is significant because it is this FBI connection that is the likely source for H.L. Hunt's private copy, for Hunt was not only a close associate of FBI director J. Edgar Hoover, but additionally employed several former Dallas FBI agents.[125]

Whatever shenanigans occurred at the Jamieson Lab, however, probably pale in comparison to those that occurred at the CIA's National Photographic Reconnaissance Center. The CIA's film laboratory apparently obtained a copy of the film from the Secret Service, and may have even obtained the camera original.[126] The center would certainly have had the means and resources to accomplish the editing that will be catalogued in the next section, for it was, without question, the "most sophisticated film lab in the world."[127]

b. A Catalogue of Problems

A brief catalogue of the many problems of the various versions of the Zapruder film is now in order.

1) *Rotoscoping, or animation:* Rotoscoping is a technique developed by the Disney studios to combine live with animated action.[128]

---

[123] Livingston, *Killing Kennedy and the Hoax of the Century*, p. 140.
[124] Ibid, p. 116.
[125] Ibid.
[126] Ibid, pp. 118-119, 175.
[127] Ibid, p. 175.
[128] Ibid, p. 130

The Zapruder film shows clear evidence of this, where frames have been deliberately enlarged to obscure background details and other visual clues. As Livingston notes, such "'optical enhancements' of the film, or narrowing of the field of vision, eliminate a great deal of background information so the one cannot compare parts of the film to see its alteration."[129] Such realizations on the part of some early researchers into the Zapruder film led one of them, Doug Mizzer, to complain that essentially he had been analyzing "what amounts to a cartoon."[130]

2) *Image Steadying, Composites, Missing Frames and Compressions:* There are other signs of editing in many of the versions. For example, the jerking motions of the filming have been edited in many frames by steadying the image.[131] One of the clearest examples of editing is *compression*, which is found in the testimony of then Fort Worth television reporter Dan Rather, who stated that when he viewed the Zapruder film the first time, he saw a violent *forward* motion of the President's head. He later corrected his statement to say that he saw a violent *backward* motion, the now-famous left-front "kill shot" from the Grassy Knoll.[132] In fact, in the "pristine" version of the film, there *is* a violent forward head motion followed almost immediately by the now famous violent backward motion. In other words, one shot came from behind (and apparently from a *flat* trajectory), and was followed or preceded in an instant by the shot from the front. The two shots were compressed into one for the clear purpose eliminating yet *another* shooter. A shot from a flat trajectory from behind would eliminate Oswald in his "sniper's perch" on the sixth floor of the School Book Depository.[133] In some versions, whole frames and sequences of action are simply missing.[134]

3) *The "Halo" shot:* The famous "halo" shot of some versions of the film showing a spray of what is meant to be blood and brain matter occurs for only *one* frame. This is problematical in and of

---

[129] Livingston, *Killing Kennedy and the Hoax of the Century*, p. 131.
[130] Ibid, p. 136, citing Doug Mizzer and the first draft of an article Mizzer wrote at Livingston's request, Nov. 17, 1993.
[131] Ibid, p. 131.
[132] Ibid, p. 142.
[133] Ibid, pp. 142-143, 149.
[134] Ibid, p. 145.

itself, and a strong indicator that the halo was in fact "edited in", for simply put, at the eighteen frames per second at which Zapruder's Bell and Howell film camera recorded, such an effect would require at least five to six frames to record. What the "halo" frame in effect does, in other words, is to obscure any other forensic evidence that may have been recorded in the non-edited frame.[135]

4) *The Filming Speed of Zapruder's Camera and the Warren Commission's Scenario:* The "halo" frame in some versions of the Zapruder film raises the crucial issue of the speed setting that Zapruder was filming with, for in order for the Warren Commission's Oswald scenario to work, Zapruder's camera had to be set to 18 frames per second. But there are indicators that this is *two frames too fast.*[136]

5) *The Head Matter and the Lie of the Autopsy Photos:* The "halo" frame in some versions points up yet another discrepancy, in this case, concerning the head and brain matter. Doug Mizzer has shown that there is a "clear indication in the film that there was a shot at (frame 324) from in front, and in the next frame, 325, apparent head matter falls to the trunk of the car just behind the seat where Jackie is sitting."[137] In frames 326-328, this matter moves further toward the rear, giving lie to the autopsy photographs that show an intact scalp in the rear of the President's head. But the famous "halo" frame shows this matter being propelled *forward* to hit Governor Connally. But this is in contradiction to the testimony of motorcycle officer Bobbie Hargis, who, riding behind the limousine, was struck by this matter.[138]Additionally, in many versions of the Zapruder film, the resulting mess on the rear of the car is simply missing. And once again, in many versions, after the limousine emerges from behind the freeway sign, the frames are so enlarged that most of this contextual photographic evidence is simply missing.[139]

6) *Altered or Blown-up Frames and the Changing Size of the Freeway Sign*: This point also focuses attention on yet more evidence for editing, for in some versions of the film, the

[135] Livingston, *Killing Kennedy and the Hoax of the Century*, p. 132.
[136] Ibid, pp. 134-135.
[137] Ibid, p. 136.
[138]Ibid, p. 137.
[139] Ibid, p. 150, see also p. 155.

"Stemmons Freeway sign jumps around wildly and changes shape from frame to frame."[140]

7) *The "Blob":* Yet another clear indicator of deliberate alteration is the so-called "blob" seen in the film on President Kennedy's face shortly after the fatal head shot. Some have explained this as a flap of skin reflecting the sun. This, however, is in clear contradiction to the statements of the doctors at Dallas' Parkland hospital, who describe no such wound. Livingston puts the matter with his customary succinctness: "The film is imply altered to show an apparent shot from behind. They want us to think the damage is to the frontal part of his head, backed up by fake X-rays. The blob obliterates a shot from in front."[141]

8) *The Lack of a Mess in the Back Seat of the Limousine:* Such considerations raise yet another problematical point about the film, for in most versions, there is little to no "mess" in the back seat of the limousine, yet, at Parkland Hospital, Secret Service agents Kellerman and Greer, the two agents in the front of the President's limousine (Greer was the driver), covered a tarp over the rear of the automobile to cover-up the mess. There are no such indicators in the Zapruder film.[142]

9) *The Lack of Background Objects:* Last, but not least, during the famous "fatal shot," there is no background information in the film whatsoever that would indicate where this is happening vis-a-vis the rest of Dealey Plaza.[143]

As evidence, then, the Zapruder film leaves much to be desired, and its usefulness as such can only be had in accordance with the principles of jurisprudence, that is, in conjunction with the statements and testimonies of the witnesses who were there and described what they saw. Here, as we shall now see, there are even more glaring problems.

3. The Witnesses versus the Film

One of the most salient contradictions between the film and the eyewitness testimony concerns the stopping or near-stopping of the Presidential limousine after the first shot was fired, for such action is

---

[140] Livingston, *Killing Kennedy and the Hoax of the Century*, p. 150.
[141] Ibid, p. 124.
[142] Ibid, pp. 160-161.
[143] Ibid, p. 178.

never shown on the many versions of the Zapruder film. Dallas police officers Earle Brown, motorcycle officer Bobby Hargis — whom it will be recalled was riding to the rear of the limousine and was sprayed with the head matter from the fatal shot — officer James Chaney, Mrs. Earle Cabell, wife of Dallas' mayor and who was riding in the motorcade, and no less than Senator Ralph Yarborough, riding in Vice President Lyndon Johnson's limousine, all stated that the motorcade, and the President's limousine, came to a complete stop.[144] Again, the film shows none of this, and therefore, the only sound conclusion is that any frames showing this have simply been deliberately edited out, once again to deflect attention away from the fact that the Secret Service, in control of the President's limousine, was at the minimum highly derelict in its duty, or complicit in the crime.

This highlights yet another problem, for by removing such frames — possibly occurring when the limousine was behind the Stemmons Freeway sign — means that the timing in the film is short, and would have to be filled by "stretch framing," a technique where one frame is deliberately repeated in an edited version to stretch the action of a film.[145] Thus, the film's value as a "clock of the assassination" is nil.

Other witnesses that day, such as photographer Hugh Betzner, stated that he had seen what appeared to have been a firecracker that went off *inside* the limousine, and other witnesses stated that some shots "came from either close to the car or in the car."[146] Betzner also stated that he saw something like "a nickel revolver in someone's hand in the President's car or somewhere immediately around his car."[147] Even Associated Press reporter James Altgens, whose famous photograph of Lovelady or Oswald we examined earlier in this chapter, stated that the shot came from "the left side of the car..."[148]

And last, but not least, Senator Yarborough, a former Marine, and Mrs. Earle Cabell, the Dallas' mayor's wife, both stated that the smell of gunpowder on Elm Street was clear and palpable, making it *highly* unlikely that the smell wafted down from Oswald's alleged sniper's perch on the sixth floor of the School Book Depository![149]

---

[144] Livingston, *Killing Kennedy and the Hoax of the Century,* pp. 151-152.

[145] Ibid, p. 153.

[146] Ibid, p. 148. It should be noted that such statements are the ultimate origin of the myth popular in some circles that "the driver did it." (Q.v. p. 146.)

[147] Ibid.

[148] Ibid.

[149] Ibid, pp. 148-149.

At the minimum, however, we now have a clear reason for why the Secret Service in particular should have taken such an interest in the Zapruder film, and perhaps have had a hand in the creation of some of the versions of the film that erased the near-stopping or stopping of the President's limousine, for at the least such action — reported by many eyewitnesses — is dereliction of duty and a violation of normal security procedures. But as we shall see later in this book, there is a body of evidence that suggests its role was more deliberate and sinister.

F. The Structural Outlines Begin to Emerge

From all the foregoing considerations, it is now readily apparent, in the second phase of the conspiracy to place Oswald at the crime scene, and the third phase, the covering up the crime, that there has been an almost *total* obfuscation of almost every aspect of the evidence.

We may now look more closely at the structure of the conspiracy suggested by this review, by asking a simple series of questions. Who had not only the motive, but the means and opportunity to plant, modify, or suppress all this evidence? Who had not only the motive, but the means and opportunity to run Oswald and most likely one or more doubles? Who had the ability to manage his Soviet defection and subsequent easy return to the U.S.A.? Who had not only the motive but also the means and opportunity to switch rifles? Who had not only the motive, but the opportunity and means to alter the Zapruder film? Who had the not only the motive, but the means and opportunity to alter the forensic evidence of the President's body and/or the autopsy x-rays and photographs? Who had not only the motive, but the means, that is to say, the power, and opportunity to force the Navy autopsy doctors to alter their initial autopsy reports?

Clearly, these questions rule out the Mafia, Bankers, or anti-Castro Cubans as being involved at the core level of the conspiracy. We are left, at the second level of the conspiracy, the framing of Oswald by a variety of trails — the alterations of the forensic evidence of the President's body, the bullets, the planted palm prints, and so on — *with players that had to have the intelligence connections to run Oswald to, in, and from the Soviet Union, to create Oswald doubles, to ensure he was where he needed to be on November 22, 1963, and to create or falsify forensic evidence.*

At the second level of the conspiracy, we are left, in other words, with the FBI, the CIA, the Secret Service, the military, and — if one takes seriously the messages being sent by rifles of the former Axis

111

powers, and the intelligence needed to maintain covert surveillance and contact with him in Russia — the Nazis.

At the deepest level, however, that of the on-going cover-up after the crime, and the need to alter evidence, *only* those agencies within the U.S. government with the actual power over and control of the evidence are implicated: the FBI, the CIA, the Secret Service. These conclusions concerning the emerging architecture of the conspiracy may once again be summarized be recourse to our table of groups with the means, motives, and opportunity to carry out the three essential stages of the conspiracy. Our template of the architecture of the conspiracy now looks like this:

	Means	*Motive*	*Opportunity*
The Murder Itself	Anti-Castro Cubans The Mafia FBI (Hoover) CIA Big Oil The Military Bankers (Federal Reserve) Nazis	Anti-Castro Cubans The Mafia FBI (Hoover) CIA Big Oil The Military Bankers (Federal Reserve) Nazis	Anti-Castro Cubans The Mafia FBI (Hoover) CIA Big Oil The Military Bankers (Federal Reserve) Nazis
The Framing of Oswald(via doubles, planted evidence, etc)	FBI (Hoover) CIA The Secret Service The Military Nazis/Gehlenorg	FBI (Hoover) CIA The Secret Service The Military Nazis/Gehelnorg	FBI (Hoover) CIA The Secret Service The Military Nazis/Gehelnorg
The Long-term Cover-up	FBI (Hoover) CIA The Secret Service The Military	FBI (Hoover) CIA The Secret Service The Military	FBI (Hoover) CIA The Secret Service The Military

Note that our chart differs little from the conclusions reached in chapter one, save that the Secret Service is now implicated in the handing of evidence that would eventually frame Oswald and in the manipulations of the Zapruder film, for its possession of the body of the President from Dallas to Bethesda, and its role in handling the autopsy x-rays and photographs, and the evident *lack* within the Zapruder film of any indication of a slowing or stopping of the presidential limousine. The military is obviously implicated as well, since it was directly involved in the autopsy and possibly any surgical alterations done to the President's body, if Lifton's theory is true. And as we shall also discover, there are other factors that clearly indicate that someone in the military was involved in the planning of the crime itself.

It should also be noted that we have also obtained clues during our review in this chapter of who is most implicated in the third, and most important, aspect of the conspiracy, the cover-up. While it is true that *all* of the groups involved in the first level, the crime itself, would have a vested interest in the long-term cover-up of the conspiracy, no evidence has thus far been presented that they actually were involved in the practical eventualities of maintaining it, and certainly in the case of the Mafia, Big Oil and other corporate interests such as the bankers, and the anti-Castro Cubans, they simply lacked the means to do so, and therefore, the opportunity.

It should be noted however, that the argument and evidence that remains to be presented may change the listed groups in the third component of the conspiracy. If such evidence is to be had that any of the missing groups — the Mafia, Big Oil, the Bankers, the Nazis — were involved in maintaining the cover-up, that evidence can only be had by looking closely at another category of cover-up activity: the convenient murders, suicides, and deaths by natural causes of some of the "dead witnesses."

3

Skeletons in the Closet:
Some of the Dead "Witnesses"

"A study of the dead witnesses and their backgrounds will
develop many connections between the various individuals....
and why they might have been eliminated."
Craig Roberts and John Armstrong[1]

The uniqueness of the category of the dead "witnesses" to the Kennedy assassination and to the conspiracy behind it has not been readily appreciated by most assassination researchers. While it is true that they understand these witnesses clearly testify to the *existence* of a conspiracy, most researchers do not realize that they also form the basis for significant insights into unraveling its *structure and its participants' designated roles and spheres of activity.* The mere existence of this strange class of "evidence" in the case thus affords the basis from which to peer into the third component of the conspiracy — the long-term cover-up — and to see exactly how it functioned in relationship to the other two. It allows us to see which groups were *behind* the planning committee for the crime itself, and also allows us to see the messages being sent to that committee via the deaths of the witnesses themselves.

The term "witnesses" is, however, somewhat misleading, though we continue its use here simply because of its common usage in other assassination research to designate that category of persons who, *having some connection* to the assassination, die under such circumstances and in such *numbers* as to indicate that the cover-up required their deaths. This implies that, whatever they knew, it somehow threatened the long-term interests of those involved in the conspiracy. In some cases, we can easily see what interests were threatened, and why they had to be silenced, and what group most likely silenced them. In other cases, the threatened interest has to be carefully reconstructed and argued from the evidence in order to see which group is connected to the assassination, *how* it is connected, and why the specific witness had to be silenced. While it would be impossible in the course of this review to cite *every* such witness, every effort has been made to select as wide a sampling as possible.

---

[1] Craig Roberts and John Armstrong, *JFK: The Dead Witnesses* (Tulsa, Oklahoma: Consolidated Press International, 1995), p. 177.

115

A. The Dead Witnesses and Government Investigations, or, A Funny Thing Happened While I was On My Way to Testify ...I Died

The first and most obvious thing about this category of evidence in the Kennedy assassination is the sheer *number* of people that have died under mysterious circumstances and at unusual *times*, for the timing of these deaths is not random according to authors Craig Roberts and John Armstrong:

> Of particular interest is the fact that the greatest number of deaths coincided with the four main investigations conducted by government entities: The Warren Commission (1964-65); the Jim Garrison investigation of the New Orleans connection, and later, Clay Shaw (1965-69); the Senate Committee investigation (1974-76), and the House Committee on Assassinations investigation (1976-79). By graphing out the dates of death, the authors discovered that they peaked in the months leading up to, and during, the above named inquiries — sometimes with an important witness being killed, or "committing suicide" only days or hours prior to their scheduled testimony.[2]

Roberts and Armstrong base this conclusion on a study of 143 dead witnesses in the Kennedy assassination.

Of the 106 witnesses who died between 1963 and 1982, 28 were murdered (16 were shot, 2 were poisoned), 23 suffered heart attacks, 13 committed suicide, 12 died of "natural causes," 9 suffered accidents (including 4 gunshot accidents), 7 died in auto accidents, 5 in airplane crashes, and only 9 had no cause of death indicated.[3]

With that, it is time to survey the cases of some of the witnesses themselves, why they were killed, and who might have done it. In doing so, our assumption is that in ambiguous cases — where the death cannot be known to be coincidental — that the death was intentional. In such cases, we shall extrapolate a possible motivation if there is sufficient reason from what is known about the case to do so. This method arises from a very simple contextual consideration, for a great number of the dead witnesses die having been obviously murdered, or in such mysterious ways that their deaths are hardly coincidental. These

---

[2] Craig Roberts and John Armstrong, *JFK: The Dead Witnesses* (Tulsa, Oklahoma: Consolidated Press International, 1995), p. iv.

[3] Ibid, pp. iv-v.

witnesses thus form a context in which to interpret more ambiguous cases.
In fact, our very first dead witness demonstrates this method very clearly.

B. The Dead Witnesses
1. Captain Michael D. Groves

Captain Michael D. Groves commanded the military honor guard during President Kennedy's funeral. Seven days later, while eating dinner, he "took a bite of food, paused briefly as a pained look came over his face, then passed out and fell face down into his plate. He died instantly."[4] As Roberts and Armstrong point out, this military honor guard had actually been *practicing* for a presidential state funeral for three full days prior to the assassination![5]

1) Cause of death: From the description of Captain Grove's death, and given the methodological assumption noted above, poison seems the likely method of death.

2) Motivation for death: If the military honor guard was actually drilling for a presidential funeral, then it seems obvious that the motivation for the murder is twofold:

(1) he had *a limited foreknowledge* of the assassination; and
(2) could have indicated whence his orders to practice for a funeral came. Following these orders back up the chain of command could have *exposed actual personnel involved in the plot*, and have also exposed a *documentary paper trail, consisting of the orders themselves,* indicating that there was a plan to assassinate the President prior to the event in Dallas.

3) Implicated Group(s): The military.

2. Jack Zangretti

Jack Zangretti is another crucial "dead witness." A Mafia figure based near the town of Altus, Oklahoma, 200 miles northwest of Dallas, Zangretti owned and operated "The Red Lobster" on Lake Lugert. According to Roberts and Armstrong, this restaurant and resort rivaled Las Vegas facilities, and specialized in illegal drinking and gambling

---

[4] Roberts and Armstrong, *JFK: The Dead Witnesses,* p. 3.
[5] Ibid, p. 3.

facilities, at a time when *both* were still illegal on Oklahoma. The resort played host to high ranking mobsters and often was the venue for their meetings.[6]

On the day after the assassination, Zangretti allegedly informed friends that the next day Oswald would be murdered by "a man named Jack Ruby" and that a few days after that, a member of Frank Sinatra's family would be kidnapped in order to divert attention away from the assassination and its aftermath. Sure enough, Ruby did kill Oswald, and Sinatra's son was kidnapped. As for Zangretti, he was found floating in Lake Lugert with multiple gunshot wounds to his chest. His resort and restaurant was demolished, "and all traces of its existence were removed."[7]

1) Cause of death: This is a clear case of murder, so there is no ambiguity about the witnesses having been intentionally killed in connection with the assassination.

2) Motivation for death: Clearly, the motivation for his murder is twofold once again:

1) He clearly had *foreknowledge* of the conspiracy, which, moreover, was clearly wide-ranging and complex, since he intimated that the Sinatra kidnapping was part of a well-thought-out and wide-ranging plan to divert and dilute the attention and trauma of the nation away from the assassination; and

2) he clearly was in a position *to expose personnel and implicate groups.* Since both Sinatra and Ruby were known to have Mafia connections, there is the possibility that he, like Captain Groves, might have been able to provide links that would have led back up the chain of command and exposed some of the plotters themselves. Moreover, since Ruby was also involved in gun-running operations into Cuba, and since these were Mafia operations carried out in conjunction with the CIA, such exposure might conceivably have implicated the agency as well.

3) Implicated Group(s): The Mafia definitely, the CIA possibly.

3. Maurice Brooks Gatlin

In May 1964 Maurice Brooks Gatlin died from a conveniently fatal fall from the roof of a tall building. According to Roberts and Armstrong,

---

[6] Roberts and Armstrong, *JFK: The Dead Witnesses*, pp. 3-4.
[7] Ibid, p. 4.

Gatlin was a member of the World Anti-Communist League, The Anti-Communist League of the Caribbean, was an associate of New Orleans private detective Guy F. Bannister, and was a "bag man" for Bannister and New Orleans businessman Clay Shaw, whom Jim Garrison indicted and brought to trial for his part in the conspiracy to murder President Kennedy. He once transported $100,000 in cash to Paris to agents of the OAS to fund yet another assassination attempt on French President Charles de Gaulle.[8]

While we have not yet delved into the association between the OAS and Permindex, and their mutual associations with the post-war Nazi International, it should be noted that The World Anti-Communist League was known to be one of the fronts for the post-war Nazi organization under the auspices of the CIA.[9]

1) Cause of death: Convenient fall from a tall building.

2) Implicated Group(s): Here we invert our normal order of exposition, since there is no known statement by Gatlin that would indicate possible motives for his death. Here, it is the groups implicated in the connections that spin out from him that provide a clue to the motivations for his possible murder. Gatlin is connected to the following groups via the channels indicated:

1) *To the Nazi International* via:
   a) The World Anti-Communist League;
   b) The Permindex-OAS connection;
   c) Clay Shaw, who in turn is a member of Permindex
2) *To the FBI* via:
   a) Former FBI agent and New Orleans private detective Guy F. Bannister;
3) *To the CIA* via:
   a) The World Anti-Communist League;
   b) Clay Shaw;
4) *To the Mafia* via:

---

[8] Roberts and Armstrong, *JFK: The Dead Witnesses*, p. 11.

[9] Q.v. Marin A. Lee, *The Beast Reawakens: Fascism's Resurgence from Hitler's Spymasters to Today's Neo-Nazi Groups and Right-Wing Extremists* (New York: Routledge, 2000), p. 226n, and Russ Bellant, *Old Nazis, the New Right, and the Republican Party* (Boston: South End Press, 1991), pp. 64-68, 81-83. Bellant's book should be read closely and carefully by anyone wishing to understand the connections between the CIA, its various domestic and foreign fronts, and post-war Nazi and neo-Fascist organizations such as the World Anti-Communist League.

a) Permindex corporation, which contained strong Mafia influence.

3) Motivation for death: The motivations for a possible murder are thus clear, since Gatlin could conceivably have exposed the relationship between the above groups in their involvement in the assassination, that is to say, he could have conceivably provided details that would have allowed one to uncover and reconstruct the architecture of the conspiracy itself.

4. John Garrett "Gary" Underhill

According to Roberts and Armstrong, on the night of the assassination, CIA agent John Garrett Underhill drove from Washington, D.C., to the home of his friends Robert and Charlene Fitzsimmons on Long Island. When he arrived, Robert had already gone to sleep, so he told his story to an increasingly frightened Charlene. At this juncture, there are two slightly different versions of what happened. Roberts and Craig present the following information in their book:

> Upon questioning by the now-frightened Charlene, Underhill went on to explain that he had information about the Kennedy assassination, and that "Oswald is a patsy. They set him up. It's too much. The bastards have done something outrageous. They've killed the President! I've been listening and hearing things. I couldn't believe they'd get away with it, but they did!"
>
> Underhill, emotionally distraught, continued to explain "They've gone mad! They're a bunch of drug runners and gun runners — a real violence group. God, the CIA is under enough pressure already without that bunch in Southeast Asia."....
>
> "...I know who they are. That's the problem," Underhill continued. "They know I know. That's why I'm here."[10]

Roberts and Armstrong state that Underhill left the Fitzsimmons' home a few hours later that night, after telling them he would return in a "couple of hours." But he never did.

He returned to his apartment in Washington, D.C. and began investigating the assassination on his own, mentioning his efforts to a friend of his, Asher Brynes, who was on the staff of *The New Republic*. Brynes found Underhill in bed, dead of a gunshot behind his left ear, and

---

[10] Roberts and Armstrong, *JFK: The Dead Witnesses*, p. 13.

laying on top of the gun on his left side. The local coroner ruled the death a suicide, even though Underhill was right-handed.[11]

A slightly different version of Underhill's convenient suicide was uncovered by the Garrison investigation, which in turn had run down the original story of Underhill's "suicide" to an article in *Ramparts* magazine. I present a typed version of the document in the National Archives, preserving notations and stamps, for ease of reading, followed by pictures of the document itself:

CIA HISTORICAL REVIEW PROGRAM
RELEASE AS SANITIZED
1998

~~SECRET~~
~~RYBAT~~

19 JUL 1967

MEMORANDUM

SUBJECT: Ramparts: John Garret UNDERHILL Jr:
Samuel George CUMMINGS, and
INTERARMCO

1. Ramparts of June 1967, Vol. 5, No. 12, pp. 28-29, contains the following passage about Subjects:

"The day after the assassination, Gary Underhill left Washington in a hurry. Late in the evening he showed up at the home of friends in New Jersey. He was very agitated. A small clique within the CIA was responsible for the assassination, he confided, and he was afraid for his life and probably would have to leave the country. Less than six months later Underhill was found shot to death in his Washington apartment, The coroner ruled it suicide.
(...)
"The friends whom Underhill visited say he was sober but badly shook. The say he attributed the Kennedy murder to a CIA clique which was carrying on a lucrative racket in gun-running, narcotics and other contraband, and manipulating political intrigue to serve its own ends. Kennedy supposedly got wind that something was going on and was killed before he could "blow the whistle on it." Although the friends had always known Underhill to be perfectly rational and

---

[11] Roberts and Armstrong, *JFK: The Dead Witnesses*, p. 14.

objective, they at first didn't take his account seriously. 'I think the main reason was,' explains the husband, 'that we couldn't believe that the CIA could contain a corrupt element every bit as ruthless — and more efficient — as the mafia.'

"The verdict of suicide in Underhill's death is by no means convincing. His body was found by a writing collaborator, Asher Brynes of the New Republic. He had been shot behind the left ear, and an automatic pistol was under his left side. Odd, says Brynes, because Underhill was right-handed. Brynes thinks the pistol was fitted with a silencer, and occupants of the apartment building could not recall hearing a shot. Underhill had obviously been dead several days."[12]

The discrepancies, though minor, should be noted, for in Roberts' and Armstrong's account, the home of Underhill's friends was on Long Island, whereas the *Ramparts* magazine article places it in New Jersey. Additionally, the timing of Underhill's drive is different. In the Roberts and Armstrong version, it occurs on the evening of the assassination, though no time is given. In the *Ramparts* article, the drive occurs the next day.

However, there are significant agreements. In both versions, Underhill is obviously in fear of his life; in both versions, he blames a rogue element within CIA as having had a hand in the President's assassination, a rogue element that in both versions is running drugs and guns in Southeast Asia. The significant difference between the two accounts is that in the Roberts-Armstrong version, Underhill states that he knows the names of the people involved.

1) **Cause of Death:** Convenient "suicide" by gunshot.

2) **Motivation for Death:** Once again, the motivation is clear: it is to protect the names and operations of a rogue group within the CIA

3) **Implicated Group(s):** CIA and rogue groups within it.

---

[12] National Archives and Records Administration, Document 1993.07.26.11:20:02:900620, Box JFK37, Garrison Investigation: John Garret Underhill, Jr., June 19, 1967.

NARA IDENTIFICATION AID

Document Print Date	7/26/1993
AgencyName	
AgencyNumber	0
DiskNo	0
ControlNo	0
Document id number	1993.07.26.11:20:02:900620
Recseries	JFK
Agfileno	80T01357A
JFK Box #	JFK37
Vol/Folder	F12
Title	GARRISON INVESTIGATION: JOHN GARRETT UNDERHILL JR.
Tirest	N
Document Date	6/19/1967
Whofrom	PRATT, DONOVAN E., DC/CI/R&A
Fromrest	N
Whoto	D/DOMESTIC CONTACT SERVICE
Torest	N
Numpg	1
Originator	CIA
Daterev	
Classify	U
Curstat	SAN
Doctype	PAPER
RC1	0
RC2	1
RC3	0
RC4	0
RC5	0
RC6	0
RC7	0
Comment	
Keywords	RAMPARTS
	UNDERHILL, JOHN

National Archives and Records Administration cover-sheet for Garrison investigation document on John Garrett Underhill

123

**CIA HISTORICAL REVIEW PROGRAM
RELEASE AS SANITIZED
1998**

~~SECRET
RYBAT~~

1 9 JUL 1967

MEMORANDUM

SUBJECT: <u>Ramparts</u>: John Garrett UNDERHILL Jr:,
Samuel George CUMMINGS, and
INTERARMCO

1. <u>Ramparts</u> of June 1967, Vol, 5, No. 12, pp. 28-29, contains
the following passages about Subjects:

"The day after the assassination, Gary Underhill left
Washington in a hurry. Late in the evening he showed up
at the home of friends in New Jersey. He was very agitated.
A small clique within the CIA was responsible for the assassination, he confided, and he was afraid for his life and
probably would have to leave the country. Less than six
months later Underhill was found shot to death in his
Washington apartment. The coroner ruled it suicide.

"J. Garrett Underhill had been an intelligence agent
during World War II and was a recognized authority on limited warfare and small arms. A researcher and writer on
military affairs, he was on a first-name basis with many of
the top brass in the Pentagon. He was also on intimate terms
with a number of high-ranking CIA officials--he was one of
the Agency's 'un-people' who perform special assignments.
At one time he had been a friend of Samuel Cummings of
Interarmco, the arms broker that numbers among its cus-
tomers the CIA and, ironically, Klein's Sporting Goods of
Chicago, from whence /sic/ the mail-order Carcano allegedly was purchased by Oswald.

Page one of Garrison investigation of John Garrett Underhill

124

~~SECRET~~
~~RYBAT~~

2

"The friends whom Underhill visited say he was sober but badly shook. They say he attributed the Kennedy murder to a CIA clique which was carrying on a lucrative racket in gun-running, narcotics and other contraband, and manipulating political intrigue to serve its own ends. Kennedy supposedly got wind that something was going on and was killed before he could 'blow the whistle on it'. Although the friends had always known Underhill to be perfectly rational and objective, they at first didn't take his account seriously. 'I think the main reason was,' explains the husband, 'that we couldn't believe that the CIA could contain a corrupt element every bit as ruth-less--and more efficient--as the mafia.'

"The verdict of suicide in Underhill's death is by no means convincing. His body was found by a writing collaborator, Asher Brynes of the New Republic. He had been shot behind the left ear, and an automatic pistol was under his left side. Odd, says Brynes, because Underhill was right-handed. Brynes thinks the pistol was fitted with a silencer, and occupants of the apartment building could not recall hearing a shot. Underhill obviously had been dead several days.

'Garry Underhill's chilling story is hardly implausible. As a spy apparatus the CIA is honeycombed with self-contained cliques operating without any real central control...."

2. A check of Agency records has yielded the following information about John Garrett UNDERHILL Jr.

    a. DPOB: 7 August 1915, Brooklyn.

    b. Attended high school in Brooklyn and was graduated from Harvard in 1937.

    c. Died 8 May 1964.

~~SECRET~~
~~RYBAT~~

Page two of Garrison investigation of John Garrett Underhill

5. Guy F. Banister, Jr.

Guy Banister, Jr. has already been encountered in the previous pages, but like many others with a connection to the JFK assassination, he too died in June of 1964 — before he could testify to the Warren Commission - of what was becoming a pathological disorder unique to those with such connections: the convenient heart attack.[13] As Banister's widow told the investigation of New Orleans District Attorney Jim Garrison, the FBI or Secret Service (she could not remember exactly whom) showed up within an hour of Banister's death and removed all his locked filing cabinets from his office, leaving only a few papers behind.[14] (Apparently the Federal agencies had been monitoring Banister's heart, waiting for the moment!)

Well might these agencies have wanted to clean Banister's office out, and well might they, or the CIA, have had something to do with his timely death before he could testify to the Warren Commission, for Banister's employee, Jack Martin,[15] stated to the Garrison investigation that he had seen Banister, Oswald, David Ferrie (who was training anti-Castro pilots for the Bay of Pigs invasion, and was involved in training anti-Castro guerillas as late as 1963)[16], and several anti-Castro Cubans together, and moreover, Martin made it clear that Banister was the one "running the circus."[17]

Bannister was not only a former FBI agent, as we have seen, but was also a former officer of Naval Intelligence, that is, had some connection to the Office of Naval Intelligence (ONI),[18] and his offices were conveniently located quite close to New Orleans' FBI, CIA, and ONI field offices.[19] In his memoirs of his investigation and the trial of Clay Shaw, Garrison states his belief that it may have been possible that Oswald was acting as an ONI or CIA informant, via his association with Banister.[20]

---

[13] Roberts and Armstrong, *JFK: The Dead Witnesses*, p. 20.

[14] Jim Garrison, *On The Trail of the Assassins*, p. 41.

[15] Martin was played by Jack Lemmon in Oliver Stone's celebrated movie, *JFK*, with Ed Asner playing Banister.

[16] Garrison, op. cit., p. 50. The training was being conducted at covert paramilitary camps north of Lake Pontchartrain(see p. 112).

[17] Ibid, p. 35.

[18] Ibid, p. 50.

[19] Ibid, p. 29. The closeness of Banister's offices to the CIA, FBI, and ONI field offices on New Orleans is well-dramatized in Stone's *JFK*.

[20] Jim Garrison, *On the Trail of the Assassins*, p. 264.

The possibility is not nearly as remote as it sounds, for Garrison not only had a witness — Jack Martin — who placed Oswald and David Ferrie in Banister's company on numerous occasions, he had something else, something quite significant, that indicated a definite connection between Banister and Oswald, or at least, a connection between Banister and someone *claiming* to be Oswald. Two men, a Latin and a younger Caucasian man, showed up at the Bolton Ford Dealership on January 20, 1961, claiming to represent an organization called The Friends of Democratic Cuba and talked to the salesmen, Oscar Deslatte and Fred Sewall:

> The two men indicated that they wanted to buy ten Ford pickup trucks. They wanted a bid from Bolton Ford on the price. The Latin identified himself as "Joseph Moore" but said that the bid had to be in the name of "Oswald." The young Anglo-Saxon confirmed this, explaining that "Oswald" was his name and that he was the one with the money. Instead of asking the buyers to sign, Deslatte himself printed the name "Oswald" on the form. Of course, as all the world now knows, **the real Lee Oswald was in the Soviet Union that day and would be for more than another year.**
>
> Following President Kennedy's assassination,...Deslatte remembered "Oswald's" visit and called the F.B.I. When the F.B.I. agents saw the bid form with Oswald's last name on it, according to the two salesmen, they picked it up carefully with solenoid tongs.
>
> After hearing of the Bolton Ford incident, I became very interested in Friends of Democratic Cuba. I obtained a copy of its articles of incorporation. There, among the organizations incorporators, was the ubiquitous name of *Guy Banister.*
>
> I pondered the implications of this staggering information. In the very month that John Kennedy was inaugurated, an intelligence project being run by Guy Banister was using the name "Oswald" in bidding for pickup trucks for apparent use in the Bay of Pigs invasion. More important, the thin young American who had done the bidding either knew Lee Oswald or knew his name. In either case, Oswald was far off in the Soviet Union at the time. **At the very least, this strange incident seemed to make Oswald's actual appearance at Guy Banister's operation in the summer of 1963 something less than sheer happenstance.**[21]

---

[21] Ibid, boldface emphasis added, italicized emphasis Garrison's.

In short, Guy Banister clearly was involved in CIA preparations for the Bay of Pigs invasion, was clearly connected both to the *real* and to a *double* Oswald, was a former ONI and FBI agent who, according to his employee Jack Martin, was "running the circus" of anti-Castro Cubans in New Orleans. And finally, as we saw in chapter one, Banister was at one time stationed in the northwest, and filed FBI reports on UFO activities, a fact that will eventually assume its own bizarre significance.

1) Cause of Death: Convenient heart attack before he could testify to the Warren Commission.

2) Motivation for Death: Banister was in a position, like so many others, to name names and draw connections between various aspects of the plot, specifically between the CIA, the anti-Castro Cubans, and very possibly the FBI and ONI as well. Additionally, since we have seen that Oswald's fellow employees at the Reilly Coffee Company were able to obtain jobs at NASA — an unusual career move to say the least! — and since Oswald himself thought that he would also be able to obtain a position at NASA, one cannot rule out that Banister, a key figure in all these other machinations, may have had a hand in this as well.

3) Implicated Group(s): CIA, Anti-Castro Cubans, and possibly the ONI, FBI, and NASA.

6. Mary Pinchot Meyer

No survey of the dead JFK witnesses would be complete without a mention of Mary Pinchot Meyer, one of President Kennedy's alleged mistresses. Meyer, who had been married to Cord Meyer, Jr., the "*chief of the covert action staff of the CIA,*"[22] had moved into a Georgetown apartment in Washington, D.C., and became President Kennedy's mistress in the spring of 1962. She was known to have kept a diary, which, needless to say, went completely missing after she was shot on a jogging trail within months of the assassination.[23]

1) Cause of Death: Shot to death

2) Motivation for Death: The most obvious motivation is to keep her silent about whatever she may have learned from the President himself and recorded in her diary, and additionally, whatever she may have learned from her former husband and CIA agent Cord Meyer.

---

[22] Roberts and Armstrong, *JFK: The Dead Witnesses,* p. 26, emphasis in the original.

[23] Ibid, pp. 26-27.

3) Implicated Group(s): CIA

7. Rose Cheramie

Two days before the assassination, on November 20, 1963, Rose Cheramie, whose real name was Melba Christina Marcades, was picked up in Eunice, Louisiana by state trooper, Lieutenant Francis Fruge, to convey her to the Louisiana State Hospital in Jackson. She appeared to be under the influence of drugs, and had sustained minor abrasions after she had literally been thrown from a moving car. During the trip to Jackson, Cheramie told Lieutenant Fruge a very interesting story. She had, she said, been travelling to Dallas with two men whom she said were *Italians*, or who *resembled* Italians.[24] Fruge asked her what she intended to do once she got to Dallas, and she replied that she wanted to get some money, pick up her child, and "kill Kennedy."[25]

But that was not the end of the saga. Once she arrived at the state hospital in Jackson she informed the doctors there that the President was to be murdered in Dallas during his impending visit. Worse, it was discovered that she had once worked for Jack Ruby, and hence, it appeared that her knowledge of the impending assassination came through Ruby's contacts.[26]

When the assassination occurred, Lieutenant Fruge returned to the State Hospital to take Cheramie into custody for her apparent foreknowledge of the murder and the clear indicators of a conspiracy involved with it. During her questioning she again reiterated her story, this time adding that the two men who had pushed her out of the car were travelling from Florida, and that she was to get $8000 for her part in the operation, a part that has never been fully revealed nor told.[27] Fruge contacted Dallas police captain Will Fritz and informed him of Cheramie's claims, but was told that the Dallas police department was not interested. He then stopped his investigation of the matter.[28] While the House Select Committee on Assassinations found not FBI records of Cheramie's foreknowledge of the assassination, it did discover that Cheramie had attempted to tip the FBI off that she "was travelling to

---

[24] Jim Marrs, *Crossfire*, p. 401.
[25] Ibid.
[26] Ibid, p. 402.
[27] Ibid.
[28] Ibid.

Dallas to deliver heroin to a man in Oak Cliff, then to Galveston to pick up a shipment of drugs."[29]

Cheramie made one last attempt in August of 1965 to tell the FBI of a similar drug shipment, but was ignored. On September 4, 1965, she was found dead on a roadside after apparently having been tossed from a moving car *again*, and then having been run over by a man from Tyler, Texas, who told police that in his attempt to avoid her body which was lying in the middle of the road, he had accidentally driven over her head. Police could find no connection between the driver and Cheramie and her death was ruled accidental (if indeed she had not been dead before he ran over her). The case was dropped.

Lieutenant Fruge, however, investigated further, and discovered that the address in Tyler that the driver had given did not even exist.[30]

Cheramie's claims are worth looking at closely, for two reasons: (1) her obvious foreknowledge of the assassination, and (2) her claim that the two men she was with were travelling to Dallas for the express purpose of murdering the President, and that they were either *Italians* or that they *resembled* Italians.

Let us deal with the issue of the resemblance to Italians first. As is now well-known, Miami, Florida was the headquarters of a large and powerful anti-Castro community and also one of the CIA's largest domestic bases and field offices at that time. Consequently, it is entirely possible that Cheramie was travelling in the company of anti-Castro Cubans.

On the other hand, Miami was also the home base of Mafia gun-running operations into Cuba, and under the direction of Santos Trafficante, as we have seen, and thus, Cheramie might indeed have been travelling with Italians, just as she said, with members of a mob hit team dispatched to commit the assassination. Such a role for the Mafia in the assassination does indeed make sense, for with the Mafia-CIA connections vis-a-vis the anti-Castro movement, both groups would be served by the elimination of the President, with the Mafia acting as the "cut-out" for the CIA to provide "plausible deniability" should any of the assassins actually have been apprehended by law enforcement after the murder.

However, there is a final, even more sinister involvement that the two "Italians" might signify, and that is yet another connection to

---

[29] Jim Marrs, *Crossfire*, p. 402.
[30] Ibid.

Permindex and through it, deeper connections to the Fascist and Nazi International, and yet more connections to the CIA.

1) Cause of Death: Death by being thrown from a moving car and subsequently run over by a driver whose address did not exist.

2) Motivation for Death: Foreknowledge of the assassination and the ability to indicate who was involved.

3) Implicated Group(s): The CIA, the Mafia, anti-Castro Cubans and possibly deeper connections to a Fascist and Nazi International.

8. Dorothy Mae Kilgallen

I well remember Dorothy Kilgallen. A regular panelist on the old 1960s TV game show "What's My Line," hosted by John Dailey, Kilgallen was a well-known syndicated columnist in the country, and a New York City socialite. Oddly enough, like another witness, Guy Banister, she has a connection both to the Kennedy assassination, and to the subject of UFOs, having written articles on the latter subject in the mid-1950s.

Kilgallen was found at 2:45 PM in her New York City apartment on November 8, 1965, by her hairdresser, dead, apparently, of an overdose of barbiturates which she had taken with alcohol, causing her heart to fail. She had appeared the night before in her role as a regular panelist on "What's My Line."[31]

Kilgallen had done something, however, that even the Warren Commission had not. Following Jack Ruby's trial and conviction, in March 1964 Kilgallen journeyed to Dallas and managed to obtain a private interview with Ruby. After this interview, she travelled back and forth between Dallas and New Orleans, tracking down leads. Upon her return to New York, she confided to a few friends that she "had discovered information that would blow the whole Kennedy assassination story 'wide open.'"[32]

Given that she travelled to New Orleans to investigate whatever leads Ruby had given her, we may assume that she uncovered a similar murky trail as New Orleans District Attorney Jim Garrison would begin to uncover only two years later, and possibly more. We may assume, therefore, that she discovered the deep connections between anti-Castro Cubans, the Mafia, and the CIA, and may also have uncovered evidence

---

[31] Armstrong and Roberts, *JFK: The Dead Witnesses*, p. 31.
[32] Ibid, p. 32.

of two Oswalds. Exposure of *those* connections would inevitably have led to other deep players as well.

1) Cause of Death: Overdose of barbiturates with alcohol

2) Motivation for Death: Knowledge of CIA, Mafia, anti-Castro operations in New Orleans, with possible knowledge of more than one Oswald.

3) Implicated Group(s): CIA, Mafia, anti-Castro Cubans

9. Mrs. Earl E.T. Smith

Smith, who was Kilgallen's best friend, was found dead in her home of a brain hemorrhage a mere three days after Kilgallen was found dead.[33] Roberts and Armstrong note that "It was rumored that Mrs. Smith was the recipient of Dorothy Kilgallen's notes. If this is true, she may have had knowledge concerning just exactly how Kilgallen planned to 'bust the Kennedy assassination wide open.'"[34]

1) Cause of Death: Brain hemorrhage.

2) Motivation for Death: Knowledge of CIA, Mafia, anti-Castro operations in New Orleans, with possible knowledge of more than one Oswald.

3) Implicated Group(s): CIA Mafia, anti-Castro Cubans

10. Lee Bowers, Jr.

Lee Bowers Jr. was working in the railroad yard control tower behind the Grassy Knoll on the day of the assassination. From this vantage point, Bowers later testified to the Warren Commission that he saw three cars enter the railroad yard, and then circle around his control tower. Bowers stated that the second of these was occupied solely by the driver who was apparently speaking into a radio telephone. The last car, a muddy Chevrolet Impala, arrived a few minutes before the President's motorcade, and parked behind the concrete wall of the memorial.[35]

Bowers saw more. At the eastern end of the area behind the Knoll, he saw two other men wearing uniforms "similar to those custodians at the courthouse."[36] Additionally, there was a man wearing dark clothes who was standing in the bushes and trees behind the picket fence. Another

[33] Roberts and Armstrong, *JFK: The Dead Witnesses*, p. 32.
[34] Ibid, p. 33.
[35] Marrs, *Crossfire*, pp. 75-76.
[36] Ibid, p. 77.

man was near him wearing a white shirt.[37] Bowers then stated that after the last shot had been fired, the Chevy Impala reappeared from behind the wall where it had been parked.[38] As if that were not bad enough for the emerging cover story of Oswald the "Lone Nut" shooting from the Depository, Bowers stated in a subsequent filmed interview that he had seen either a flash of light or puff of smoke from the area of the picket fence on the Grassy Knoll.[39]

To put it bluntly, Bowers had seen both the shot from, and the shooter on, the Grassy Knoll as well as perhaps members of his team.

On August 6, 1966, Lee Bowers died in a single car accident near Midlothian, Texas.[40] But the local medical examiner had a rather different cause of death in mind, for he maintained

> that when Bowers died, he was in some kind of "strange shock." It should be noted that at this time the intelligence services world-wide had access to drugs that produced various mental conditions ranging from a catatonic state to grogginess and death.[41]

Following our methodology, and assuming that Bowers' death was indeed a deliberate act of murder, then a very interesting scenario is implied. Bowers would have had to have been under surveillance for some time, in order to administer any drugs surreptitiously to him. It seems possible that the drug or drugs — whatever it or they may have been — were administered precisely to cause the accident. In any case, this probable surveillance and the highly unusual manner of death points to those groups with access to them and the means to administer them, namely, the CIA, the Mafia, and possibly even the Nazi element.

1) Cause of Death: Suspicious one car accidental death in which drugs are indicated.

2) Motivation for Death: The motivation for the death here is clearly because Bowers could potentially identify the people behind the picket fence on the Grassy Knoll. Successful identification of these individuals could in turn lead to groups and connections involved in the assassination that the conspirators wished to keep silent. Those connections might very likely have disclosed much about the actual

---

[37] Marrs, *Crossfire*, p. 77.
[38] Ibid.
[39] Ibid.
[40] Roberts and Armstrong, *JFK: The Dead Witnesses*, pp. 38-39.
[41] Ibid, p. 39.

architecture of the conspiracy itself. Bowers, accordingly, had to be silenced.

3) Implicated Group(s): Mafia, CIA and other intelligence groups, including the Nazi element.

11. Lt. Cmdr. William Bruce Pitzer

Lieutenant Commander William Bruce Pitzer was one of those involved in taking photographs, and perhaps even film, of President Kennedy's "autopsy" in Bethesda, Maryland. On Saturday, October 29, 1966, Pitzer was found dead in his office at Bethesda Naval Hospital. He had been shot in the right temple. The Navy, of course, immediately ruled it a suicide, but Pitzer's family, and especially his widow, questioned the finding. She maintained that her husband "had parts of the autopsy that they wanted destroyed," meaning that they wanted certain photographs he had taken destroyed. Pitzer had refused. His widow also stated that after his "suicide" she had been visited by four Navy intelligence agents who told her not to talk.[42] According to Roberts and Armstrong, all government records showing Pitzer's presence at the autopsy have been sanitized and his name removed.[43]

1) Cause of Death: Gunshot to right temple, ruled suicide by the Navy, but showing the signature of a professional execution or "hit."

2) Motivation for Death: As noted in the previous chapter, there is strong evidence to suggest that either the President's body had been surreptitiously altered at some point between Dallas and Bethesda, or that the photographs and x-rays of the autopsy in Bethesda were forgeries and fabrications, or both. This alone would be cause to have him murdered. But there are also two other potential reasons for the murder. Pitzer was in a position to name the people that had ordered him to destroy evidence, and thus, potentially was in a position to expose aspects of the conspiracy's chain of command and therefore, to expose aspects of its structure. Additionally, it is possible that Pitzer may have made personal copies of the photos and films that he was ordered to destroy.

3) Implicated Group(s): The Military, Office of Naval Intelligence. There are possibly other intelligence connections involved in the murder itself, as Pitzer's mode of death shows the clear signature of a

---

[42] Livingstone, *Killing Kennedy and the Hoax of the Century*, p. 336n.
[43] Roberts and Armstrong, *JFK: The Dead Witnesses*, p. 41.

professional hit, or execution. This would even suggest that the Mafia may have been ordered to murder Pitzer.

12. General Charles Peare Cabell

As Deputy Director of Operations in the CIA from 1953 to 1961,[44] General Charles Peare Cabell was one of those generals who, along with others such as Generals Krulak, Ed Lansdale, and others, while appearing to be military, were in fact a significant "CIA military" coterie, a private army, navy, and air force created for the express purpose of covert paramilitary action.[45] On the day of the Bay of Pigs invasion, it was in fact General Cabell, and not President Kennedy, who initially froze the airstrikes that were to have eliminated Castro's air force and provided air cover to the invading Cuban brigade.[46] In the wake of the Bay of Pigs disaster, President Kennedy fired CIA Director Allen Dulles, and his two right-hand men who oversaw cover operations and planning: Richard M. Bissell and General Charles Cabell.

Cabell, in an interesting career move, then became a member — along with General Richard Secord of Iran-Contra fame - of the board of directors for Pacific Corporation, a subsidiary for the notorious CIA front, "Air America" that is now known to have been involved in smuggling opium out of southeast Asia during the Vietnam War. In other words, General Cabell never really left the CIA at all.[47]

There is yet another connection well-known to assassination researchers, and that is that General Cabell's brother, Earle, was the mayor of Dallas at the time of the murder, and in that capacity, had been instrumental in establishing the route of President Kennedy's motorcade that changed at the last minute, to take the detour down Houston on to Elm, past the School Book Depository, and into the kill zone.[48] Cabell died of "natural causes" while on a visit to Fort Meyers, Virginia for a routine physical, when he suddenly collapsed and expired.[49]

---

[44] Roberts and Armstrong, *JFK: The Dead Witnesses*, p. 70.

[45] See L. Fletcher Prouty, *The Secret Team: The CIA and Its Allies in Control of the United States and the World* (New York: Skyhorse Publishing, 2008), pp. 13-15.

[46] Roberts and Armstrong, op. cit., pp. 76-78.

[47] Ibid, p. 82.

[48] Ibid.

[49] Ibid.

1) Cause of Death: No known or publicly stated caused of death other than his collapse at Fort Myers. Cabell's brother Earle died ten years after the assassination, also of "natural causes."

2) Motivation for Death: Following the methodological principle that "two deaths is a coincidence," but "several is a pattern," the motivation for Cabell's elimination seems clear, given the relationship between him and his brother, the Mayor of Dallas, who changed the motorcade route. The Cabells seem to be involved, at some level, in the planning of the mechanical details of the operation, and would thus be in a position to expose those higher up in the structure.

3) Implicated Group(s): CIA, the Military.

13. Roscoe Anthony White

Roscow Anthony White is beyond doubt one of the more crucial and problematic "dead witnesses" to have emerged in recent years. White was a Dallas police officer assigned to the Dallas police laboratory as a photographic technician. He also had ties to Jack Ruby since his wife, Geneva, worked at Jack Ruby's nightclub, the Carousel Club, in Dallas.[50]

His wife later claimed that White was in fact a hit man, "and told of hearing Ruby and her husband discuss plans to assassinate the President."[51] She also maintained that White and Oswald were friends. Indeed, their association ran very deep:

> It was later discovered that Roscoe White and Lee Harvey Oswald had served in the Marines together and had reportedly been on a small unit joint exercise in the Philippines at the same time. Some photographs of the period purportedly show Oswald and White in the same picture. It is Roscoe White, who was built similar to Oswald (though more muscular) that is thought to be a stand-in on some of the *Life* magazine published photos of Oswald holding a rifle and newspaper.[52]

There was more to White than merely a suspicious resemblance to Oswald — and how many "suspicious resemblances" does that add up to now?

After White's very suspicious death due to burns suffered in an explosion, his son Ricky discovered a secret diary among his father's

---

[50] Roberts and Armstrong, *JFK: The Dead Witnesses*, p. 83.
[51] Ibid.
[52] Ibid.

effects, inside a "water tight artillery canister."[53] The canister also contained "three secret teletypes addressed to (or mentioning an operation codenamed) 'Mandarin.'"[54] The first message, dated September 1963 was ominous:

> "Remarks — Mandarin: Foreign affairs assignments have been canceled. The next assignment is to eliminate a national security threat to worldwide peace. Destination will be Houston, Austin or Dallas. Contacts are being arranged now. Orders are subject to change at any time. Reply back if not understood."[55]

According to Roberts and Armstrong, the message was typed on a "rough newsprint quality teletype paper", was typed in blue ink, and was signed "C. Bowers, OSHA." At the bottom of the message there was a line that read "Re-rifle: Code AAA: destroy/on/"[56]

The next two messages were equally ominous:

> The next message, addressed in similar fashion, was dated October, 1963. It also referenced "Mandarin," and went on to state that: "Dallas destination chosen. Your place hidden within the department. Contacts are within this letter. Continue as planned."
>
> Again, the signatory was C. Bowers," and it referenced "rifle."
>
> The third message, as were the others, was "signed" C. Bowers, OSHA, and referenced "rifle." The wording is quite unmistakable: "Stay within department[.] Witnesses have eyes, ears, and mouth. You [had nothing] to do of the mix-up. The man will be in to cover all misleading evidence soon. Stay as planned (and) wait for further orders."[57]

Once White's son Ricky read these messages and portions of his father's secret diary, he, of course, attempted to make the matters public.

And that is where things began to get complicated, for the messages were immediately decried by various federal agencies as being complete and utter hoaxes. The problem, as Roberts and Armstrong correctly observe, is that "No motive for a hoax could be determined — after all

---

[53] Roberts and Armstrong, *JFK: The Dead Witnesses*, p. 83.
[54] Ibid.
[55] Ibid.
[56] Ibid.
[57] Ibid, p. 84. Roberts and Armstrong note that the brackets denote "missing or faded words that were not deciphered until 1992 by Kennedy researcher Gary Shaw."

who would want to go down in history as the son of one of the men who shot Kennedy..."[58] Ricky White maintained that when he read the actual diary itself, it stated that his father had been *one* of the shooters on the Grassy Knoll, and that his father had also been ordered to eliminate twenty-eight other witnesses to the assassination. Finally, the diary, according to Ricky White, also placed his father with murdered Dallas police officer J.D. Tippit, the officer whom Oswald was initially arrested and charged with murdering.[59]

As for the diary itself, "soon after Ricky's revelations the diary vanished, taken by the FBI and never returned."[60] When queried about the diary, the FBI has given curiously inconsistent response, maintaining that it never even existed, or that it was brought to Washington where it was subsequently given to the House Select Committee on Assassinations, where it subsequently disappeared, or, finally, that the FBI had examined the diary, determined it to be a hoax, and "weren't interested."[61] But if a hoax, why not return it to Ricky White? And why go to the bother to give out such conflicting statements as to its whereabouts?

There were other potent arguments that the messages, and White's wider role in a conspiracy, were probably genuine:

> Roscoe White was in Lee Harvey Oswald's platoon in the Orient; they traveled to Japan on the same ship; both were from Texas; Roscoe and Oswald both worked in the Intelligence community; he had access to a Dallas police uniform complete with badge; his serial number matched that of the message addressee number; and finally, the messages were of standard military format down to the last detail.[62]

However, perhaps the most potent argument for the authenticity of the strange messages and the now missing diary, is the way that Roscoe Anthony White perished.

White died on September 24, 1971 after sustaining severe burns from the explosion of a welding tank with which he was working.[63]

1) Cause of Death: Severe burns suffered during the explosion of a welding tank.

---

[58] Roberts and Armstrong, *JFK: The Dead Witnesses*, p. 84.

[59] Ibid, p. 85.

[60] Ibid.

[61] Ibid.

[62] Ibid, p. 84.

[63] Ibid, pp. 82, 86.

2) Motivation for Death: White's alleged obvious knowledge of the operational details of the plot, and possible ability to connect the "mechanics" of the operation to higher-ups in the chain of command, and thus expose its real structure.

3) Implicated Group(s): CIA, the Military, and at a subsidiary level, elements within the Dallas Police Department.

14. Congressman Hale Boggs

Exactly ten years to the day after President Kennedy's assassination, on November 22, 1973, the *Los Angeles Star* ran an article on the death of Louisiana Congressman Hale Boggs in an airplane accident in Alaska. The article maintained that the Congressman "had startling revelations on the Watergate and the Assassination of President Kennedy."[64] Boggs' flight disappeared over Alaska on October 16, 1972, one month after the break-in at Democratic Party Headquarters in the Watergate complex in Washington, D.C.

Boggs was, of course, one of the seven commissioners appointed to the Warren Commission by President Lyndon Johnson, and of that seven, he was one of a "strange quadrinity" of three that had some unusual connections in his own right. A closer look at those seven men is now in order, to reveal those three men and their unusual connections, and therefore, the possible motivation behind their selection by President Johnson to be on the Warren Commission.

The seven commissioners are pictured in the following photograph. From left to right, they are:

1) Congressman Gerald Ford (R-Michigan);
2) Congressman Hale Boggs (D-Louisiana);
3) Senator Richard Russell (D-Georgia);
4) Chief Justice Earl Warren;
5) Senator John S. Cooper (R-Kentucky);
6) John J. McCloy, a lawyer with prominent business contacts to Wall Street, one time American High Commissioner for Germany, a role in which he was instrumental in "pardoning" known Nazis and bringing many of them to this country under

---

[64] Roberts and Armstrong, *JFK: The Dead Witnesses*, p, 94.

Operation Paperclip, and American counsel for the giant German cartel, I.G. Farben prior to World War Two;[65]

7) Allen Dulles, former CIA Director, fired by President Kennedy for his role in the Bay of Pigs invasion;

8) Warren Commission chief counsel J. Leo Rankin.

The Seven Commissioners of the Warren Commission, With Chief Counsel J. Leo Rankin;
Seated, Left to Right, are:
Congressman Gerald Ford, Congressman Hale Boggs, Senator Richard Russell, Chief Justice Earl Warren, Senator John S. Cooper, John J. McCloy, Allen Dulles, and Chief Counsel J. Leo Rankin

Let us look carefully now at two members of the "strange triumvirate" *and the interests they represent*: John J. McCloy, and former CIA director Allen Dulles.

When one looks at the interests that these two men alone represent, it will be discovered that they represent some of the major groups with "coalescing interests" with the means and motives, and in some cases, the opportunity to commit the crime. These groups are:

---

[65] For these facts, see my *The SS Brotherhood of the Bell: NASA's Nazis, JFK, and Majic-12* (Kempton, Illinois: Adventures Unlimited Press, 2006), pp. 394-396. I note there that McCloy shared Hitler's box at the 1936 Berlin Olympics by dint of the fact that he was Farben's chief American counsel.

1) The CIA and its operations and plans divisions (Dulles);
2) Banking and finance (McCloy);
3) The Nazis, via Operation Paperclip and I.G. Farben (McCloy);

It is worth noting that when President Johnson initially discussed the proposed Commission members with FBI Director Hoover, that the list originally included all these men, plus General Lauris Norstad. Norstad somehow managed to avoid appointment to the Commission.[66] Had Norstad eventually have been persuaded to accept appointment to the Commission, he would have symbolized the *military's* interests.

So where does Congressman Hale Boggs fit into this "strange triumvirate"? Boggs, as it turns out, had his own interesting connections, and represents yet another group with the motives and means to commit the crime itself:

> His chief financial backer during his election bids was none other than New Orleans Mafia don Carlos Marcello. This fact also did not surface during the Commission hearings or selection *due to the fact that Hoover never let it be mentioned even though he knew it.*[67]

Additionally, it was Boggs himself who had the most difficulty with the Commission's findings concerning Oswald the "Lone Nut," and it was Boggs who first directed New Orleans District Attorney Jim garrison's attentions to a possible CIA connection to the conspiracy.[68]

Given Hoover's complicity in withholding information about the connections between Boggs and Marcello, and given Boggs' role as a Commissioner, we now have the following group interests represented on the Warren Commission, and therefore the following groups' connections to the development of the cover-story of the Warren Report:

1) The CIA and its operations and plans divisions (Dulles);
2) Banking and finance (McCloy);

---

[66] L. Fletcher Prouty, *JFK: The Cia, Vietnam, and the Plot to Assassinate John F. Kennedy*, p. 139.

[67] Roberts and Armstrong, *JFK: The Dead Witnesses*, p. 94, emphasis added.

[68] Ibid.

3) The Nazis, via Operation Paperclip and I.G. Farben (McCloy);
4) The Mafia (Boggs);
5) The FBI (via Hoover's conferral with Johnson on the latter's proposed Commission members).

Boggs' presence as a Congressman from Louisiana, with deep connections to all the suspicious activities surrounding New Orleans surveyed earlier, is hardly coincidental, given the presence of Dulles and McCloy on the same Commission. *The interests represented on the Warren Commission are clues to the deep architecture of the conspiracy, if only because these groups would apparently have some long term vested interest jeopardized if a conspiracy were ever exposed.*

In this light, Boggs' subsequent behavior in *exposing* aspects of the plot to District Attorney Garrison must be scrutinized rather carefully. While it is entirely possible and indeed probable that Boggs' suspicions and actions in directing Garrison to the CIA were legitimate concerns and altruistically motivated, it is equally possible that they were intended to divert attention away from the deep Mafia connections with the plot.

But there is also a third, and final possibility, and that is that the exposure of the conspiracy was *itself* part of the *design* of the conspiracy, a disturbing possibility that will be examined more closely in chapter five.

1) Cause of Death: Suspicious disappearance by airplane accident in Alaska one month after the Watergate break-in, under circumstances that one major newspaper suggested connected the JFK assassination to the Watergate burglary.

2) Motivation for Death: Probable knowledge of the connections of the major groups with vested interests in the on-going cover-up.

3) Implicated Group(s): The CIA, FBI, Banks and major corporate interests, Nazis, the Mafia.

15. President Lyndon Baines Johnson

It may seem unusual or even impertinent to include President Lyndon Johnson in this list of "dead witnesses," especially as one intention of this book is to scrutinize rather closely his probable role at some level within the conspiracy. However, in the truest sense, Lyndon Johnson *was* a witness, for he was in the motorcade in Dallas on a trip that he had personally helped to plan and organize, heard the shots that killed his predecessor, the shots that impelled him into the Presidency and into a role that, at the minimum, forced him to act in behalf of the cover-up as an accessory after the fact.

Johnson came from a family that, on his father's side, suffered a long history of heart ailments. Johnson himself had suffered a nearly fatal heart attack in the 1950s when he was the Democratic Majority Leader in the United States Senate. On January 20, 1973, Johnson was found dead of a heart attack on his ranch in Texas.

Giving a President with a history of chronic heart ailments a heart attack is a very convenient way to get rid of a problem without drawing suspicion to the death itself. But was Johnson, like so many others, silenced for his role in and knowledge of aspects of the conspiracy?

On April 24, 1975, on the *CBS Nightly News*, then-anchorman Walter Cronkite aired a portion of an interview he had conducted with President Johnson on his ranch in September, 1969. Cronkite asked very directly if Johnson thought the assassination could have been the work of a conspiracy. In a short answer of little over a minute's length, Johnson replied that he did think it could have been such. Later, Johnson asked CBS to edit out that portion of the interview for national security purposes.[69]

The fact that Johnson would first talk on record, and then later "request" CBS not to air that portion of the interview, may have sent shock waves through the groups that had a possible role within the plot. For one thing, Johnson was directly connected to almost all of them. As Senate Majority leader, he had direct hands in the passing of the law that created NASA, and not only was a close friend of Hoover, but also a close friend to "former" Nazi rocket scientist Wernher Von Braun. He was a close political associate of Texas oil magnates H.K. Hunt, and Clint Murchison, both of whom were heavy financial contributors to his political campaigns. Through his aide Bobby Baker, Johnson also had direct ties to the Mafia. And in his various public statements concerning the Kennedy conspiracy, Johnson fingered or implicated almost every possible group: the CIA, anti-Castro Cubans, and so on.[70] By the time Johnson talked to Cronkite, and then rescinded his on-the-record comments, it was clear that Johnson was beginning to buckle under pressure, and wanted to talk.

1) **Cause of Death:** Convenient heart attack.

---

[69] This portion of the interview, as it was aired on CBS on April 24, 1975, may be viewed at http://www.youtube.com/watch?v=oF4_7_Emzy0.

[70] Roberts and Armstrong, *JFK: The Dead Witnesses*, p. 97.

2) Motivation for Death: Possible exposure of the highest echelons of the conspiracy architecture, of which he himself was a member, at some level.

3) Implicated Group(s): The Mafia, CIA, anti-Castro Cubans, Big Oil, Nazis... just about everyone.

16. Clay Shaw

Clay Shaw has the distinction of being the only man ever charged and brought to trial for a direct role in the Kennedy assassination, for Shaw ultimately became the focus of New Orleans District Attorney Jim Garrison's investigation of the assassination. Shaw's career as a spy began during World War Two, shortly after his enlistment in 1941, when he was recruited by General Donovan's Office of Strategic Services (OSS), the predecessor to today's CIA. He soon found himself in the high octane atmosphere of being the liaison officer to Prime Minister Winston Churchill's headquarters.[71]

Settling in New Orleans after the war, Shaw by the 1960s had become entangled with a number of post-war CIA proprietary fronts, including Centro Mondiale Commerciale in Italy, the International House-World Trade Center in New Orleans, and the yet-to-be discussed Permindex Corporation.[72] The connections of Centro Mondiale Commerciale and Permindex are, however, worth noting here:

> The European connections of Permindex and Centro Mondiale Commerciale ran the gamut of former Nazis, princes, aristocrats from both Germany and Italy, and even members of the former Italian royal family. The president of Permindex was Ferenc Nagy, former premier of Hungary and a leading anti-Communist.[73]

This is just scratching the surface, but the deeper, murkier connections are perhaps best summarized here by noting that Nagy was one of the principal members of the pro-Nazi puppet government of Hungary during the Second World War, and a leading figure in the post-war émigré societies established as fronts for post-war Nazi activity, with strong ties to General Reinhard Gehlen's "organization."

Shaw was a close confidant of David Ferrie in New Orleans, and additionally, former CIA Director Richard Helms finally admitted that

---

[71] Roberts and Armstrong, *JFK: The Dead Witnesses*, p. 103.
[72] Ibid.
[73] Ibid, p. 104.

both Shaw and Ferrie were CIA operatives. Additionally, Shaw also knew the CIA's General Charles Cabell.[74] Finally, both Shaw and David Ferrie were prominent members of New Orleans' homosexual underground community of the day.[75]

As the Garrison investigators probed Shaw's effects after his arrest, they discovered in his address book the name "LEE ODOM, P.O. Box 19106, Dallas, Texas."[76] This exact same citation also appeared in Lee Harvey Oswald's notebook.[77] On one of the unused pages in Shaw's address book, the notations "Oct" and "Nov" appeared, followed by "an indecipherable scribble" and then the simple word, "Dallas."[78]

Not surprisingly, Shaw died on August 15, 1974, under circumstances that even for the dead witnesses can only be categorized as bizarre. Shaw had just given an interview to a columnist for the *Washington Post*. Shortly thereafter, a neighbor reported seeing an ambulance drive up to Shaw's home, remove a stretcher from the back with a body under a sheet, and carry it into his house. A few minutes later, they returned with the stretcher, but no body. Hours later, Shaw was "found dead in his home alone."[79] Shaw's death certificate listed "lung cancer" as the cause of death, but the parish coroner demanded exhumation of Shaw's body for an autopsy. A media campaign was whipped up against the exhumation, and the coroner dropped the demand.[80]

1) Cause of Death: convenient "lung cancer"

2) Motivation for Death: Clearly Shaw was connected to the CIA via a number of its proprietary fronts, including Centro Mondiale Commerciale and Permindex, both with strong ties to the post-war Nazi and Fascist International. Additionally, since Shaw's connections to Guy Bannister, David Ferrie, Lee Oswald and the New Orleans anti-Castro Cubans is a matter of some documentation,[81] those groups are implicated as well.

3) Implicated Group(s): CIA, Nazis, anti-Castro Cubans.

---

[74] Roberts and Armstrong, *JFK: The Dead Witnesses*, p. 105.

[75] Ibid, p. 106.

[76] Jim Garrison, *On the Trail of the Assassins*, p. 170.

[77] Ibid.

[78] Ibid, p. 172.

[79] Roberts and Armstrong, *JFK: The Dead Witnesses*, pp. 106-107.

[80] Ibid, p. 107.

[81] See Jim Garrison, *On the Trail of the Assassins*, pp. 100-104, 122-124, 136-145, 176-181, and Jim Marrs, *Crossfire*, pp. 498-515.

17. Dallas Deputy Sherriff Roger Dean Craig

We have already met Deputy Sherriff Roger Dean Craig previously in these pages. Here it will be recalled that there are two significant, though very distinct, features of what Craig saw and later testified to that day in Dallas: (1) Craig maintained he saw someone like Oswald get into a Nash Rambler station wagon being driven by a Latin-looking man, and drive away from the Book Depository. This conflicts completely with the "escape" route advocated by the Warren Commission; and (2) Craig and two other deputies stated that the rifle found in the Book Depository was the very accurate high-powered 7.65 German Mauser, not the cheap and inaccurate Italian 6.5 Mannlicher-Carcano that was eventually sold as the alleged murder weapon.

Craig was convinced there was a conspiracy in Dallas on November 22, 1963, and spent the rest of his life trying to expose it, even going so far as to meet with Jim Garrison in New Orleans to discuss it. On his return to Dallas, someone attempted to shoot him in the head, but ended up only grazing it. Then while driving in West Texas in 1973, he was forced off the road and experienced a severe accident, injuring his back and forcing him to retire from law enforcement. In 1974, Craig answered a knock at his back door, only to find himself facing a man with a shotgun pointed at his chest.[82]

Craig was found dead in his father's home in Dallas on May 15, 1975, dead from a gunshot wound *fired from a rifle*. The death, not surprisingly, was ruled a suicide.[83]

1) Cause of Death: Suicide by rifle shot.

2) Motivation for Death: Craig has been selected because of the very difficulty of assigning a motivation for his death. Clearly, Craig's testimony concerning Oswald, the Nash Rambler, and the Mauser, are problematic to the official cover story. But beyond the symbolic value of the Mauser and Mannlicher-Carcano rifles, there are really no implicated groups.

3) Implicated Group(s): Theadbare possible Nazi connection, Dallas police department complicity and corruption is also implied.

---

[82] Roberts and Armstrong, *JFK: The Dead Witnesses*, p. 116.
[83] Ibid, p. 117.

18. Mafia Don Sam Giancana

Sam Giancana was at the time of the Kennedy assassination one of four Mafia dons who, along with Meyer Lansky in New York, Santos Trafficante in Miami, and Carlos Marcello in New Orleans, controlled the criminal underground in the United States.[84] There was one common interest that in the early 1960s united these men and their "families" and that was their common participation in CIA sponsored Mafia operations against Castro. This Mafia-intelligence relationship, as we saw in chapter one, went back to World War Two and the agreement between the CIA's predecessor, the OSS, and Mafia don Lucky Luciano. Due to Giancana's position as the Chicago don, it is most likely that there was some direct association with Jack Ruby, who was also from Chicago, as well as an indirect one through New Orleans don Carlos Marcello.[85]

June 19, 1975, Giancana was gunned down in his fortress-like Chicago home while cooking a dinner. Roberts and Armstrong are worth citing extensively here:

> According to both (sic) his daughter and the police, who stated that Giancana was invulnerable in his own home due to the security systems and impregnability of the structure, only someone he knew or trusted could have gotten to him. Gianaca would have to have let them in, gone back to cooking, then been surprised when the assailant, or assailants, pulled a .22 pistol.
>
> From the crime scene, it appeared that Giancana had turned his back on the gunman, whereupon the assassin produced his pistol, shot him in the back of the head six times, then rolled his body over, reloaded, and shot several bullets around his mouth. The M.O. matched that of a standard Mafia hit, and the message sent by the mouth shots was quite clear: Giancana had already said too much — and would never talk again.[86]

Giancana was murdered just as the Senate Intelligence Committee was preparing to question him.[87]

---

[84] Roberts and Armstrong, *JFK: The Dead Witnesses*, p. 117.
[85] Ibid., p, 119.
[86] Ibid., p. 120.
[87] Ibid., p. 119.

1) Cause of Death: There is no ambiguity with Giancana; his death was clearly a murder with all the M.O. of a standard Mafia hit, by someone whom he apparently knew.

2) Motivation for Death: The motive in Giancana's murder also seems more or less clear, it was to prevent him from testifying to the Senate Intelligence Committee on what he knew about the CIA and anti-Castro operations, and what he may have known about the Kennedy assassination.

3) Implicated Group(s): The Mafia, CIA, anti-Castro Cubans and oeprations.

C. Patterns, Spheres of Responsibility, and Emerging Structures

We are now in a position to draw some conclusions. There is one clear pattern that emerges from these various "dead witnesses," and that is that *it appears that each of the implicated groups within the Kennedy assassination was responsible for cleaning up loose ends within its own group.* In the clear cases of Giancana and Zangretti, for example, the mode of death fits the M.O. of a Mafia hit. In other cases of more suspiciously convenient deaths by "heart attack" or other means of death, it would appear that a more sophisticated player is involved, players with the means to engineer convenient deaths by drugs (Kilgallen), automobile accidents (Bowers and Craig), heart attacks or deaths by other "natural causes."

This implies a certain structure to the conspiracy to perpetuate a cover-up:

1) It implies that there exists a network of surveillance to inform the various involved groups when one of their own has stepped "off the reservation" and needs to be silenced. It implies, in other words, *some enduring structure* or network to maintain close watch on such people, and to inform the respective group to take care of the loose end when it arises. This may be an ad hoc or informal group, but nonetheless it is an intricate and necessary component and a semi-permanent one in order to make the conspiracy work and maintain it in power long enough to consolidate its gains, *its semi-permanence thus implies some sort of structure; it implies an intelligence connection*;

2) It implies that such groups as the Mafia had some long-term vested interest in maintaining a cover-up, and that were therefore involved at some deep stage of the planning of the crime itself;

148

3) It also implies, however, that the central core of the cover-up could *not* have come from the Mafia, and the other dead witnesses and their strange modes of death indicate that there is a deeper layer involved in the structure of the cover-up. As seen from the strange case of Congressman Boggs, there are clear indicators that the deep planners of the crime are in other groups that had the means and long term interests to do so, namely, High Finance, the CIA, and, unbelievably, the Nazis (McCloy and Dulles).

4) We are thus able to tentatively conclude that the architecture of the conspiracy had a planning committee that at the minimum included representatives of *or liaisons to* these groups, with possibly a Mafia connection or representative or liaison. In other words, *the composition of the Warren Commission itself is a significant clue into the structure of the "planning committee" for the assassination and the conspiracy to cover it up.*

Our architecture now looks like this, reflecting the structure of the Warren Commission's "Strange triumvirate" back upon the conspiracy itself:

The Murder Itself	Anti-Castro Cubans The Mafia FBI (Hoover) CIA Big Oil The Military Bankers (Federal Reserve) Nazis	Anti-Castro Cubans The Mafia FBI (Hoover) CIA Big Oil The Military Bankers (Federal Reserve) Nazis	Anti-Castro Cubans The Mafia FBI (Hoover) CIA Big Oil The Military Bankers (Federal Reserve) Nazis
The Framing of Oswald (via doubles, planted evidence, etc)	FBI (Hoover) CIA The Secret Service The Military Nazis	FBI (Hoover) CIA The Secret Service The Military Nazis	FBI (Hoover) CIA The Secret Service The Military Nazis
The Long-term Cover-up	FBI (Hoover) CIA (Dulles) Bankers (McCloy) Nazis (McCloy) *Secondary Level:* Mafia (Boggs)	FBI (Hoover) CIA (Dulles) Bankers (McCloy) Nazis (McCloy *Secondary Level:* Mafia (Boggs)	FBI (Hoover) CIA (Dulles) Bankers (McCloy) Nazis (McCloy) *Secondary Level:* Mafia (Boggs)

What is now gradually emerging is the architecture of the conspiracy, for it is evident that in the commission of the crime itself, at the level of the "mechanics" that had to carry it out, virtually everyone had the motives, means, and opportunity. The *deep* structure of the assassination cabal is revealed by the second and third elements of the conspiracy, the ability to place the patsy at the designated scene, and the ability to control the cover-up in all its aspects, from the alteration of forensic evidence, to the silencing of inconvenient witnesses. It is here, at the stage of the cover-up itself, that the deepest components of the architecture have begun to reveal themselves. The only questions remaining are, what roles and functions within it did they each play?

Thus, of all the architecture of the conspiracy thus far suggested, it is the connection to the CIA and to the Nazis that still remains to be documented more fully. The CIA's role and interest seems abundantly clear, but the Nazis seems to be the most murky, perhaps even ludicrous. Did they even *have* a real role, or is too much being read into McCloy's presence on the Commission?

The answer to this question leads us to the most bizarre triumvirate of "dead witnesses" of them all, and to some truly bizarre and astonishing connections.

4
THE HANDLER, THE DOCTOR, D. FERRIE, AND OTHER SKELETONS IN THE CLOSET

"Perhaps the most intriguing person in the entire cast of characters connected with the Kennedy assassination was oil geologist George S. DeMohrenschildt — a man who was friends with both Jackie Kennedy's family and the alleged assassin of her husband, Lee Harvey Oswald."[1]

"If anyone was guiding Oswald's activities during late 1962 and early 1963, it would have been DeMohrenschildt."[2]
Jim Marrs

Second only to President Lyndon Baines Johnson himself, the strangest dead "witness" in the whole tragic opera of the assassination, and the one who, like Johnson, had the most connections to the groups involved in it, is George DeMohrenschildt, the first of a very bizarre trinity of dead witnesses, and probably by anyone's lights, the most bizarre of the three in their consubstantial bizarrerie.

The other two dead "witnesses" in this macabre libretto are David Ferrie, the obscure former Eastern Airlines pilot, member of New Orleans' homosexual underground along with Clay Shaw, self-styled cancer researcher, and CIA intelligence asset heavily involved in the anti-Castro Cuban community of Louisiana. The final dead "witness" in this trio is an oncologist and physician in New Orleans, Dr. Mary Sherman, whose connection to the assassination via David Ferrie is seldom discussed, for the reason that it is little understood, but it is in fact from her and her associates that the connections lead, like those of George DeMohrenschildt, to the corporate logo of the swastika and to the deepest foundations in the architecture of the conspiracy, the "Murder Incorporated" at the heart of it.

---

[1] Jim Marrs, *Crossfire*, p. 278.
[2] Ibid, p. 199.

George De Mohrenschildt

A. The Key Dead Witness: George S. De Mohrenschildt
1. His Background and Byelorussian Connection

According to assassination researcher Edward Jay Epstein, George De Mohrenschildt had been under investigation by various U.S. intelligence agencies since 1941.[3] A quick biographical sketch will show why:

> The FBI investigation went on for more than seven years, but all that was known about him for certain was that he had arrived in the United States in May 1938 on the SS *Manhattan*, carrying a Polish passport issued in Belgium, which identified him as Jerzy Sergius von Mohrenschildt and stated that he had been *born in Mozyr, Russia,* in 1911. Some three years later, when he was briefly detained for *sketching a naval installation in Port Aransas, Texas,* an examination of his personal papers revealed that *he was carrying two different*

---

[3] Edward Jay Epstein, *Legend: The Secret World of Lee Harvey Oswald* (New York: McGraw-Hill, 1978), p. 177.

biographical sketches of himself. The first identified him as being of "Swedish origin, born April 17, 1911"; the second portrayed him as a "Greek Catholic,"[4] born in 1914. The résumés indicated that he had been educated in Belgium and held either a business or philosophy degree. He also claimed such diverse occupations as insurance salesman, film producer, newspaper correspondent and textile salesman, *although the FBI was able to establish that he was not actually earning money from any of these occupations. Moreover, British mail intercepts in Bermuda at the start of World War II indicated that he was closely associated with intelligence agents working against the Allies.*[5]

Note that his activity in sketching naval bases, his possession of two different biographical legends, and his wide range of occupations from which he is deriving no income, are all activities deeply suggestive of an intelligence background. Additionally, note that there is strong evidence from British intelligence that he was working "with intelligence agents working against the Allies," i.e., with agents of the Axis powers. As Epstein observes, "from his pattern of associations it was not clear for whom, if anyone, 'Von Mohrenschildt' was working, though he seemed to have large financial resources at his disposal."[6]

Finally, note where he claims to have been born: Mozyr, in Belorussia, an odd fact, since Belorussia was, of course, where Oswald ended up during his Soviet period, in the Belorussian capital of Minsk. This will assume some significance when our examination turns to his Dallas connections.

2. DeMorenschildt's Strange Intelligence Connections and Activities
a. To WW2 German Intelligence, and French Counter-Intelligence

While in the U.S.A. and as World War Two was raging, before the attack on Pearl Harbor and when the Axis was at the height of its power, De Mohrenschildt joined French counter-intelligence, working in the country for the Deuxième Bureau for France, but even then he would subsequently admit to his wife that he was "playing a double game."[7]

---

[4] "Greek Catholic," i.e., an Eastern Orthodox Christian.

[5] Edward Jay Epstein, *Legend: The Secret World of Lee Harvey Oswald*, p. 178, emphasis added.

[6] Ibid, p. 178.

[7] Ibid, p. 179.

Indeed he *was* playing a double game, and it is here that De Mohrenschildt's probable Nazi connections run very deep:

> By 1941, De Mohrenschildt had also joined forces with Baron Konstantin Von Maydell in a propaganda venture called "Facts and Film." Maydell, who had arrived in New York on an Estonian Passport about the same time as De Mohrenschildt, was, by 1941, identified by the FBI as a Nazi agent. In June of that year federal agents intercepted a letter from Maydell suggesting that De Mohrenschildt obtain credentials from Nelson Rockefeller, who was then coordinator of information for Latin America, to distribute films in Latin America. The venture came to an end in September 1942, when Maydell was arrested on a presidential warrant as a "dangerous alien" and interred for four years in North Dakota. The suspicion that De Mohrenshildt was involved with Maydell in an espionage ring was heightened when it was learned that De Mohrenschildt was corresponding with Germany through Saburo Matsukata, the son of a former Prime Minister of Japan, who was alleged at the time to be coordinating German and Japanese intelligence activities in the United States. His name was also found written in the address book of a woman in Washington, D.C., who was under suspicion as a Nazi agent.[8]

De Mohrenschildt even attempted to join the wartime precursor to the CIA, America's OSS or Office of Strategic Services, but was turned down for his suspected ties to Nazi intelligence.[9]

Of course, the problem of playing a "double game" means simply that no one was ever sure of just who ultimately controlled De Mohrenschildt nor where his loyalties ultimately reposed. Was he working for French counter-intelligence, ingratiating himself with Axis espionage rings to spy on them? Was he working for British intelligence? Or was he in fact an Axis, Nazi agent?[10] De Mohrenschildt eluded internment in America during the war because the FBI was never able to determine the answers to these questions.

De Morhenschildt, however, learning of the continuing FBI interest, went into Mexico — center of Axis espionage activities in the Western hemisphere during the war — and claimed to be a film producer,

---

[8] Eward Jay Epstein, *Legend: the Secret World of Lee Harvey Oswald*, p. 179.

[9] Ibid, p. 180.

[10] Ibid, pp. 179-180.

cultivating many high contacts in the neutral Mexican government.[11] From there he returned to the U.S.A. in 1944, changed his name from "Von Mohrenschildt" to "De Mohrenschildt" and registered at the University of Texas where he obtained a master's degree in petroleum engineering in a mere year. It was during this period that he was under investigation by the Office of Naval Intelligence (ONI).[12]

b. The CIA Investigation and Connection

With his petroleum engineering degree in hand De Mohrenschildt then worked after the war in the Caribbean for a number of American oil companies,[13] ultimately being recommended in 1957 by the U.S. government as a consulting geologist to be sent to Marshal Tito's Yugoslavia. It was at this juncture that the CIA became interested in De Mohrenschildt.[14] Despite the agency's misgivings about De Mohrenschildt's ultimate loyalties, he was approved for the mission, but denied access to classified material.

To top off this picture of an active intelligence agent whose loyalties were unclear, De Mohrenschildt actually attempted to reach Marshal Tito's private island by boat while he was in Yugoslavia, claiming to be interested only in sketching the island's fortifications.[15] Traveling extensively up and down the Yugoslavian Adriatic coast, De Mohrenschildt returned to the U.S.A., "where he was debriefed by J. Walter Moore of the CIA's Domestic Contact Service. The information De Mohrenschildt provided the CIA became the basis for at least ten reports that were circulated within government agencies."[16]

These facts have led many investigators to conclude — in my opinion erroneously — that De Mohrenschildt worked for the CIA, i.e., that his ultimate loyalties were to this country and its intelligence services. But this conclusion ignores significant facts and associations that began to emerge in the 1960s, during the fateful period between the Bay of Pigs debacle and the JFK assassination itself. It is here, in De

---

[11] Ibid, p. 180. For the other possible connection of Mexico to post-war Nazi activities inside this country, see my *Roswell and the Reich* (Adventures Unlimited Press, 2010), pp. 350-358.

[12] Edward Jay Epstein, *Legend: The Secret World of Lee Harvey Oswald,* p. 180.

[13] Ibid.

[14] Ibid, p. 181.

[15] Ibid, p. 182.

[16] Ibid.

Mohrenschildt's activities during this period and the pattern of associations displayed in them, that we discover what is his most intriguing set of associations, associations that strongly suggest that his loyalties were with the Axis and Nazi Germany all along.

The first of these activities concerns De Mohrenschildt's spying on the very country that some claim he was now loyal to.

> In the summer of 1960 De Mohrenschildt disappeared from sight for almost a year, after telling friends in Dallas that he was going on an 11,000-mile walking trip along Indian trails from Mexico to South America. Jeanne accompanied him to the ranch on the Mexican border of Tito Harper, who flew them both to central Mexico. The De Mohrenschildts reemerged in April 1961 in Guatemala, just as the Cubans trained by the CIA were being marshaled for the Bay of Pigs invasion of Cuba. De Mohrenschildt had been in Gautemala for approximately four months, and his route took him within a few miles of the CIA training bases...[17]

When the Warren Commission questioned De Mohrenschildt's son-in-law Gary Taylor it asked "if he believed the DeMohrendschildts (sic) may have been spying on the invasion preparations, Taylor replied, 'Yes.'"[18]

While De Mohrenschildt's son-in-law's opinion is only an opinion, it is significant that De Mohrenschildt's walking tour route took him so close to the CIA's Gautemalan training base for the Bay of Pigs operation. If De Mohrenschildt *was* spying on the CIA's operation, this raises once again the question of just who he was working for and where his ultimate loyalties were. If indeed he was working for America, then his activity would represent a case of one agency spying on another, perhaps the FBI spying on the CIA. Or else it might represent a case of one faction of the CIA spying on another.

Or it might be that all along De Mohrenschildt was working for someone else entirely, and not America at all.

This is the possibility that emerges as the strongest candidate when his other associations and activities are examined. Before we get to those, however, one more, and very strange, De Mohrenschildt connection must be mentioned.

---

[17] Edward Jay Epstein, *Legend: The Secret World of Lee Harvey Oswald,* pp. 182-183.

[18] Jim Marrs, *Crossfire: The Plot that Killed Kennedy,* p. 200.

c. To Jacqueline Bouvier Kennedy's Family

This connection is De Mohrenschildt's acquaintanceship with the family of Mrs. Kennedy herself, Jacqueline Bouvier Kennedy. In his testimony to the Warren Commission, George De Mohernschildt stated that he had met Jackie Kennedy's mother, Janet Bouvier, as well as her father John V. Bouvier, and that he had known Jackie Kennedy when she was a little girl.[19]

d. Big Oil, and "Murder Incorporated:" Permindex

The connection that exposes De Mohrenschildt's ultimate loyalties is his connection via his petroleum engineering background to the Texas oil magnates Clint Murchison and H. L. Hunt in Dallas, De Mohrenschildt's hometown.[20] As noted in chapter one, Hunt in turn had a private intelligence network, drawing upon former FBI agents, right wing American generals, and some hitherto unknown connection to the West German intelligence service, the *Bundesnachrichtendienst* or BND. As is now well-known, the BND was, especially at that time, nothing but the old World War Two German military intelligence unit on the Eastern Front and in Eastern Europe, the *Fremde Heere Ost*, headed by Nazi General Reinhard Gehlen, who was, at the time of the assassination, still the head of West German intelligence.

One of those connections between Hunt and the Texas oil interest on the one hand, and that group of post-war Nazi interests and intelligence networks on the other, must surely have been the notorious "Murder Incorporated," the Permindex corporation. We have mentioned this entity in previous chapters, but delayed discussion of it until now. While most assassination researchers are aware of it and its role somewhere within the foggy and murky architecture of the conspiracy, few have really

---

[19] Jim Marrs, *Crossfire: The Plot that Killed Kennedy*, p. 278.
[20] Craig Roberts and John Armstrong, *JFK: The Dead Witnesses*, p. 136. Roberts and Armstrong also state that De Mohrenschildt was also within the circle of Oklahoma oilman, Senator Robert Kerr of Kerr-McGee, and that as an associate of Murchison and Hunt, he also knew Paul Raigorodsky. Roberts and Armstrong provide no substantiation for these statements, although, at least in the case of Murchison and Hunt, it would have been a virtual impossibility for De Mohrenschildt, an oil geologist, not to have had some dealings with these two Texas oilmen who, like De Mohrenschildt himself, were both based in Dallas.

paused to consider it in detail. Jim Marrs notes toward the end of his encyclopedic study of the assassination that "in recent years, several studies of Shaw and his associations indicate a man who — through the shadowy company Permindex — was connected to the CIA, European Nazis and Fascists, and international criminals. This cloudy area of Garrison's investigation deserves closer scrutiny."[21] We now intend to provide some of that "closer scrutiny" in order to answer the question of why Texas oil magnates such as H.L. Hunt would be associated with a group of European Nazis and the West German BND and why that association through Permindex is so important. Once that context is elaborated, we shall then turn to take a closer and final look at De Mohrenschildt, to see if indeed he fits the wider pattern represented by Permindex.

(1) The "Torbitt Document"

No discussion of the Permindex corporation, however, can proceed without a consideration of the principal source document upon which knowledge of it exists, the famous "Torbitt Document," a pseudonymous compilation of some of the more obscure and sensational details of District Attorney Jim Garrison's investigation. The document's actual title was *Nomenclature of an Assassination Cabal*, and its author was the pseudonymous "William Torbitt," a south Texas lawyer[22] with alleged connections to the Texas oil industry, and a close follower of Garrison's investigation. Torbitt composed the document in 1970.

In his introduction to the document, "deep politics" researcher Kenn Thomas notes that opinions on the document's utility as a source for JFK assassination research *initially* ran the whole spectrum, from those advocating that it was nothing but a piece of clever CIA disinformation, to those advocating that it was "a kind of Rosetta stone to understanding the event."[23] The reason for this wide spectrum of evaluations stems from the contents of the document itself:

---

[21] See, for example, Jim Marrs, *Crossfire: The Plot that Killed Kennedy,* p. 516.

[22] Kenn Thomas, "Introduction: Furtive Winks, Flying DISCs and the Torbitt Document," *NASA, Nazis, and JFK: The Torbitt Document and the JFK Assassination* (Adventures Unlimited Press, 1996), p. 5. This book is the only complete version of the Torbitt Document available, edited by Kenn Thomas who meticulously reconstructed it from various photocopied versions in which it had been circulated underground.

[23] Ibid.

It makes connections to such then-unknown governmental spy agencies as Defense Industrial Security Command and Division Five of the FBI; it suggests that a former prime minister of Hungary was the infamous "umbrella man" seen in the Zapruder film; it introduces to the assassination lore such personalities as Fred Crisman (spelled "Chrismon" by Torbitt) as one of the railroad tramps behind the grassy knoll. The Torbitt Document contains a lot to tempt a reader into dismissing it as lunacy.[24]

Yet, as assassination researchers probed deeper and deeper into the crime, many of its most bizarre assertions were subsequently validated, such that the Torbitt Document now forms a source even for such prestigious investigators as professor Peter Dale Scott and others:

> Yet, it has a real air of authenticity. It ties together indisputable parts of the Warren Commisssion and testimony (of) Jim Garrison's case. Few now doubt the existence of DISC(Defense Industrial Security Command) or the FBI's Division Five.... Every major study of the assassination cites the Torbitt Document; some support or expand upon its conclusions; even studies of the files released since the establishment of the government's Assassinations Material Review Board. It is clearly the pivotal document of JFK assassination research.[25]

The reason for the Torbitt Document's growing influence — and it took nearly forty years for it to achieve this status — is due to the conclusions on the nature of the architecture of the conspiracy that it reached. Thomas summarizes these conclusions this way: "It reflects a dialectic of spies, international fascism, multi-national corporate conspiracy, bank malfeasance, Mafia crime and space-age cover-up that is still at work."[26]

In other words, the Torbitt Document was the *first* analysis of the JFK assassination that had concluded that no *one* particular group was responsible for the murder, but that *all* of them were, and that operating in the deepest layers of that architecture, as a semi-permanent feature of

---

[24] Kenn Thomas, "Introduction: Furtive Winks, Flying DISCs and the Torbitt Document," *NASA, Nazis, and JFK: The Torbitt Document and the JFK Assassination*, p. 6.

[25] Ibid.

[26] Ibid, p. 17.

American para-political life, were organized crime, multi-national corporate power, NASA, and, oddly enough, some sort of post-war Nazi or Fascist organization.

All of these various interests gathered and coalesced in the corporation known as Permindex.

(2) Permindex Corporation

Permindex stood for "Permanent Industrial Expositions," the official name of the corporation. Founded in 1958 in Switzerland by Montreal lawyer L.M. Bloomfield, a "long time friend and confidant of J. Edgar Hoover,"[27] fully one half of Permindex's stock was held by Bloomfield, who was in overall charge of its European, African, and North and South American operations.[28] One should not, on this basis, leap to the conclusion that Bloomfield was really the man in control, simply because of the amount of shares he held. It must be remembered that those wishing to conceal or cloak their involvement in the corporation and its activities could easily hold "hidden guns" to the heads of its publicly known officers and figures. Torbitt states unequivocally that Bloomfield "was the top coordinator for the network planning the assassination."[29]

The Permindex Corporation was closely allied to an Italian counterpart, also a subject of Garrison's investigation: Centro-Mondiale Commerciale, or World Trade Center, an Italian subsidiary of the World Trade Center Corporation and a CIA front. The man ultimately indicted by Jim Garrison, Clay Shaw, was a member of the boards of both corporations.[30] The ostensible purpose of Permindex was "to encourage trade between nations."[31] But according to Torbitt, the actual purposes were far more sinister:

> (Their) actual purpose was fourfold:
>
> 1. To fund and direct assassinations of European, Mid-East and world leaders considered threats to the Western World and to petroleum interests of the backers.

---

[27] "Nomenclature of an Assassination Cabal," *NASA, Nazis, and JFK: The Torbitt Document and the JFK Assassination*, p. 52.
[28] Ibid.
[29] Ibid, p. 26.
[30] Ibid, pp. 47-48.
[31] Ibid, p. 48.

2. To furnish couriers, agents, and management in transporting, depositing and re-channeling funds through Swiss banks for Las Vegas, Miami, Havana and (the) international gambling syndicate.
3. To co-ordinate the espionage activities of the Solidarists and Division Five of the FBI with groups in sympathy with their objectives and to receive and channel funds and arms from the financiers to the action groups.
4. To build, acquire and operate hotels and gambling casinos in the Caribbean, Italy and at the other tourist areas.[32]

The rationalization for the involvement of various intelligence agencies and of the international Fascists with gambling and gun-running and therefore with Mafia operations as exemplified in this list becomes rather obvious, for implied in this activity is a degree of "sanction and protection" to these Mafia activities given by the intelligence agencies and presumably by the international Fascists as well. This, as we saw in chapter one, was indeed part of a pattern that began during World War Two and the covert arrangement between America's wartime OSS and Lucky Luciano. In return for such protection, the agencies and international Fascists would have received a "cut" in the action, and thus a nearly inexhaustible supply of steady and covert funding for black projects of all sorts, from intelligence operations to secret research projects.

Thus, while the name "Permindex" officially stood for "Permanent Industrial Expositions," there might be a more sinister significance to its abbreviated name as a kind of "permanent index" of people to be target for assassination.

In any case, it is when one looks closely at the members of the board and financial contributors of Permindex that the connections between American petroleum interests and post-war Nazis and Fascists deepens considerably. We have already noted that Clay Shaw was on the boards both of Permindex and Centro-Mondiale Commerciale. But there were other more intriguing members:

---

[32] "Nomenclature of an Assassination Cabal," *NASA, Nazis, and JFK: The Torbitt Document and the JFK Assassination*, pp. 48-49. Torbitt cites for these assertions: "Basel, Switzerland Publication A-Z, August, 1961; Canadian Le Devoir Publication, March, 1967; Rome Paesa Sera Publication, March, April, 1967, also 1959 thru (sic) 1960 files: Il Gornia of Milan, Italy, 1967-1968 files; Il Tempe, Rome, 1967-1968 files; New Orleans District Attorney Records; Swiss Intelligence, J.F. Kennedy files." Torbitt gives no indication how he acquired access to the files of Swiss Intelligence.

The other members of the Board include a publisher of the Fascist National-Zeitung in West Germany, an Italian industrialist who married into the family of Adolph (sic) Hitler's finance minister, and a woman lawyer, the Secretary of the Fascist Party. (Public Corporations Records office, Berne, Switzerland)

Also on the Board of Permindex was *Ferenc Nagy, a Solidarist and Prime Minister of Hungary from 1946 to 1947; George Mandel, alias Mantello, a Hungarian fascist who supervised attempts to purchase national monuments for real estate development in Italy,* and Munir Chourbagi, an uncle of King Farouk....

The ruling clique of Permindex and its two subsidiaries. (sic) The Italo American Hotel Corporation and Centro Mondiale Commerciale, in addition to the sophisticated Nazis and Fascists heretofore named, were Gutierz di Spadofora, who was under-secretary of agriculture in Mussolini's Fascist regime and who was also a ruling lord in the Mafia with Italy and Southern Europe as his land area; Enrico Mantello (Henry Mandel, brother of George Mandel); Giuseppe Zigotti, the head of the Italian political party, Fascist Nationalist Association for Militia Arms; and Hungarian *emigre* and former Nazi, H. Simonfay...[33]

The Torbitt Document's list of heavy financial contributors to Permindex is even more revealing of deep political connections:

The principal financiers of Permindex were a number of U.S. oil companies, *H.L. Hunt of Dallas, Clint Murchison of Dallas,* John DeMenil, *Solidarist* director of Houston, *John Connally* as executor of the Sid Richardson estate, Haliburton Oil Co., Senator Robert Kerr of Oklahoma, Troy Post of Dallas, Lloyd Cobb of New Orleans, *Dr. Oechner of New Orleans,*[34] George and Herman Brown of Brown & Root, Houston, Attorney Roy M. Cohn, Chairman of the Board for Lionel Corporation, New York City, Schemley Industries of New York City, *Walter Dornberger, ex-Nazi general and his company, Bell Aerospace,* Pan American World Airways, and its subsidiary, Intercontinental Hotel Corporation, *Paul Raigorodsky of Dallas through his company, Claiborne Oil of New Orleans,* Credit Suisse of Canada, Heineken's Brewery of Canada and a host of other munition

---

[33] "Nomenclature of an Assassination Cabal," *NASA, Nazis, and JFK: The Torbitt Document and the JFK Assassination*, pp. 47-48, emphasis added.

[34] Pay attention to that Dr. Oechner, for we will encounter him later. Torbitt misspells his name, and he was in fact the famous physician Albert Oechsner, about whom there is more later in this chapter.

(sic) makers and *NASA contractors directed by the Defense Industrial Security Command.*

The *gambling syndicate and Mafia contracting agents* who handled the transactions with Permindex were ex-president Carlos Prio Socarras of Havana, Miami and Houston, Clifford Jones of Laz Vegas, Morris Dalitz of Las Vegas, Detroit, Cleveland and Havana, former head of the Cleveland mob and Roy Cohn, L.J. McWillie of Las Vegas, a gambling partner with Cliff Jones, *Bobby Baker of Washington, DC,* Ed Levinson of Law Vegas, Benny Siegelbaum of Miami, Henry Crown of Chicago, associate of the Mafia, Patrick Hoy of the controlling clique in General Dynamics and Joe Bonanno of Lionel Corporation of New York.[35]

Note what we have represented in this list, as indicated by the italicized names and groups in the two previous quotations; there are:

1) *The Petroleum Interests,* represented by the specific mention of Texas oil tycoons H.L. Hunt and Clint Murchison, and Paul Raidgorodsky, a close associate of George De Mohrenschildt, and future Texas Governor John Connally;

2) *The Fascists and Nazi Interest,* represented by Ferenc Nagy, Nazi puppet prime minister of Hungary, Nazi H. Simonfay, Italian Fascist and former Mussolini government member Gutierz di Spadofora; Nazi "Paperclip" scientist and General Walter Dornberger; and a group called "Solidarists" about whom we shall say more later;

3) *The Mafia Interest* represented by the most famous in the list, *Lyndon Baines Johnson's personal aid, Bobby Baker,* about whom we shall have much more to say in part two of this book;[36]

4) *The Space Interest* represented by various NASA contractors all of which are coordinated by something called the Defense Industrial Security Command, or DISC.

All of these were organized, according to "Torbitt," into five groups with Permindex forming the institutional connection between them:

> 1. The Czarist (sic) Russian, eastern European and Middle East exile organization called SOLIDARISTS, headed by Ferenc Nagy, ex-Hungarian premier, and John DeMenil, Russian exile from

---

[35] Nomenclature of an Assassination Cabal," *NASA, Nazis, and JFK: The Torbitt Document and the JFK Assassination,* pp. 49-50.

[36] Torbitt also points out that New Orleans mobster Carlos Marcello was also a member of Permindex's board! Q.v. p. 117.

Houston, Texas, a close friend *and supporter of Lyndon Johnson* for over thirty years.[37]

2. A section of the AMERICAN COUNCIL OF CHURCHES headed by H.L. Hunt of Dallas, Texas.[38]

3. A Cuban exile group called FREE CUBA COMMITTEE headed by Carlos Prio Socarras, ex-Cuban president.

4. An organization of United States, Caribbean, and Havana, Cuba gamblers called the Syndicate headed by Clifford Jones, ex-lieutenant governor of Nevada and Democratic National Committeeman, and Bobby Baker of Washington, DC. This group worked closely with a Mafia family headed by Joe Bonanno.

5. The SECURITY DIVISION of the National Aeronautics and Space Administration (NASA) headed by Werner Von Braun, head of the German Nazi rocket program from 1932 through 1945. Headquarters for this group was the DEFENSE INDUSTRIAL SECURITY COMMAND at Muscle Shoals Redstone Arsenal in Alabama...[39]

The assassination, in other words, at its deepest level represented a coalescence of the interests of the Mafia, American intelligence (and

---

[37] For a recent update of this group of exile East European fronts, their deep connections to post-war Fascism and Nazism, see Russ Bellant, *Old Nazis, The New Right, and the Republican Party: Domestic Fascist Networks and their Effect on U.S. Cold War Politics* (Boston: South End Press, 1991). This network was represented within Republican Party politics beginning during the Reagan Administration by the Republican Heritage Groups Council (p. xvii). Bellant states explicitly that "the foundation of the Republican Heritage Group Council lay in *Hitler's networks into East Europe before World War II*. In each of those Eastern European countries, the German SS set up or funded political action organizations that helped form SS militias during the war."(p. 4, emphasis added). These groups were coordinated by General Reinhard Gehlen's *Fremde Heere Ost*, or "Foreign Armies East" which, of course, later became the West German *Bundesnachrichtendienst*.

[38] Nomenclature of an Assassination Cabal," *NASA, Nazis, and JFK: The Torbitt Document and the JFK Assassination*, p. 54, notes that an individual known only was "Dimitri" was associated with the Hunts' American Council of Christian Churches... this may or may not be a significant clue, for one might have to look for a Dimitri or Dmitri (1) with ecclesiastical connections indicative of the Slavic character of his name, and (2) with personal or professional links to the Texas oil industry. George De Mohrenschildt, a member of the Dallas White Russian exile community and an oil geologist, might thus point to other hitherto uninvestigated areas of the assassination. There is, in fact, such an individual whose sister was an oil geologist...

[39] Ibid, pp. 26-27, italicized emphasis added, uncial emphasis in the original.

specifically the intelligence and security connected with, of all things, NASA), anti-Castro Cubans, and big petroleum interests, especially those of the Texas oilmen.

Of these, the NASA interest may seem the most unusual, and its connection to Garrison's JFK assassination investigation even odder, until one looks closely at facts that first found mention in the Torbitt document, but that are now more or less common knowledge. Torbitt states that "immediately upon arriving in the United States," Von Braun

> made close personal friends with J. Edgar Hoover and Lyndon B. Johnson; and the relationship remained close with Von Braun working with Hoover in security in the Tennessee Valley Authority and the Redstone Arsenal; and later, beginning in 1958, they worked together in the security of the National Space Agency (sic).[40]

Worse yet, when the Nazi rocket scientists led by Von Braun surrendered themselves to the American armies overrunning their country, it was then that Von Braun and his associates encountered another player in the drama, Clay Shaw:

> Von Braun first met Clay Shaw in 1945 when he, Walter Dornberger and about 150 other Nazi rocket scientists abandoned Peenemünde and traveled south to join the American forces in Germany close to the French border. The Nazis were brought to the Deputy Chief of Staff's headquarters where Major Clay Shaw was aide-de-camp to General Charles O. Thrasher.[41]

And as if all this were not bad enough, in the process of secretly sanitizing these Nazis' past in order to bring them to this country covertly and employ them in America's most sensitive military and space projects, the assistance of — you guessed it — General Reinhard Gehlen's Nazi military intelligence network was vital to the Nazi scientists, who thus maintained a relationship with it after the war was over.[42]

That this oddball group of Nazis, Fascists, Mafiosi, space scientists, Eastern European émigré communities (themselves with deep Nazi and Fascist connections), Texas oilmen and intelligence agents that was Permindex was involved with assassinations is attested by the fact that it

---

[40] Nomenclature of an Assassination Cabal," *NASA, Nazis, and JFK: The Torbitt Document and the JFK Assassination*, p. 141.

[41] Ibid, p. 142.

[42] Ibid, pp. 143, 144

is this group that was consistently funneling money and other assistance to the right-wing French opposition to President Charles De Gaulle and its repeated attempts to assassinate him.[43]

But the piece-de-resistance of the Torbitt document is in the form of an actual detailed list *of the names involved in the planning of the assassination itself.* I cite this in its entirety, though for our purposes only the first two paragraphs will concern us throughout the remainder of this book:

> At the top was (sic) JOHNSON, HOOVER, BLOOMFIELD, NAGY, DE MENIL, PRIO, JENKINS, HUNT, BAKER, JONES, McWILLIE, VON BRAUN, COHN, KORTH, CONNALLY and MURCHISON.
>
> L.M. Bloomfield was in overall charge responsible only to Hoover and Johnson.
>
> The second layer of participants with supervisory and working assignments under Bloomfield and the first group were Walter Dornberger, ex-Nazi General, Guy Bannister....
>
> There were others involved also, but the published evidence up to 1969 is such that it would be unfair to name them.
>
> Substantially the same management under Bloomfield of Montreal and J. Edgar Hoover planned and carried out the execution of Martin Luther King and Robert Kennedy. Albert Osborne had his riflemen in Memphis and one of his professionals fired the fatal shot at King. Ray was used as Oswald had earlier been used.[44]

Oddly enough, as will be discovered in part two, a very strong prima facie case can be made that Lyndon Johnson, J. Edgar Hoover, and Texas Governor John Connally were at some level involved in the assassination. As for the rest on Torbitt's list, as we shall see in subsequent chapters, Von Braun, representing NASA, and Bobby Baker, Johnson's personal aide, can also be seen to have some motive, at least, for possible involvement.

Before leaving the subject of Permindex and returning to a consideration of De Mohrenshildt's possible role in all these activities, it is worth pausing to consider the strange alliance between the Mafia, the intelligence agencies represented in Torbitt's account, and the post-war Nazis, and Fascists from another angle, for in doing so we will see yet more motivations for these groups to be involved in the assassination.

---

[43] Nomenclature of an Assassination Cabal," *NASA, Nazis, and JFK: The Torbitt Document and the JFK Assassination*, pp. 74-75.

[44] Ibid, pp. 54-55, uncial emphasis in the original.

In an intriguing book whose title says it all — *The Great Heroin Coup: Drugs, Intelligence, and International Fascism* — author Henrik Krüger documents a fascinating case for international Fascism's penetration into the international narcotics traffic during a massive restructuring that pitted America's and Latin America's intelligence agencies and Mafia along with representatives of a host of International Fascist organizations, against the standard European traffic controlled through more traditional Mafia channels via Marseilles in France. In his Foreword to this seminal work, JFK assassination researcher Peter Dale Scott notes that at the very minimum, the alliance between these various intelligence agencies and Fascist organizations on the one hand, and the American Mafia on the other, stood to gain from the dual role that drug couriers would have as intelligence agents channeling information back.[45]

But besides containing intriguing bits of information on the organization of the Nazi or Fascist International — such as the Gehlen organization's refusal to tip off French intelligence about the plans to assassinate President DeGaulle, plans which it knew intimately,[46] or the infamous World Anti-Communist League's ability to draw on the resources of Gehlen's organization,[47] or the role of SS Colonel Otto Skorzeny's *International Fascista* in Madrid,[48] or (best of all) the continued post-war contact between General Gehlen's organization and the Latin American Nazi hierarchy[49] (which this author believes included the infamous Nazi Party *Reichsleiter* Martin Bormann himself)[50] — beyond all this, there is little to no indication of what this alliance and the vast sums of money that each party stood to gain from it was used for.

However it takes but a little thought to see what the intelligence agencies would use it for, for these funds represented a virtually bottomless pit of money that could be kept off the books and used to fund their various black projects and covert operations. Similarly, on the side of the Nazi International, such funds would be a similar bottomless pit of money to fund their own ongoing secret research projects and covert operations.

---

[45] Henrik Krüger, *The Great Heroin Coup: Drugs, Intelligence, and International Fascism* (Boston: South End Press, 1980), p. 3.

[46] Ibid, p. 56.

[47] Ibid, p. 192.

[48] Ibid, pp. 209-210.

[49] Ibid, p. 205.

[50] See my *The Nazi International* (Adventures Unlimited Press, 2009), pp. 84-136.

In this context it is thus now quite crucial to realize what Permindex really was: *it was the one corporate and institutional entity where the coalescing interests and groups and the deep politics in the assassination were each represented: the Mafia, Big Oil, rogue right wing groups in American intelligence, and post-war Fascists and Nazis, or "the Nazi International."* It is thus a crucial and often-overlooked institutional clue to the architecture of the conspiracy.[51]

Given its significant overlap and intersection with prominent representatives of the Anglo-American corporate elite represented by Bloomfield, its association with Mafia gambling and narcotics trafficking, represented by Bonanno, Marcello, Bobby Baker, Roy Cohn and others, and with the post-war Nazi International, whose representatives are too numerous to be reiterated here, one may also conclude that Permindex represents yet another institution created, like the Bilderberger Group before it,[52] to liaise between that post-war Nazi International and the deep parapolitical structures of Anglo-American corporate and underground power, including Big Oil.[53]

e. De Mohrenschildt's Post-war Pattern of Alliances and His Probable Ultimate Loyalties to the Post-War White Russian Exilee Community: the Gehlenorg and Nazi International

So how does George De Mohrenschildt fit into the wider pattern of activity and relationships represented by Permindex?

---

[51] We shall leave the discussion of what common interests could have bound big oil to the other groups to chapter six.

[52] See my *Babylon's Banksters: The Alchemy of Deep Physics, High Finance, and Ancient Religion* (Feral House, 2010), pp. 65-73.

[53] Torbitt states his own assessment of Permindex in less guarded terms: "...Permindex in Switzerland (was) basically a NATO intelligence front using the remnants of Adolph (sic) Hitler's intelligence units in West Germany and also, the intelligence unit of the Solidarists headquartered in Munich, Germany." (p. 75). General Gehlen's organization was indeed headquartered just outside of Munich in the town of Pullach, and it was Gehlen's organization, once again, that headed and coordinated the activities of the Eastern European militias loyal to the Nazis, the very groups that became the exile groups known as Solidarists. Torbitt is, in effect, saying that Permindex ultimately was the intelligence front for that vast postwar network of Nazis by which they made common cause with the other interests represented in the corporation.

He fits, as by now is rather obvious, rather *neatly* and *tightly*, for his activities are almost a mirror-image of Permindex and its deep corporate, big oil, and international Fascist connections. De Mohrenschildt:

1) had connections to the oil industry and most likely would have known Permindex Board members H.L. Hunt and Clint Murchison, and it is known that he personally knew Hunt associate and Permindex Board member Paul Raigorodsky;

2) had connections to the Dallas White Russian (Belo-Russian) and Russian exile communities, which communities, as representatives of the Solidarist fronts of Gehlen's old Nazi military intelligence group and its continued existence as the West German intelligence agency, the BND, formed part of the network of Fascist penetration into American politics and culture. De Mohrenschildt is thus *the most likely liaison between Hunt and his known connections to West German intelligence discussed in chapter one;*

3) spied on the CIA's Bay of Pigs preparations in Guatemala, according to his son-in-law Gary Taylor, which, if true, meant he was not working for the CIA but for someone else;

4) was strongly suspected to have espionage connections with Axis espionage rings, and left the U.S.A. and fled to Mexico — a hotbed of Nazi intelligence activity during World War Two and after — when he came under suspicion by the FBI during the war;

5) reacted cordially to Lee Harvey Oswald — a former defector to the Soviet Union — when the rest of the Dallas Russian exile community, which was staunchly anti-Communist, did not.[54] If indeed Oswald was "run" as a double agent inside the Soviet Union, then it was most likely West German intelligence — General Gehlen's "organization," that maintained surveillance on and contact with Oswald, that may have prepared him *for* the defection — recall that Oswald's Marine buddy Delgado reported hearing Oswald speak German — and that may have helped him *back* from the Soviet Union — and that may have actually been handling Oswald in Dallas via De Mohrenschildt. De Mohrenschildt's reaction to Oswald and attempts to assist him in Dallas perhaps signify that he held privileged information on the alleged assassin;

---

[54] Jim Marrs, *Crossfire: the Plot that Killed Kennedy*, p. 281.

169

6) died of a shotgun blast to the head in March 1977, after being contacted to testify for the House Select Committee on Assassinations. The blast was, of course, ruled a suicide.[55]

Given all this, it is reasonable to conclude that De Mohrenschildt's positioning in Dallas, and his handling of Lee Harvey and Marina Oswald, was no accident. Additionally, it is reasonable to conclude that there is a strong possibility that De Mohrenschildt was the liaison, the Dallas representative, of Permindex and was the liaison between Hunt and German intelligence.

1) **Cause of Death:** "suicide" by shotgun blast to the head
2) **Motivation for Death:** probable intimate knowledge of the relationships between Texas petroleum interests, German intelligence, the Mafia, and the Nazi connections of German intelligence. Moreover, De Mohrenschildt may have had detailed knowledge of some of the personnel actually involved in the planning of the assassination.
3) **Implicated Group(s):** Texas oil interests, Solidarist émigré groups, Nazi International and other intelligence groups.

3. DeMohrenschildt Associate Paul M Raigorodsky

Mention has been made of Paul M. Raigorodsky in the previous pages, and it is worth taking a brief look at him as well, since he was yet another member of the Dallas White Russian exile community that befriended the Oswalds in addition to De Mohrenschildt. Moreover, he was himself "a close friend of George DeMorenschildt(sic)."[56] Raigordsky was an oil millionaire and, as has been seen, a Board member of the Permindex corporation, and a director of the Tolstoy Foundation, a key CIA front in the network of the various émigré and exile communities from Eastern Europe, which also places him in the orbit of groups with relationships to General Gehlen's organization. Raigorodsky conveniently died of "natural causes" in the same month as his friend, George De Mohrenschildt.[57]

1) **Cause of Death:** convenient "natural causes."

---

[55] Roberts and Armstrong, *JFK: The Dead Witnesses*, p. 138.
[56] Ibid, pp. 138-139.
[57] Ibid, p. 139.

2) **Motivation for Death:** probable intimate knowledge of the relationships between Texas petroleum interests, German and America intelligence use and manipulation of émigré groups.
3) **Implicated Group(s):** Texas oil interests, Solidarist émigré groups, Nazi International and other intelligence groups.

The Founding of Permindex.
Note the association of the corporation with the World Trade Centre Corporation

171

Permindex Shareholder Meeting.
Note again the association of the company with
Centro Mondiale Commerciale
or World Trade Center Corporation

B. Dr. Mary Sherman, David Ferrie, Jack Ruby, and " the Cancer
Connection"

1. Dr. Mary Sherman, David Ferrie, Tulane University, and Cancer
Induction

In an article in *Playboy* magazine in October 1967, New Orleans District Attorney Jim Garrison mentioned a very peculiar aspect of the JFK assassination case he was building:

PLAYBOY: Penn Jones, Norman Mailer and others have charged that Ruby was injected with live cancer cells in order to silence him. Do you agree?
GARRISON: I can't agree or disagree since I have no evidence one way or the other. But we have discovered that David Ferrie had a rather curious hobby in addition to his study of cartridge trajectories: cancer research. He filled his apartment with white mice — at one point he had almost 2,000, and neighbors complained — wrote a medical treatise on the subject and worked with a number of New Orleans

172

doctors on means of inducing cancer in mice. After the assassination, one of these physicians, Dr. Mary Sherman, was found hacked to death with a kitchen knife in her New Orleans apartment. Her murder is listed as unsolved. Ferrie's experiments may have been purely theoretical and Dr. Sherman's death completely unrelated to her association with Ferrie; but I do find it interesting that Jack Ruby died of cancer a few weeks after his conviction for murder had been overruled in appeals court and he was ordered to stand trial outside of Dallas — thus allowing him to speak freely if he so desired. I would also note that there was little hesitancy in killing Lee Oswald in order to prevent *him* from talking, so there is no reason to suspect that any more consideration would have been shown Jack Ruby if *he* had posed a threat to the architects of the conspiracy.[58]

That's not the half of it.

Dr. Mary Sherman around the time of her murder

---

[58] Jim Garrison and Eric Norden, "Playboy Interview," *Playboy,* Oct. 1967, p. 59, cited in Edward T. Haslam, *Dr Mary's Monkey: How the Unsolved Murder of a Doctor, A Secret Laboratory in New Orleans and Cancer-Causing Monkey Viruses are Linked to Lee Harvey Oswald, the JFK Assassination, and Emerging Global Epidemics* (Walterville, Oregon: Trine Day, 2007), p. 60.

Dr. Mary Sherman's murder was not only unsolved in Garrison's day, it remains officially unsolved to this day.[59] And Garrison was being unusually vague about Dr. Sherman's death and the numerous problems associated with it, for in fact, she had been discovered with her entire right arm missing,[60] her stab wounds were of a precise surgical nature,[61] and to top it all off, the homicide report for her murder states that her murderer "set fire to her bed and piled underclothing on her body, setting it afire" and burning her body.[62] But her body, according to the homicide report, sustained more than the normal burns one would expect from merely piling unclothing on her and setting them afire:

> The body was in a supine position, the head in the direction of the river, the feet in the direction of the lake, and both legs were outstretched and parallel to each other... The left arm was outstretched and parallel to the left side of the body. *The right side of the body from the waist to where the right shoulder would be, including the whole right arm, was apparently **disintegrated** from the fire, yielding the inside organs of the body...* The body was nude: however there was clothing which had apparently been placed on top of the body, mostly covering the body from just above the pubic area to the neck. *Some of the mentioned clothes had been burned completely, while others were still intact but scorched.*[63]

Needless to say, the word "disintegrated" is not normally a word one would expect to encounter in an official homicide report.

The official explanation for all this was that it was a simple burglary gone horribly and tragically wrong. But there were no signs of a struggle between Dr. Sherman and her murderer, nor was anything out of place in her bedroom.[64] How could someone do all of this damage to someone else, in an apartment surrounded by other people, and none of the apartment residents heard *a thing.*[65]

---

[59] Edward T. Haslam, *Dr. Mary's Monkey*, p.1

[60] Ibid, p. 3.

[61] Ibid, p. 127.

[62] Ibid, p. 124.

[63] Ibid, p. 129, citing the official homicide report, all emphasis added.

[64] Edward T. Haslam, *Dr. Mary's Monkey*, pp. 129. Haslam also notes that the door of her apartment had not been forced open nor was a box of jewelry taken, which could easily have been removed from her apartment, all of which strongly suggests that burglary was not a motive(p. 121). Haslam mentions other strange oddities of the case on pp. 122-123.

[65] Ibid, p. 227.

It gets worse.

For example, how would an ordinary fire explain the *complete disintegration* of the upper right side of Dr. Sherman's body, including a completely missing right arm and totally exposed interior organs? How would such a fire explain why some of the clothing was completely burnt, while the rest was merely scorched?[66] Questions such as these about Dr. Sherman's murder led researcher Edward T. Haslam on a long quest to find the answers, and when he did, they opened up yet another labyrinthine aspect of the JFK assassination.

When he consulted an expert on the cremation of human remains, Haslam discovered that the heat required to burn bones completely away was between 1,600 and 2,000 degrees Fahrenheit, and even then, it took several hours of exposure to such a fire to reduce bones to powder.[67] Yet, clothing found on her body was said to be only scorched! Haslam came to a conclusion that set him off on an odyssey of discovery about Dr. Sherman and some very sinister research that connects her, David Ferrie, Lee Harvey Oswald, and a famous physician whom we shall encounter in a moment, to the assassination:

> If Mary's entire apartment building had been burning out of control and had caved in on top of her body, it could not have produced the type of damage described in the police report. The smoky mattress and the smoldering pile of clothes with their less-than-500 degree temperature were certainly not capable of destroying the bones in Mary's right arm and rib cage. The critical point hit me: *The crime scene did not match the crime.* It was impossible to explain the damage to Mary's right arm and the right side of her body with the evidence found in her apartment.
>
> Or to put it even more bluntly, the damage to Mary's right arm and thorax *did not occur* in her apartment.[68]

But if it did not occur there, where *did* it occur, and more importantly, *why*?

The answer to those questions probably lies with Dr. Sherman's associates, and what she was doing with them, among them the notorious David Ferrie - ex-pilot, associate of Guy Bannister and Lee Harvey Oswald, a leader in the anti-Castro Cuban community, and a member of New Orleans' homosexual sub-culture — and the internationally

---

[66] Ibid, pp. 228-229.

[67] Ibid, p. 230.

[68] Edward T. Haslam, *Dr. Mary's Monkey*, p. 231, emphasis in the original.

175

renowned physician, surgeon, and New Orleans luminary, Dr. Alton J. Ochsner.

We have already cited the Garrison interview in *Playboy* magazine of October 1967, in which the famous district attorney mentioned in passing the association between Dr. Mary Sherman and David Ferrie, a self-styled cancer researcher. But the association itself raises serious questions, for Dr. Mary Sherman was no local country doctor; she was an internationally-known cancer researcher whose published medical articles were standard reference material in medical science. Local newspapers referred to her as in internationally known bone specialist when they reported her murder. "She was an Associate Professor at a prominent medical school engaged in monkey virus research,[69] a director of a cancer laboratory at an internationally famous medical clinic,[70] and Chairman of the Pathology Committee of one of the most elite medical societies in America. The medical articles she wrote were quoted for half a century."[71] For Haslam, this posed an interesting set of questions:

> What was a highly trained medical professional with impeccable credentials doing in an underground medical laboratory run by a political extremist with no formal medical training?
> This question is so vexing that it puts enormous importance on this one passage (of Garrison's *Playboy* interview). What other evidence of the Ferrie-Sherman experiments do we have?[72]

What indeed was someone like Dr. Mary Sherman doing with someone like David Ferrie?

The question becomes more important when one considers David Ferrie himself, and his apartment, which he had converted into a medical laboratory: "His medical equipment included microscopes, syringes, surgical tools, and a medical library." His previous landlords "told of a full-scale laboratory" containing "thousands of mice in cages." While Ferrie claimed publically that he was looking for a cure for cancer, Garrison and his investigators "thought that he was trying to figure out a way to use cancer as an assassination weapon, presumably against Castro and his followers."[73]

---

[69] Tulane Univerity.
[70] The Ochsner Foundation Hospital.
[71] Edward T. Haslam, *Dr. Mary's Monkey*, p. 64.
[72] Ibid.
[73] Ibid, p. 46, see also Haslam's discussion on pp. 87-89.

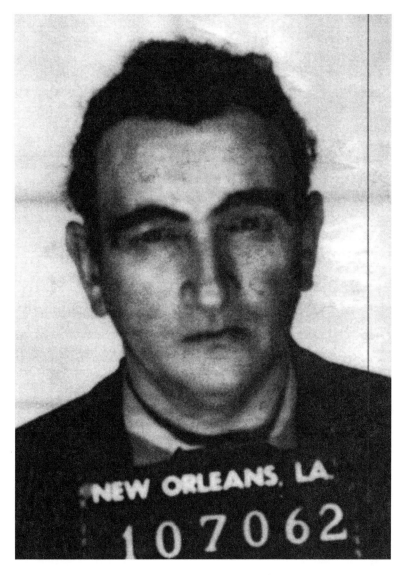

Mug shot of David Ferrie; note the artificial eyebrows and toupé

But again, why would Dr. MarySherman, a famous pathologist and cancer researcher, be involved with such a man?

The answer lies at the *other* end of the spectrum of her associations, this time with Tulane University, and with the even more famous physician and surgeon Alton J. Ochsner, and his Ochsner Foundation

Hospital in New Orleans, and with the indications that more was going on in those institutions than just simple research.

At the time of her death, Tulane University was researching exotic monkey viruses from Africa.[74] This would not be so extraordinary if it were not for the fact that this may not have been ordinary medical research. Louisiana's congressional delegation — which at the time included subsequent Warren Commission member Congressman Hale Boggs — saw to it that Tulane received massive grants from the National Institute of Health, an institution often fronting for CIA black projects.[75] Indeed, some of the viral research conducted by Tulane and other universities around the world at the time included research *in the induction of cancer* by injection with exotic simian viruses.[76] In fact, one of the earliest reported cases of an AIDS-like disease comes from the early 1960s, and precisely from Tulane University,[77] an odd fact, since Garrison suspected David Ferrie's real interest in medical matters was not to cure cancer, but to find a deadly biological weapon.[78] And of course, given Ferrie's activities with Guy Bannister, the New Orleans anti-Castro Cubans, his known association with Lee Harvey Oswald, it is highly probable that Ferrie was some sort of intelligence asset.

Given this supposition, Ferrie's "medical research" activities are worth a closer look, since these lead back through Sherman, and through her, to her other professional associates and their activities. To begin, let us recall one thing that Garrison mentioned in his 1967 *Playboy* interview: "But we have discovered that David Ferrie had a rather curious hobby in addition to his study of cartridge trajectories: cancer research. He filled his apartment with white mice — at one point he had almost 2,000, and neighbors complained — *wrote a medical treatise on the subject and worked with a number of New Orleans doctors on means of inducing cancer in mice.*" Haslam determined to find Ferrie's "medical treatise" and through JFK assassination researcher Jim DiEugenio obtained a copy of it from the U.S. National Archives.[79]

What Garrison's investigators had found in David Ferrie's apartment was not a complete document but "fragments of a much larger document."[80] But what they found was significant enough. For one thing,

---

[74] Edward T. Haslam, *Dr. Mary's Monkey*, p. 14.
[75] Ibid, pp. 30-31.
[76] Ibid, p. 20.
[77] Ibid, p. 47.
[78] Ibid, p. 5.
[79] Ibid, pp. 193-194.
[80] Ibid, p. 194.

it was a complete review of the medical literature from 1901 to 1955 on the theory of the viral origins of cancers.[81] A review of the document's contents was even more darkly revealing:

Page 1. Jim Garrison's memo describing David Ferrie's unintentional xeroxed personal notations.

Page 2. *A description of a viral cancer experiment which transferred cancer tumors from animal to animal.*

Page 3. *A discussion of the work of a doctor who developed an experimental antibiotic for treating cancer.*

Page 4. A chart showing different types of cancers and their tissue of origin.

Page 5. The first page of a bibliography.

Page 6. The second page of the bibliography.

At the top of each reproduced page we find:

REPRODUCED AT THE NATIONAL ARCHIVES
Collection: HSCA (RG 233)[82]

This is darkly revealing because the treatise clearly implies that in the race to *cure* cancer, medical researchers had discovered the means to *reproduce it, to induce it* in their test animals. Indeed, the document states quite specifically that "Extracts were made from the malignant tumors which appeared in the test group. These extracts were then injected into other animals of the test group. A variety of malignancies appear: leukemia, chorioepitheloma (cancer of the uterus) among them."[83] It is also darkly revealing because it suggests that a successful antibiotic had been developed for the treatment of cancer — based on the theory of its viral origins — as early as 1960! The technicality of the document, plus its frequent reference to sophisticated equipment and procedures, quite clearly meant that David Ferrie simply could not have authored the document.[84]

And what of the antiobiotic? Haslam notes that whoever authored the document quite clearly conducted tests with an experimental antibiotic called Antivin, a drug developed from a mold, with "happy results," and noting that "Antivin has not as yet been released for general trial."[85] Clearly something was going on in the New Orleans medical research

---

[81] Edward T. Haslam, *Dr. Mary's Monkey*, p. 195.

[82] Ibid, p. 194, italicized emphasis added.

[83] Ibid, pp. 195-196.

[84] Ibid, p. 197.

[85] Ibid, p. 198.

community involving the induction of cancer, and experimental anti-cancer drugs.

And this brings us back to Dr. Mary Sherman, her strange association with David Ferrie, and even stranger professional associations.

2. Dr. Mary Sherman, Dr. Alton J. Ochsner, and Some Strange Latin American Connections

In the early 1950s Dr. Mary Sherman was at the University of Chicago, doing serious and respected cancer research. It was because of this that her life would soon change, and set her on the path that would lead to her eventual murder.

> Her cancer work at the University of Chicago had attracted the attention of a famous and wealthy doctor who was president of the American Cancer Society, president of a famous medical clinic which bore his name, and Chief of Surgery at Tulane Medical School, one of the most respected medical schools of the day. The doctor was Alton Ochsner, M.D., of New Orleans.
>
> Oschner's offer to Dr. Sherman was considerable. She would be a partner in Ochsner's clinic, the head of her own cancer laboratory, and, to keep her place in the academic side of medicine, she would be an Associate Professor at Tulane Medical School. Additionally, she would also have the personal support of one of the most politically powerful and well-connected doctors in America, a conduit for a constant flow of research funds.[86]

Just how well-connected Ochsner was politically will be seen in a moment, for it is an important part of the story.

---

[86] Edward T. Haslam, *Dr. Mary's Monkey*, p. 118.

Dr. Mary Sherman ca. 1953, with some of the Ochsner Foundation hospital staff

Alton J. Ochsner was born in Kimball, South Dakota in 1896. He was a typical over-achieving child of the Germans who so populate that state, speaking both English and German from childhood, graduating from the University of South Dakota and then completing his medical training at Washington University in St. Louis, Missouri.[87] By 1927 he counted among his best friends William J. Mayo, founder of the famous Mayo Clinic in Rochester, Minnesota, and had travelled to Europe where his proficiency with the then-emerging technique of blood transfusions saved two lives. A later article in a European medical journal, written by Ochsner in German, established his international reputation.[88] Ochsner married into a wealthy American family while in Switzerland, and he and his wife soon set off touring Europe's medical clinics. By 1927, the 31 year-old Ochsner was appointed the head of surgery at Tulane Medical School in New Orleans, selected both for his skill and his connections over several older doctors, a post which Ochsner occupied for the rest of his life.[89]

---

[87] Ibid, p. 170.
[88] Edward T. Haslam, *Dr. Mary's Monkey,* p. 171.
[89] Ibid, p. 172.

A young Dr. Alton J. Ochsner

By 1949 Ochsner had become President of the American Cancer Society, and a member of its Board of Directors along with General William Donovan, the founder of America's World War Two espionage service, the OSS, predecessor to the CIA.[90] This is probably where Ochsner's connections to America's intelligence agencies and covert projects began. Earlier, in 1942, he founded the now world-famous Ochsner Clinic and Foundation Hospital, a project that was deliberately meant to cater to Latin America's wealthy right-wing political elites.[91]

Ochsner's politics reflected the extreme right-wing leanings of his Latin American clients. Ochsner founded and became the president an organization called INCA, the Information Council of the Americas,[92] an organization with deep ties to the CIA for which it "almost certainly did work..."[93] INCA in turn represented the corporate interests of the Standard Fruit Company, a corporation with heavy investments in Latin America threatened by Castro's revolution, and by the Reily Coffee Company, Oswald's New Orleans employer.[94] Standard Fruit was also a corporate sponsor of Ochsner's clinic,[95] and to top all this off, Ochsner was also a consultant for the U.S. Air Force for "the medical side of

---

[90] Ibid, p. 175.
[91] Ibid, p. 177.
[92] Ibid, p. 160.
[93] Peter Dale Scott, *Deep Politics and the Death of JFK*, p. 94.
[94] Ibid, pp. 94-95.
[95] Ibid, p. 97.

subversive matters."[96] One witness uncovered by Haslam even maintained that Ochsner was working on a virus to assassinate Castro.[97] While it is unreasonable to assume that Ochsner was working on such a project to get Castro *specifically*, it is not unreasonable to assume that the technologies and techniques for the induction of cancer in animals would have been of interest to the CIA for covert operations, nor is it unreasonable to assume that Ochsner, with his connections to other intelligence fronts such as INCA, might have been involved with black medical research projects as well.

Dr. Alton J. Ochsner was thus no ordinary wealthy physician. As his INCA membership attests, he was a deep, but also highly visible, component of the New Orleans anti-Castro covert operations of the CIA, operations that included Guy Bannister, David Ferrie, and of course, Lee Harvey Oswald.

Dr. Alton J. Ochsner in Later Life

All of this would be only a kind of inferential "guilt by association" were it not for the fact that a witness — Judith Vary Baker — who was involved in these projects with Ochsner and Sherman, stepped forward to tell her story.[98] Baker stated that she and Oswald had carried on an affair while the latter was in New Orleans. Moreover, given her medical training in handling carcinogenic viruses, she was the one who was the technician for David Ferrie's underground laboratory, helping to develop

---

[96] Peter Dale Scott, *Deep Politics and the Death of JFK*, pp. 96-97.
[97] Edward T. Haslam, *Dr. Mary's Monkey*, p. 145.
[98] For the full account of this witness see Haslam, pp. 283-307.

a biological weapon to kill Castro.[99] She had, she stated, visited Ferrie's underground laboratory *with* Oswald. But there was more:

> To put the icing on the cake, the entire project was secretly directed by the famous Dr. Alton Ochsner... and supervised by a prestigious cancer researcher named Dr. Mary Sherman, who worked for Dr. Ochsner at his hospital.
> Further, she said, after successfully killing numerous monkeys with their new biological weapon, this group had tested it on a human subject in a mental hospital, killing the human.[100]

So now we have a tapestry of relationships that includes Ferrie, Ochsner, Oswald, and Dr. Mary Sherman, all connected to a biological weapons project seeking to develop cancer as a biological weapon. Judith Baker also accompanied Oswald to an appointment with Ochsner, during which she stated that Oswald went in first to see Ochsner alone. She also accompanied Oswald to Dr. Sherman's apartment "for a private dinner, whose only other guest was David Ferrie." She maintained that Dr. Mary Sherman was the "operational director" of the covert project.[101] Given all these associations of Dr. Ochsner, it should not be surprising that there are some allegations that Jim Garrison was planning to arrest Dr. Ochsner as part of his investigation into the JFK assassination.[102]

As noted previously, Ochsner's clinic and hospital was founded in part for the express purpose of catering to Latin America's wealthy political elite, an elite which shared Ochsner's right-wing political views. But oddly, Dr. Ochsner seemed to have been even more selective within that elite of the patients he served. For example, he numbered former Nicaraguan dictator Anastasio Somoza and none other than Argentina's Juan Péron as his patients.[103] Worse yet, one witness informed Haslam that "Ochsner was part of an international fascist group and had been very close to Nazi scientists who fled to South America at the end of

---

[99] Edward T. Haslam, *Dr. Mary's Monkey*, p. 284.

[100] Ibid, pp. 284-285.

[101] Ibid, p. 299.

[102] Ibid, p. 62. Haslam notes, however, that such a move would have been politically costly to Garrison, given Ochsner's enormous popularity and fame within the city.

[103] Ibid, pp. 178-179.

World War II, particularly in Paraguay."[104] Haslam thought nothing of this, ascribing the allegation to liberal anti-right-wing hysteria.

This author is not so sure, having documented in previous books that the Nazi presence in South America was more than just the disorganized affair of remote and isolated enclaves clinging to survival, but actually a highly organized, well-run international network with extensive independent intelligence and research capabilities of its own.[105] Given Ochsner's links to Latin America *and* to American anti-communist covert operations and intelligence, he would be a prime candidate for a liaison position between this post-war "Nazi International" and American intelligence.[106]

We have seen how Dr. Mary Sherman fit into this dark and murky network of CIA covert operations and secret medical research, but how did she die?

Haslam notes that Tulane had a large particle accelerator that was used in its secret medical research, and speculates that Sherman, for whatever reason, was killed away from her apartment, by being subjected to the severe burning — recall her homicide report's statement that her right arm had been completely disintegrated — by exposure to that

---

[104] Ibid, p. 78, see also pp, 285-286. Paraguay at the time was under the regime of dictator Stroessner, who eventually allowed Péron into that country following his ouster in Argentina.

[105] See my *The Nazi International: The Nazis' Postwar Plan to Control Finance, Conflict, Physics and Space* (Adventures Unlimited Press, 2009), pp. 85-205; 249-350; *Roswell and the Reich: The Nazi Connection* (Adventures Unlimited Press, 2010), pp. 342-371. For other studies of the extent, power, influence, and deep penetration of this organization into western intelligence and organized crime and drug trafficking, see Martin A. Lee, *The Best Reawakens: Fascism's Resurgence from Hitler's Spymasters to Today's Neo-Nazi Groups and Right-Wing Extremists* (Routledge, 2000); Michael Schmidt, *The New Reich: Violent Extremism in Unified Germany and Beyond* (Pantheon Books, 1993); this last work is especially revealing of the close association of the government of Chancellor Helmut Kohl with Nazi and Neo-Nazi front groups in Germany and elsewhere prior to and during the reunification.

[106] There is also yet another, though slim, possibility for Ochsner's association with this group, and that is he may have been involved in medical research with it in Latin America. A recent study by Latin American journalist Jorge Camarasa has disclosed a hitherto unknown project of the infamous Nazi "doctor of death," Dr. Josef Mengele in Brazil where, in a remote Indian village, beginning in the late 1970s, a large number of blonde-haired blue-eyed twins were suddenly being born into the native population. Camarasa traces this to Megele's post-war research activities in behalf of this "Nazi International."

185

particle accelerator, and then placed into the completely faked "crime scene" of her apartment.[107]

The motive for her murder seems clear: she knew enough to tie Oswald, Ferrie, and one of America's most famous doctors and surgeons, to the network of covert operations that were linked to the Kennedy assassination. And lest it be forgotten, Jack Ruby himself came down with a sudden and very virulent cancer after his conviction for murder was overturned in appeals court and the trial venue changed. Ruby always maintained that he could never talk openly and freely in Dallas about what he knew, and the order for him to be re-tried outside of Dallas would have given him the opportunity to do so. Ruby himself maintained that he was given cancer by injection, so perhaps there is a connection between Ochsner, Mary Sherman, and Ruby as well. We will never know.

In any case, is should also be noted, that Dr. Sherman's unsolved murder — whether it was murder by surgically placed stab wounds, or by particle accelerator, or even, as some allege, by gunshot[108] — occurred in March 1967, only a couple of weeks after the "suicide" of David Ferrie by drug overdose. Howsoever she ultimately died — she was after all stabbed, burned, and probably baked in a particle accelerator for good measure — someone wanted Dr. Sherman to be quite dead.

Dr. Mary Sherman:
1) **Cause of Death:** stabbing, burned (possibly in a particle accelerator)
2) **Motivation for Death:** Intimate knowledge of CIA covert medical research and covert operations, connections to Ochsner, Oswald, and Ferrie
3) **Implicated Group(s):** CIA definitely, Nazis very distantly (through Ochsner), anti-Castro Cubans (through Ferrie and Oswald).

As for David Ferrie, Dr. Sherman's erstwhile collaborator in this covert project, so much has been and could be said about him that it is clear that his "suicide" by a drug overdose-induced hemorrhage mere weeks before Dr Sherman's murder suggests the two deaths are closely related. Ferrie, with direct ties to Guy Bannister, Lee Harvey Oswald, the

---

[107] Edward T. Haslam, *Dr. Mary's Monkey*, p. 232.
[108] Roberts and Armstrong, *JFK: The Dead Witnesses,* p. 52.

New Orleans anti-Castro Cubans, and even New Orleans Mafia boss Carlos Marcello, also knew too much, and had to be silenced.

David Ferrie:
1) **Cause of Death:** brain hemorrhage by drug overdose, ruled a "suicide."
2) **Motivation for Death:** Intimate Knowledge of CIA covert anti-Castro operations, including secret medical research, probable knowledge of details of the architecture of the conspiracy.
3) **Implicated Group(s):** CIA, anti-Castro Cubans, Mafia.

And while we're at it, we may as well add Jack Ruby to this list:

Jack Ruby:
1) **Cause of Death:** Convenient and sudden onset of virulent cancer weeks before his second trial was to begin
2) **Motivation for Death:** Ruby's repeated statements that he wanted to tell the whole truth but could not do so in Dallas for fear of his life
3) **Implicated Groups:** CIA, given the fact that the CIA was, per the research of Drs. Ochsner and Sherman, researching means to induce cancer in humans as a biological weapon

The "suicide" of David Ferrie and the still unsolved murder of Dr. Mary Sherman are perhaps the least understood aspects of the JFK assassination, for from them, as from De Mohrenschildt, the connections run very deeply into the world of intelligence and post-war international Fascism.

C. Motives, Patterns, and Clues

One thing that emerges from these three murders and "suicides" is that the pattern discussed in the previous chapter appears to hold: each group involved in the assassination was responsible for cleaning up its own loose ends within its own sphere of responsibility: Ferrie and Sherman appear to have been murdered by those with access to the sophisticated technologies or medicines to do them in. In De Mohrenschildt's case, suicide by shotgun blast appears to be unlikely, and given his network of associations almost anyone could have done it.

There are two elements, however, that have changed in this picture. First, it is apparent that the role of Texas "big oil" and the Nazi connection — via General Gehlen's West German intelligence — is much more prominent a feature in the group interests coalescing around the assassination. This relationship is reflected in the shadowy Permindex corporation, a nexus of intelligence, Mafia, petroleum, and international Fascist connections in and of itself. De Mohrenschildt personalizes this nexus, for if he was in fact working for *American* intelligence, it is highly unlikely that he would be spying on its activities in preparation for the Bay of Pigs invasion. It is more likely that De Mohrenschildt in reality represents the liaison between Texas Big Oil and its connection to West German intelligence and via that connection, the relationship to international Fascism; De Mohrenschildt, in other words, *was* that connection. His "suicide" may therefore have been the work either of the Texas petroleum interests, international Fascism, or both.

In short, the Texas petroleum interests and the Fascist International probably had a hand in the aspects of the cover-up dealing with such "loose ends" as De Mohrenschildt.

Drs. Ochsner and Sherman also oddly personalize this nexus represented by Permindex, with their own murky connections to American intelligence, covert ops, and black projects and, in Ochsner's case, the even more foreboding connections to Latin America were accompanied by allegations of connections to its exiled Nazis. The brutal murder of Dr. Sherman, however, points to a different culprit, given her strong connections to Ochsner's work for the CIA, and given her probable "death by particle accelerator." This would have required someone with access, and in this case, the hands of American intelligence are implicated. The same must be said of David Ferrie and his suicide. Both Sherman and Ferrie point to threatened US intelligence interests.

In the previous chapter we reproduced the following table of represented interests on the Warren Commission:

The Murder Itself	Anti-Castro Cubans The Mafia FBI (Hoover) CIA Big Oil The Military Bankers (Federal Reserve) Nazis	Anti-Castro Cubans The Mafia FBI (Hoover) CIA Big Oil The Military Bankers (Federal Reserve) Nazis	Anti-Castro Cubans The Mafia FBI (Hoover) CIA Big Oil The Military Bankers (Federal Reserve) Nazis
The Framing of Oswald(via	FBI (Hoover) CIA	FBI (Hoover) CIA	FBI (Hoover) CIA

doubles, planted evidence, etc)	The Secret Service The Military Nazis	The Secret Service The Military Nazis	The Secret Service The Military Nazis
The Long-term Cover-up	FBI (Hoover) CIA (Dulles) Bankers (McCloy) Nazis (McCloy) *Secondary Level:* Mafia (Boggs)	FBI (Hoover) CIA (Dulles) Bankers (McCloy) Nazis (McCloy) *Secondary Level:* Mafia (Boggs)	FBI (Hoover) CIA (Dulles) Bankers (McCloy) Nazis (McCloy) *Secondary Level:* Mafia (Boggs)

If we now take into consideration the interests represented or threatened by De Mohrenschildt, Sherman, and Ferrie, the following groups may now be added as possible players to the second and third layers of the structure, as follows:

The Murder Itself	Anti-Castro Cubans The Mafia FBI (Hoover) CIA Big Oil The Military Bankers (Federal Reserve) Nazis	Anti-Castro Cubans The Mafia FBI (Hoover) CIA Big Oil The Military Bankers (Federal Reserve) Nazis	Anti-Castro Cubans The Mafia FBI (Hoover) CIA Big Oil The Military Bankers (Federal Reserve) Nazis
The Framing of Oswald(via doubles, planted evidence, etc)	FBI (Hoover) CIA The Secret Service The Military Nazis (De Mohrenschildt) Texas Big Oil (De Morhenschildt)	FBI (Hoover) CIA The Secret Service The Military Nazis (De Mohrenschildt) Texas Big Oil (De Mohrenschildt)	FBI (Hoover) CIA The Secret Service The Military Nazis (De Mohrenschildt) Texas Big Oil (De Mohrenschildt)
The Long-term Cover-up	FBI (Hoover) CIA (Dulles) Bankers (McCloy) Nazis (McCloy) *Secondary Level:* Mafia (Boggs) Nazis Texas Big Oil (De Mohrenschildt)	FBI (Hoover) CIA (Dulles) Bankers (McCloy) Nazis (McCloy) *Secondary Level:* Mafia (Boggs) Nazis Texas Big Oil (De Mohrenschildt)	FBI (Hoover) CIA (Dulles) Bankers (McCloy) Nazis (McCloy) *Secondary Level:* Mafia (Boggs) Nazis Texas Big Oil (De Mohrenschildt)

It will also be noted from this table that Permindex embodies most of the coalescing interests at all levels of the conspiracy. Indeed, one has to wonder whether the abbreviated name "Permindex," which stood officially for Permanent Industrial Expositions, was not also chosen to convey the darker and sinister purpose that Garrison and "William Torbitt" alleged for it: the planning and execution of assassinations, putting people on a kind of "permanent index."

The murder of this strange trinity — DeMohrenschildt, Ferrie, and Sherman — and their close associates at these relatively late dates from the assassination itself, indicates that the motives and groups behind the crime were still in place at the times of their deaths, and that a long-term agenda was put into play on November 22, 1963, which could potentially be hurt, crippled, or completely derailed by revelations from any of these three or their associates. In Dr. Mary Sherman's case it may even be that not only did she have to be silenced, but that her death was used to send a message and ensure the silence of her boss, Dr. Alton J. Ochsner, whose prominence would have assured an investigation should he too mysteriously die.

Not for nothing, perhaps, did Jack Ruby write in a letter to a fellow prisoner, that Lyndon Johnson "is a Nazi in the worst order."[109] Just how true or false those allegations may be, will be seen later on.

For now, however, there are even deeper motivations behind the assassination. Just what those motivations were, however, can only be grasped by peering into the abyss of the occult aspects of the murder, and into the abyss of deep space, which we now undertake in the next two chapters.

---

[109] Jim Marrs, *Crossfire: The Plot that Killed Kennedy*, p. 430.

5

THE ALCHEMY OF THE ASSASSINATION:
RITUAL MAGIC AND MASONIC SYMBOLISM OF THE COUP D 'ÉTAT

*"...the ultimate purpose of that assassination was not political or
economic but sorcerous..."*
James Shelby Downard and Michael A. Hoffman II[1]

R itual magic seems the least likely motivation for the assassination of President Kennedy, yet, in the deepest sense, it holds the key to it all, and in so doing, points a clear finger to the deep politics, and deepest players, in the whole alchemical "psychodrama" played out, with all the deliberate exactitude of an occult ritual, in Dallas on November 22, 1963, for that is exactly what it was: a ritual of sacrifice, an alchemical working, the heartbeat of black magic at the center of the century's most daring coup d'état.

To describe the assassination as an alchemical act is not as odd as it might at first seem, for one of the goals of esoteric alchemy is the transformation of mankind himself,[2] that is, to create, via a magical operation, a transformation of consciousness in a group of individuals, in this case, the psyche of the American people and culture themselves. Today we would simply call "esoteric alchemy" nothing but "social engineering." But the alchemical, magical effect is the same regardless of the terms one uses. In normal alchemical doctrine, this esoteric transformation is understood to be an operation of white, or "good," magic to elevate and illuminate the consciousness of an individual, to make them more compassionate, more *human.* The JFK assassination, conversely, has all the hallmarks of black magic, of the evil searing, scarring, and dehumanizing debasement of the American people.

But why call it a coup d'état? Many assassination researchers have in fact referred to it as such, but does the assassination bear the *actual signatures* of a coup d'état? And if so, how does the ritual magic, the alchemical element, fit in?

---

[1] Michael A. Hoffman II, *Secret Societies and Psychological Warfare* (Coeur d'Alene, Idaho: Independent History and Research, 2001), p. 84.

[2] For a brief discussion of this aspect of alchemy, see my *The Philosophers' Stone: Alchemy and the Secret Quest for Exotic Matter* (Port Townsend, Washington: Feral House, 2009), pp. 31-36.

These are important questions, for if indeed the assassination bears the signatures of *both* kinds of operation, of a magical operation *and* of a coup d'état, then indeed it was a potent magical working on the soul of America, and for that reason, we shall carefully examine both aspects.

A. The Alchemy of the Assassination:
1. The Ultimate Aims of Socio-Alchemy

Michael A. Hoffmann II is one of the few researchers to have delved into the ritual magic aspects of modern social engineering in general, and the Kennedy assassination in particular, in a seminal little book entitled *Secret Societies and Psychological Warfare.*[3]

There are three essential alchemical workings, each of which is also designed to bring about a transformation of consciousness in addition to the goal of each working:

1) the bringing of the Philosophers' Stone, the *materia prima*, from heaven to earth and embodying it in material form within this three dimensional existence;
2) the creation and destruction of that Philosopher's Stone, the *materia prima*; and,
3) The Killing or Sacrifice of the King.[4]

Each of these three workings are designed, says Hoffman, with the goal of planting certain "memes" into the social consciousness, and in the case of the Kennedy assassination — the Sacrifice of the King — the memes to be implanted, says Hoffman, were clear:

> The virus embedded within the ritual murders of John F. Kennedy... are in the trickery, punning lingo of the Hermetic fraternity's Camelot, "once-and-future" tales possessing the intention of self-fulfilling prophecy; what I term "inevitablism."...
> The "virus" containing this *meme* ("contagious" idea pattern), infects the host with the sense that it is:
> • Useless to resist central, establishment control.

---

[3] The other researcher to do so is Peter Levenda. See his three-volume study of the role of the occult within American politics: *Sinister Forces: A Grimoire of American Political Witchcraft*, Book One: *The Nine*; Book Two: *A Warm Gun;* and Book Three: *The Manson Secret* (Walterville, Oregon: Trine Day, 2005, 2006, and 2006, respectively).

[4] Hoffman, *Secret Societies and Psychological Warfare*, p. 80.

- Or it posits a counter-cultural alternative to such control which is actually a counterfeit, covertly emanating from the establishment itself.
- That the blackening (pollution) of earth is as unavoidable as entropy.
- That extinction ("evolution") of the species human being is inevitable.
- That the reinhabitation of the earth by the "old gods" (Genesis 6:4), is our stellar scientific destiny.[5]

The Kennedy assassination was, in other words, one of the magical workings in modern times designed to implant these "memes." One need hardly question the role that evolutionary theory has played in implanting the meme that the human species is destined as a species to die, to be replaced by "something better" in the name of "survival of the fittest." Indeed, the whole quest for the Nietzschean *Übermensch* is writ large within 20th century history, from the Nazi eugenics and sterilization programs to the Soviet Union's Stalinesque obsession to create "New Soviet Man" to more recent calls from geneticists and cybernetics researchers to create the ultimate genetic chimera, the "manimal" hybrid of human and animal genes, or the "cyborg," the human implanted with computer interfaces and other machines to "enhance" his capabilities.

But what of Hoffman's assertion that this is all in aid of a covert and deep agenda to reinvoke the presence of "the old gods?" And why indeed make such an outlandish statement at the beginning of a book which has as one of its major themes the assassination of President Kennedy? Hoffman gives a hint of his reasoning in the following quotation:

> This humanoid-beast creature prepared in the gleaming laboratories and research-hospitals, fulfills the occult mandate for the return of the legendary, god-like "beast with reason," Oannes, an animal with a human head, reputed to have been the bringer of civilization to Sumer, in the dimmest reaches of antiquity.[6]

---

[5] Hoffman, *Secret Societies and Psychological Warfare*, p. 8.

[6] Ibid., p. 11. Oannes is described in the Babylonian priest Berossus' three volume *Babylonaica*, a work lost to history. Fragments of the work, however, survive in quotations from the early church historian Eusebius(citing Alexander Polyhistor), in Apollodorus, and in Abydenus. Alexander Polyhistor produced this lengthy quotation: "At Babylon there was (in these times) a great resort of people of various nations, who inhabited Chaldæa, and lived in a lawless manner like the beasts of the field. In the first year there appeared, from that part of the

The reference to Oannes, ancient god and civilizer of Sumeria, part man, part fish, is deliberate, for in the deepest sense, the idea of such chimeras implants the meme of barbarism, of bestiality, into society, producing at least the "chimerical consciousness," part human, part beast.

Erythræan sea which borders upon Babylonia, an animal destitute of reason, by name Oannes, whose whole body (according to the account of Apollodorus) was that of a fish; that under the fish's head he had another head, with feet also below, similar to those of a man, subjoined to the fish's tail. His voice too, and language, was articulate and human; and a representation of him is preserved even to this day.

"This Being was accustomed to pass the day among men; but took no food at that season; and he gave them an insight into letters and sciences, and arts of every kind. He taught them to construct cities, to found temples, to compile laws, and explained to them the principles of geometrical knowledge. He made them distinguish the seeds of the earth, and shewed them how to collect the fruits; in short, he instructed them in everything which could tend to soften manners and humanize their lives. From that time, nothing material has been added by way of improvement to his instructions. And when the sun had set, this Being Oannes, retired again into the sea, and passed the night in the deep; for he was amphibious. After this there appeared other animals like Oannes, of which Berossus proposes to give an account when he comes to the history of the kings. Moreover Oannes wrote concerning the generation of mankind; and of their civil polity; and the following is the purport of what he said:

"There was a time in which there existed nothing but darkness and an abyss of waters, wherein resided most hideous beings, which were produced of a twofold principle. There appeared men, some of whom were furnished with two wings, others with four, and with two faces. They had one body but two heads: the one that of a man, the other of a woman: and likewise in their several organs both male and female. Other human figures were to be seen with the legs and horns of goats: some had horses' feet: while others united the hind quarters of a horse with the body of a man, resembling in shape the hippocentaurs. Bulls likewise were bred there with the heads of men; and dogs with fourfold bodies, terminated in their extremities with the tails of fishes: horses also with the heads of dogs: men too and other animals, with the heads and bodies of horses and the tails of fishes. In short, there were creatures in which were combined the limbs of every species of animals. In addition to these, fishes, reptiles, serpents, with other monstrous animals, which assumed each other's shape and countenance. Of all which were preserved delineations in the temple of Belus at Babylon."

The assassination of President Kenneday, to put it succinctly, was also done in aid of a deeply occult agenda, and a very old one.[7]

The goal of this occult working, this ritual immolation, was to produce the three conditions of a totally passive population:

> What we observe in the population today are the three destructive symptoms of persons whose minds are controlled by alien forces: 1. Amnesia, i.e., loss of memory. 2. Abulia, i.e., loss of will. 3. Apathy, i.e., loss of interest in events vital to one's own health and survival. Amnesia, abulia, and apathy are nearly-universal among us today and gaining a greater foothold with each passing day.[8]

Crucial to this magical working is the fact that it must be — as a matter of occult principle — clearly communicated to its intended targets or victims, in this case, by the open parade of symbolism indicating the true significance of the act and its dark motivations and perpetrators, by a series of deliberate "leaks":

> This alludes to the process wherein murderous deeds and hair-raising conspiracies involving wars, revolutions, decapitations, secret archaeo-astronomic deity cult-worship, and every manner of horror show are first buried beneath a cloak of secrecy... and then, when finally accomplished and secured, slowly revealed to the unsuspecting populace who watch...deep-frozen...as the hidden history is unveiled... In the circulation of...(anti-Academy) manuscripts...the revelation of the method is accomplished.[9]

Indeed, for any researcher engaged in such exposure, the thought must be ever-present that "in exposing the conspirators he is probably serving the final dictum (in their alchemical formula)..."[10]

The reason for this is simple, because "such revelations may only serve to strengthen the cryptocracy's mental hold."[11] Again, it is a

---

[7] Hoffman states "To process a population of *goyim* sufficiently depraved to devour unborn children for the benefit of the elderly, mix races and species and rebuild the Tower of Babel, it was necessary to immerse the people of the West in an era that would idolize the material world and deny the spiritual."(Hoffman, *Secret Societies and Psychological Warfare*, p. 17). Hoffman's own quiet agenda is evident from his remarks, and needless to say, this author does *not* agree with the idea that a mixing of the races is inherently materialistic or evil.

[8] Ibid, p. 20.

[9] Ibid, p. 53.

[10] Ibid.

populace of two minds, and hence, completely passive, that is the goal. The purpose of these activities it to reinforce the notion that "there is nothing that we can do about it but accept it." It is here however, that I believe that Hoffman is to a certain extent in error, for by changing the perception of the key players and their motivations, a wider mistrust of their institutions and methods of power is engendered.

But in any case, Hoffman's meaning is clear: by parading their power in a clear act of ritual murder, and then "explaining" that murder with an explanation that was self-evidently ridiculous and untrue, and wrapping it in the purple of official sanction, the population was reduced to confusion, to two minds, to abulia, amnesia, and apathy. We shall see how this "consent in the status quo" and these states of minds in populations are crucial elements — viewed in another way — of all coups d'état.

2. Some of the Ritual Symbolism of the JFK Assassination

So how does the assassination of President Kennedy fit into all of this deep politics of the occult?

One need only to consider the blatant facts, the "obvious things," to see how.

America's first, and only, Roman Catholic President's motorcade takes him through Dealey plaza, a plaza dedicated to the memory of the first Masonic Grand Master of Texas. Thus is met in Dealey plaza an old animosity, that of the Roman Church and Freemasonry, that of a "catholic" religion for the masses versus a Gnostic hermetic sect, preserving its secrets for the initiate of "higher consciousness and degrees."

Even in this there is Masonic significance, for the builder of the "temple of Man," in Masonic initiatory ritual, Hiram Abiff, is murdered by three treasonous servants. Kennedy in his limousine is riding, like the king in the Masonic ritual, into a trap.

And the trap itself has symbolic significance, for the layout of the three streets converging in Dealey Plaza, when viewed from above, form a trident, the symbol of Poseidon, the god of the sea, a symbolism full of "Atlantean" references to the "old gods" and to their vanished civilization and all its technologies, with their secret societies preserving their secrets.

---

[11] Hoffman, *Secret Societies and Psychological Warfare*, p. 53.

It is onto *this* darkly occult stage, carefully prepared, that John F. Kennedy's motorcade rides.

Masonic Dealey Plaza with Poseidon's Trident

Nothing is left to chance, nothing can be left to chance, in any act of ritual such as this. So accordingly, Hiram Abiff's three murderers are also present, and photographed as the infamous "three tramps" taken into custody by the Dallas Police, and later released, their identities unknown to this day.

The Three Tramps: Jubelo, Jubela, Jubelum
They are arrested, and later released and their identities remain
unknown

Indeed, this Masonic symbolism and its role as a method of implanting memes of helplessness, double-mindedness, and passivity within society must be grasped in its deepest significance, at work in all three of America's infamous assassinations of the 1960s:

198

One can observe a process of cryogenic, episodic revelation repeated time and again in the notorious "lone nut" assassin series (in Masonry it is known as the "three Unworthy Craftsmen"): the assassination of JFK by "lone nut" Lee Harvey Oswald; the assassination of Martin Luther King by "lone nut" James Earl Ray and the assassination of Robert Kennedy by "lone nut" Sirhan Sirhan. In each case, at the time of the murders, both the media and police officials conspired to present a united and seemingly infallible solution to these crimes centering on allegedly iron-clad and irrefutable "low temperature" evidence that Oswald, Ray or Sirhan were the sole perpetrators of these electrifying crimes which galvanized a nation.

Then, in accordance with the clockwork script, 5, 10 or 15 years later, after the trail is hopelessly cold and highly obscured, a spate of tightly documented and well-researched books and films emerge which heat us up, turning our heads 180 degrees in the opposite direction...

We learn that Oswald was a scapegoat, Ray a patsy and Sirhan an OTO cultist. And we learn of their accomplices.

If you carefully study this scenario what you'll discover is astonishing. You'll find that the after-the-fact revelations are as much a part of the assassination plot as the murder and its initial cover-up. It's a deliberate psychological process they're taking us through, a psychodrama of enormous scale....

The following is a statement which comes from within the British-intelligence wing of the Cryptocracy:

"This demonstrates one of our simpler methods. Realizing that our activities will sooner or later come to light, we structure our activities so that as conspiracy researchers unravel them, *they will release information into the public consciousness in such a way that it mirrors our initiatory procedure.* In this way, the more we are investigated, the more masses of people are psychologically processed by the very people who seek to expose us. The **meme** that constitutes our essential structure is then successfully mimicked within the consciousness of those who investigate us. Success can then be measure precisely to the extent that our work is 'exposed.'"[12]

To put all this as succinctly as possible, what Hoffman is implying is that the Warren Report itself was *not* just a cover-up; it was a deliberately contrived technique of psychological warfare, an alchemical operation

---

[12] Hoffman, *Secret Societies and Psychological Warfare*, pp. 76-77, italicized emphasis added, boldface emphasis original.

and magical working, designed to reinforce the power of the hidden elites at work in the assassination itself.

Hoffman puts it with his characteristic eloquence:

> One: the ritual murders are successfully accomplished. The principals get-away, the scapegoat conveniently rakes the blame. Two: later we learn the truth but no one is prosecuted.[13] We are mocked, disoriented and demoralized. Occult prestige and potency is heightened.
>
> This is what simplistic researchers miss: the function of macabre arrogance thumbing its nose at us while we do nothing except spread the tale of their immunity and invincibility further. That is the game plan operant here.
>
> ....
>
> The alchemical principle of Revelation of the Method has as its chief component a clown-like, grinning mockery of the victim(s) as a show of power and macabre arrogance. When this is performed in a veiled manner, accompanied by certain occult signs and symbolic words and elicits no meaningful response of opposition or resistance from the target(s), it is one of the most efficacious techniques of psychological warfare and mind-rape.[14]

So what three events fulfill the three alchemical workings, the bringing of primordial matter to earth, its creation and destruction, and the sacrifice of the king?

For Hoffman, the destruction of primordial matter was accomplished at the Trinity atomic bomb test at Alamogordo in July, 1945, when the very building blocks of all matter, the atoms themselves, were split and goldenly transubstantiated in a colossal explosion on that day. The first work — the bringing of primordial matter from heaven to earth — will have to wait the next chapter.

Here we are concerned with the third, the ritual Sacrifice of the King of Camelot. And here it is necessary to cite Hoffman at length, to gain an appreciation for the *detailed planning* that went into this aspect of the murder, for it is an important clue into the nature of yet another possible player or group at the deepest level of the assassination and its cover-up:

---

[13] Or, in Garrison's prosecution of Clay Shaw, the powers behind the assassination bend every effort to subvert the process. It is successful. Clay Shaw is acquitted as witnesses crucial to Garrison's case conveniently die and then, as we have seen, Shaw himself is murdered before he can talk openly – having already been tried for conspiring to murder the president he could not under the rule of double jeopardy be tried again, and thus was *free* to talk.

[14] Hoffman, *Secret Societies and Psychological Warfare*, p. 78.

The Killing of the King rite was accomplished at another Trinity site located approximately ten miles south of the 33rd degree of north parallel latitude between the Trinity River (in Dallas) and the Triple Underpass at Dealey Plaza in Dallas, Texas. Dealey Plaza[15] was the site of the first masonic temple in Dallas. In this spot, which had been known during the 19th century cowboy era as "Bloody Elm Street," the world leader who had become known as the "King of Camelot," President John Fitzgerald Kennedy, was shot to death.

A widely publicized image which has become perhaps the key symbol of the enigma of the Kennedy hoodwink, emerged immediately in the wake of the assassination: a photograph of the three "tramps" in official custody, who were later unexplainably released and never identified, though speculation about who they really were has reached fever pitch among investigators.

This photograph is a ritual accompaniment of the Black mass that was the ceremonial immolation of a king, the unmistakable calling card of Masonic murder, the appearance of Jubela, Jubelo, and Jubelum, the three "unworthy craftsmen" of Temple burlesque, "that will not be blamed for nothing."

....

(The assassination) is a Masonic riddle several magnitudes above the pedestrian, CIA-Mafia-Anti-Castro-pro-Castro-KGB-Texas right-wing etc political "solutions" pushed by the various books and movies which sometimes only serve to confuse and demoralize us all the more.

What ought to be unambiguous to a student of mass psychology is the almost immediate decline of the American people in the wake of this shocking, televised slaughter.

....

A hidden government behind the visible government of these United States became painfully obvious in a kind of subliminal way and lent an undercurrent of the hallucinogenic to our reality. ...

There was a transfer of power in the collective group mind of the American masses: from the public power of the elected front-man Chief Executive to an unelected invisible college capable of terminating him with impunity.[16]

In other words, Hoffman is saying that, in addition to the other groups surveyed in previous chapters with a hand in and motivation and means

---

[15] Hoffman notes that "Dea=goddess. Ley=rule. Hence 'goddess rule' plaza or more specifically, Isis plaza." (q.v. Hoffman, *Secret Societies and Psychological Warfare*, p. 83).

[16] Ibid, pp. 84-85, emphasis added.

to commit the crime, there is a deeper player, one with a much more long-term agenda, deeply rooted in ancient history and a legendary past it wants to bring into magical reality; he is saying there is a group that was involved in the planning of the murder with deep and detailed knowledge of ritual magical practice.

Of course, we have surveyed one such group in previous chapters that would have had such knowledge of deep occult practice, and that is the Nazis.

It should not therefore surprise us that, in the deeper conspiracy of the Warren Commission cover-up itself, two of the key people — J. Edgar Hoover, whose FBI led the "investigation" to frame Oswald, and Cheif Justice Earl Warren — were both Freemasons. Hoover, was a thirty-three degree Mason and one of the most highly ranking Masons in Washington, D.C. at the time,[17] and Earl Warren was founder of the *Ars Quatuor Coronati* Masonic lodge, the "research and intelligence" arm of American Masonry.[18]

In this context it is perhaps even more significant that there is not only a dark Masonic, magical symbolism operating in Dealey Plaza on November 22, 1963[19] but also the dark symbolism of the Mauser, then the Mannlicher-Carcano, rifles attributed to Oswald, pointing fingers to deeply occulted and occult powers at work.

We are now confronted by a new set of data: indications of deep Masonic principles at work in the crime, and deep Masonic principals at work in the cover-up. We have indicators even of some of the motivations for this involvement, namely, the transformation of American social consciousness.

---

[17] Jim Keith, *Mind Control, World Control"The Encyclopedia of Mind Control* (Adventures Unlimited Press, 1997), p. 139.

[18] Hoffman, *Secret Societies and Subversive Movements*, p. 57.

[19] Consider only the numerological significance of the twenty-second day of the eleventh month: 22+11=33. And of course, 1963 has its own "tetrahedral" significance. The murder was thus close to the 33rd degree north parallel, on the eleventh month and twenty-second day, with "three tramps" in attendance at Dealey, or "Isis" Plaza.

Our template of involved groups now has an added, unexpected, player or group, and now looks like this:

The Murder Itself	Anti-Castro Cubans The Mafia FBI (Hoover) CIA Big Oil The Military Bankers (Federal Reserve) Nazis	Anti-Castro Cubans The Mafia FBI (Hoover) CIA Big Oil The Military Bankers (Federal Reserve) Nazis Masons (details of the crime, motive of transformation of social conscious-ness)	Anti-Castro Cubans The Mafia FBI (Hoover) CIA Big Oil The Military Bankers (Federal Reserve) Nazis Masons (details of the crime, motive of transformation of social conscious-ness)
The Framing of Oswald(via doubles, planted evidence, etc)	FBI (Hoover) CIA The Secret Service The Military Nazis (De Mohrenschildt) Texas Big Oil (De Morhenschildt)	FBI (Hoover) CIA The Secret Service The Military Nazis (De Mohrenschildt) Texas Big Oil (De Mohrenschildt)	FBI (Hoover) CIA The Secret Service The Military Nazis (De Mohrenschildt) Texas Big Oil (De Mohrenschildt)
The Long-term Cover-up	FBI (Hoover) CIA (Dulles) Bankers (McCloy) Nazis (McCloy) Masons (Hoover and Warren) *Secondary Level:* Mafia (Boggs) Nazis Texas Big Oil (De Mohrenschildt)	FBI (Hoover) CIA (Dulles) Bankers (McCloy) Nazis (McCloy Masons (Hoover and Warren) *Secondary Level:* Mafia (Boggs) Nazis Texas Big Oil (De Mohrenschildt)	FBI (Hoover) CIA (Dulles) Bankers (McCloy) Nazis (McCloy) Masons (Hoover and Warren) *Secondary Level:* Mafia (Boggs) Nazis Texas Big Oil (De Mohrenschildt)

Note that in the level of the cover-up, the deepest players are represented on the Warren Commission by one of the members of the Commission, but at the level of the crime itself, the "Masonic" interest is present only as a motive, both in the details of the crime and in the motive itself. We will never know if any of the people actually pulling the triggers in Dallas on that day really were Masons, though, given the symbolic nature of the assassination, this author would not be surprised if it were the case.

B. The Ritual Requirements of Coups D'État
1. Prerequisites and Fundamental Aims of Coups D'État

The assassination is often said to have been a coup d'état, from everyone from Colonel Fletcher Prouty to film director and producer Oliver Stone in his movie *JFK*. But was it? Does the assassination of President Kennedy, and its aftermath, bear the hallmarks of other coups d'état? If so, how does this pattern fit with the deeper pattern of magical working surveyed in the previous section?

Since 2008 Edward Luttwalk has been a senior advisor for the Center for Strategic and International Studies in Washington, D.C. Among other posts he was been an advisor for all American military service branches, several defense ministries of NATO countries, and is a scholar of military history and grand strategy. And he is also a scholar of coups d'état, authoring the world's only "guidebook" to coups, *Coup D'État: a Practical Handbook.*

There are, according to Luttwalk, two overriding and crucial prerequisites to all coups d'état. The feasibility of staging and successfully executing a coup, says Luttwalk,

> derives from a comparatively recent development: the rise of the modern state with its professional bureaucracy and standing armed forces....
> The growth of the modern bureaucracy has two implications which are crucial to the feasibility of the *coup*: the development of a clear distinction between the permanent machinery of state and the political leadership, and the fact that, like most large organizations, the bureaucracy has a structured hierarchy with definite chains of command. The distinction between the bureaucrat as an employee of the state and as a personal servant of the ruler is a new one, and both the British and American systems show residual features of the earlier structure.[20]

Note these features, as they are quite important. There must be (1) a modern state with a professional bureaucracy with its ordinary chains of command, and (2) a standing army or military. It is obvious that the United States of America had both in abundance at the time of the assassination of President Kennedy.

---

[20] Edward Luttwalk, *Coup D'État: A Practical Handbook* (Harvard University Press, 1979), p. 19.

These features provide a second clue into the basic operational principle of coups, for rather than being confined to a small circle of revolutionaries, coups tend to be much larger, and therefore, much more carefully planned affairs:

> The *coup* is a much more democratic affair. It can be conducted from the 'outside' and it operates in that area *outside the government but within the state which is formed by the permanent and professional civil service, the armed force and police. The aim is to detach the permanent employees of the state from the political leadership,* and this cannot usually take place if the two are linked by political, ethnic or traditional loyalties.[21]

In this respect as well the Kennedy assassination fulfills the conditions outlined by Luttwalk for a coup d'état, for as we have seen in previous chapters, many of the groups with the means, motives, and opportunities to carry out the crime were essential to its cover-up. In other words, there were groups operating within the government and using its institutions of power to carry out and conduct the cover-up, as well as to lay the foundations of the crime itself.

While the assassination of a leader is not necessarily a component of coups, in the JFK case it most definitely did serve to "detach the bureaucracy" from the political leadership, and reassign its loyalties to the leadership it installed: Lyndon Johnson.

We must also pause and consider what this means in terms of Hoffman's alchemical analysis that one of the objectives of the assassination was the transformation of social consciousness into a state of bewilderment and passivity, for the professional bureaucrats would have been no less affected by such a working than anyone else. From the magical point of view, then, another aim was the transformation of the bureaucracy into a passive, if not a willing, tool of the agenda.

The reason this is such an important element is that the coup d'état must quickly seize the chain of command of the state from the political leadership it wishes to replace, and then use those chains of command to consolidate its own power and position within the state.[22] The coup in other words, relies upon the fact that the modern state is a social machine, and uses elements of the state itself to overturn its own political leadership. "A *coup* consists of the infiltration of a small but critical

---

[21] Luttwalk, *Coup D'État*, p. 20, emphasis added.
[22] Ibid, p. 21.

segment of the state apparatus, which is then used to displace the government from its control of the remainder."[23]

In this respect the JFK assassination presents some special problems, for while our templates have shown that a relatively small group of individuals had to have been involved in (1) the planning of the crime, (2) the positioning of Oswald, and (3) the cover-up, those individuals in turn are representative of much more widespread, and deeper political interests. To a certain extent then, the JFK assassination represents a coup to restore the "status quo ante" that those deep political interests perceived were threatened by the Kennedy Administration. From their point of view, it was the Kennedy machine that had infiltrated the government and staged a coup by being elected.[24]

All this brings us to a second, very obvious, but very important prerequisite condition for the staging of a successful coup: "the target state must be substantially independent and the influence of foreign powers in its internal political life must be relatively limited."[25] Closely allied to this is the fact that the nation must have a political center, that is, the controlling executive power must be clearly identifiable and its physical location and capital must be clearly identified.[26] It is easy to see that the United States fulfills both conditions.

The third essential prerequisite component of a coup is the political passivity of the majority of the people.[27] "This lack of reaction is all the *coup* needs on the part of the people in order to stay in power."[28] But here the planners had a problem, for the reaction of the American people, including the bureaucracy, could not be gauged. It is here that one must recall what happened within mere days after the assassination in order to understand the planning and architecture of the conspiracy, for the new Johnson Administration, in conjunction with behind-the-scenes consultation with J. Edgar Hoover, moved quickly to establish the Warren Commission, and as assassination researchers had more than adequately demonstrated, from the outset the FBI investigation was carefully steered by Hoover to the conclusion that Oswald was the "lone nut" assassin.

---

[23] Luttwalk, *Coup D'État*, p. 27.
[24] Ibid, pp. 85-86.
[25] Ibid, p. 44.
[26] Ibid, p. 55.
[27] Ibid, p. 34.
[28] Ibid, p. 35.

In other words, bureaucratic loyalty was insured by this tactic for a period long enough to consolidate power and secure the long-term agenda. Similarly, Hoffman's analysis now gains additional strength, for an accidental death of the President, such as a crash of Air Force One (a plan actually at one time considered), would have invited too much scrutiny; the people had to be *shocked* into passivity by a crime openly committed, and then *later* revealed to be the work of a conspiracy. The political power of the bureaucracy and the people had to be neutralized, which leads Luttwalk to another prerequisite for a coup: "The social and economic conditions of the target country must be such as to confine political participation to a small fraction of the population."[29] This too, in a certain sense, is already evident, for the groups involved in the planning and execution of each of the three stages of the assassination represent the threatened interests of deeply embedded parapolitical elites within American society, especially when one considers the interests of corporate power — Texas "big oil" and the banking community — and the interests of intelligence and underground criminal power — the various intelligence agencies, the Mafia, the Nazis, and so on. Again, it is important to note also that Hoffman's analysis again gains strength, because the shocking of the population also has as a goal to reduce the role of the population in political power to passive compliance in the face of the political situations presented to it by these elites.

As Luttwalk puts this point, "Much of the planning and execution of a *coup* will be directed at influencing the decision of the *élite* in a favorable manner."[30] That is, for those elites *not* actively involved in the planning of any stage of the assassination, the decisions of the new political leadership must be such as to win over these elites with an agenda that represents their interests. It need hardly be noted that the Johnson Administration, with its reversal of Kennedy's policies to big petroleum interests, its commitment to an expansion of the Vietnam War, and its reversal of JFK's policy of by-passing the Federal Reserve Bank and issuing debt-free United States Notes into circulation, made the "correct" decisions as far as those elites were concerned. Luttwalk's own words summarize this process adequately: "Our purpose is, however, quite different: we want to seize power *within* the present system, and we shall only stay in power if we embody some new *status quo* supported by those very forces which a revolution may seek to destroy."[31] The

---

[29] Luttwalk, *Coup D'État*, p. 37.
[30] Ibid, p. 36.
[31] Ibid, p. 58.

strategy, according to Luttwalk, is therefore very simple, and "must be guided by two principal considerations: the need for maximum speed in the transitional phase, and the need to neutralize fully the forces which could oppose us both before and immediately after the *coup.*"[32] In these respects then, the JFK assassination bears the clear hallmarks of a coup d'état, for again, the new regime moved quickly both in the areas of policy agendas and in the crucial steps it took to perpetuate a cover-up.

There is one very peculiar point that Luttwalk also raises as a potential basis of power for a coup: "Another possible substitute for the subversion of the forces of the state is the organization of a party militia."[33] While it may seem at first glance that the United States lacked this ingredient at the time — after all, neither the Democratic nor the Republican Parties then or now possessed such militias — the fact is that the Mafia and anti-Castro Cubans, the latter trained precisely as a political militia by the CIA, readily fulfill this condition and could therefore have provided the necessary on the ground "talent" to carry out the crime, providing the cover of "plausible deniability" in case something went wrong.

2. The JFK Assassination as a Coup D'État:
A Closer Look a Little-Known Details
a. Luttwalk on Operational Details

We have seen that the JFK assassination abundantly fulfills the prerequisite conditions for it to be defined as a coup d'état, but does it fulfill the conditions for a coup in terms of its tactical operational details?

A closer look at what these details are is in order. According to Luttwalk, there are four essential operational tactical details to consider:

1) *Neutralize the Forces of Coercion:* Luttwalk summarizes this important point in the following fashion:

> Because of their capability for direct intervention, the armed forces and the other means of coercion of the state must be fully neutralized *before* the actual *coup* starts; the 'political' forces can usually be dealt with immediately after the *coup*. In some situations, however, the political forces can also have an

---

[32] Luttwalk, *Coup D'État*, p. 58.
[33] Ibid., p. 59.

immediate impact on the course of events and must, therefore, be treated on the same basis as the means of coercion of the state.[34]

We shall see in the next section that distinct and definite steps were taken both to neutralize crucial elements of the American military in Texas as well as the potential political opposition from within the Kennedy Administration.

2) *Neutralize the Political Opposition and Its Means of Communication with the Bureaucratic Chain of Command:* In addition to the neutralization of the forces of coercion, it is equally important to neutralize any potential political opposition. As noted immediately above, this would include elements within the Kennedy Administration in positions to utilize the chain of command over the federal bureaucracy in the crucial hours after the assassination, when the transition of power is still underway. Luttwalk notes that there are two crucial points to this step:

a) *Neutralization of Communications and the Chain of Command:* With respect to this step, Luttwalk states "If the means of communication and the transport system are under our control, *or at any rate do not function,* the potential threat posed by the 'political forces' will be largely neutralized..."[35] As we will discover in the next section, this non-functioning communication system did in fact occur.

b) *Isolation of Crucial Personalities within the Old Regime:* A second important operational detail is the isolation of key figures within the Old Regime who might be capable of organizing and motivating a political opposition to the coup d'état. "We will, therefore, start," says Luttwalk, "by analyzing the governmental leadership in order to determine which personalities will have to be isolated for the duration of the active phase of the *coup* and which can be safely ignored."[36]

The reason that these forces must be neutralized or isolated is very simple, for firstly, "they can rally and deploy the masses, or some part of them, against the new government," and secondly,

---

[34] Luttwalk, *Coup D'État,* p. 60.
[35] Ibid, p. 110, emphasis added.
[36] Ibid, p. 111.

"they can manipulate the technical facilities under their control in order to oppose consolidation" of the coup.[37]

3) *Placing the Teams and Seizing the Physical Center of the Voice of Authority:* Closely allied with this neutralization and isolation of the potential political opposition and the seizure, or planned malfunctioning, of the means of communication is the need to seize "the voice of authority" and the physical location or locations associated with it. In standard coups, this means the seizure of state-run radio and television stations, and the presidential palace or government quarter of the capital city.[38] But within the United States, this presented special operational problems. For one thing, there were no state-run media, but three large radio and television networks, all headquartered in New York City. Needless to say, actual seizure of their headquarters would have been far too risky. Luttwalk's comment at this juncture is worth noting: "Our strategy will therefore be to seize and hold just one facility, *the one most closely associated with the voice of authority,* while neutralizing the others."[39] As will be seen below, the United States in this respect actually offers a unique opportunity to any would-be planners of a coup.

4) *"Freezing" the Situation:* The final essential operational detail is to "freeze" the situation during the crucial transitional phase of the transference of power, of that phase where the chain of command of the bureaucracies is detached from the previous political leadership and transferred to the new one. The reason for this step, once again, is clear: "If we can retain our control over what we have seized, those political forces whose primary requirement is the preservation of law and order will probably give us their allegiance. Our objective, therefore, is to freeze the situation so that this process can take place."[40] That is to say, one actually has to "freeze" the situation of *confusion* in the aftermath of a coup just long enough that those groups or bureaucracies whose interest lies in stability and calm will transfer their allegiance in order to restore a situation of apparent stability and clarity.

---

[37] Luttwalk, *Coup D'État*, p. 109.
[38] Ibid, p. 119.
[39] Ibid, emphasis added.
[40] Ibid, p. 163.

We are now in a position to take a closer look at little-known details of the Kennedy assassination.[41]

b. Col. Fletcher Prouty on the Operational Details of the Kennedy Coup D'État

Colonel Fletcher Prouty was at the time of the Kennedy assassination the Pentagon liaison officer to the CIA as well as a high White House staffer in regular contact with the Kennedy Administration. As such, he was in a unique position to view the assassination. The details provided in his book *JFK: The CIA, Vietnam, and the Plot to Assassinate John F. Kennedy* confirm the operational details of a coup.

1) *Neutralize the Forces of Coercion:*
   a) *Neutralizing the President's Cabinet by Isolation:* Prouty notes that at the exact time of the assassination that the Kennedy cabinet was en route from Hawaii to Japan. The trip to Hawaii is also noteworthy because there, at a high level meeting between the military and his cabinet secretaries, the President's own policy with respect to Vietnam was being quietly overturned and a new policy of escalation of the war was being adopted. Prouty asks the following series of questions to drive home the point that this could hardly have been accidental:

> How did it happen that the Kennedy cabinet had traveled to Hawaii at precisely the same time Kennedy was touring in Texas? How did it happen that the subject of discussion in Hawaii, before JFK was killed, was a strange agenda that would not come up in the White House until after he had been murdered? Who could have known, beforehand, that this new — non-Kennedy — agenda would be needed in the White House because Kennedy would no longer be President?
>
> Is there any possibility that the "powers that be" who planned and executed the Kennedy assassination had also been able to get the Kennedy cabinet out of the country

---

[41] These details were first popularized in cursory fashion in Oliver Stone's movie *JFK* in the section where Garrison, played by Kevin Costner, interviews "Mr. X" in Washington, D.C., played by Donald Sutherland. We present the actual basis of these statements here.

and to have them conferring in Hawaii on an agenda that would be put before President Lyndon Johnson just four days after Kennedy's death?[42]

To make matters very much worse, on the day of the assassination, that cabinet was in the air, en route to Japan, when the President was shot. The flight returned to Hawaii when it learned of the assassination. "The Honolulu trip removed most of the Kennedy inner circle — a cabinet quorum — from Washington."[43] To put it succinctly, the cabinet, which had *control over the Federal bureaucracy, was neutralized by having it out of the country at the time.*

b) *Neutralization of Military Counter-Intelligence in Texas:* There were two army counter-intelligence units available in Texas for Presidential security, and under normal circumstances, these would have been activated, the 316th and 112 Military Intelligence Groups. Instead, as Prouty discovered later, making discrete inquiries, very odd things happened *before* the assassination, exactly as stipulated by Luttwalk as a condition for a successful coup:

> The commander of an army unit, specially trained in protection and based in nearby San Antonio, Texas, had been told he would not be needed in Dallas. "Another army unit will cover that city," the commander was told.
>
> I have worked with military presidential protection units. I called a member of that army unit later. I was told that the commander "had offered the services of his unit for protection duties for the entire trip through Texas," that he was "point —blank and categorically refused by the Secret Service," and that "there were hot words between the agencies."
>
> I was told that this army unit, the 316th Field Detachment of the 112th Military Intelligence Group at Fort Sam Houston in the Fourth Army Area, "had records on Lee Harvey Oswald, before November 22." It "knew Dallas was dangerous," the commander told my associate in explaining why he had offered his services, despite a call to "stand down."...

---

[42] L. Fletcher Prouty, *JFK: The CIA, Vietnam, and the Plot to Assassinate John F. Kennedy*, pp. 280-281.

[43] Ibid., p. 291.

> This leaves an important question: Why was the assistance of the skilled and experienced unit 'point-blank refused'? Who knew ahead of time that it would not be wanted in Dallas?[44]

Note that Prouty indicates *where* this stand-down order came from: the Secret Service. This is an important clue, for the Secret Service *has no authority or chain of command over the military* under ordinary circumstances. Such a stand-down order would therefore have to come from someone in authority both over the Secret Service, and the military, and involved in the planning of the Texas trip. Someone like Lyndon Baines Johnson.

c) *Neutralization of the Secret Service by Abandonment of Normal Security Procedures:* But what of the Secret Service itself? Since it was and is responsible for presidential security, those elements within it that were not part of the conspiracy would similarly have to be neutralized. Are there any indicators that this took place? There are numerous indications not only of Secret Service complicity in the plot at some level, but of attempts to neutralize agents that were not involved by suspending its normal operational security procedures. For example, Secret Service agent Forrest Sorrels planned the motorcade route in conjunction with the Dallas Police Department, including the sharp ninety-degree turn onto Elm Street in front of the Texas School Book Depository, turns that would have slowed the motorcade much slower than the optimal 40mph minimum traveling speed.[45] Additionally, the Secret Service normally would have stationed men on the roofs of tall buildings in the vicinity if a circumstance required that a motorcade be slowed to a speed lower than 40mph, and also would have ensured that no open windows occurred over it. But on the day of the assassination, none of these normal precautions and procedures were implemented.[46] Prouty summarizes all the lapses in normal procedure as follows:

---

[44] Prouty, *JFK: The CIA, Vietnam, and the Plot to Assassinate John F. Kennedy*, p. 294.

[45] Ibid, p. 293.

[46] Ibid, p. 294.

An assassination, especially of the chief of state, can always be made easier and much more predictable if his routine security forces and their standard policies are removed and canceled. The application of this step in Dallas was most effective. A few examples serve to underscore this phase of the concept:

1. The President was in an open, unarmored car.
2. The route chosen was along busy streets with many overlooking high buildings on each side.
3. Windows in these buildings had not been closed, sealed, and put under surveillance.
4. Secret Service units and trained military units that were required by regulations to be there were not in place. As a result there was limited ground and building surveillance.
5. Sewer covers along the way had not been welded shut.
6. The route was particularly hazardous, with sharp turns requiring slow speeds, in violation of protection regulations.[47]

In short, whatever forces within the Secret Service that were not privy to the plot were neutralized by the suspension of normal procedures.

2) *Neutralize the Political Opposition:*

a) *Neutralization of Communications and the Chain of Command:* One of the most unusual and little-noted facts is that during the hour after the assassination, the phone system in Washington, D.C. went down, effectively throttling communications between Congress and the other branches of government.

b) *Isolation of Crucial Personalities within the Old Regime:* We have already noted that a quorum of the Kennedy Cabinet was out of the country, en route to Japan from Hawaii, at the moment of the assassination, thus preventing any intervention of the Old Regime via the bureaucracies that it controlled.

c) *Neutralization of Potential Opposition:* We have noted in previous chapters how Colonel Prouty was in Christ Church, New Zealand on the day of the assassination, when in the

---

[47] Prouty, *JFK: The CIA, Vietnam, and the Plot to Assassinate John F. Kennedy*, p. 316.

local newspaper, a complete biography of Oswald as the assassin appeared in the paper, *before* Oswald had even been charged with the crime of murdering the President in Dallas! The "meme" was already being planted that he was the "lone nut," thus neutralizing any potential political opposition that might arise from any revelation of evidence that a conspiracy was at work.

i) *Neutralization of Congress:* In this respect, it is important to note that the formation of the Warren Commission served a triple purpose within the alchemical architecture of the planning, not only being designed to perpetuate a cover-up, not only designed to gather all the evidence that researchers would use to overturn its own loony report and Oswald-Lone Nut theory, but also to neutralize potential political opposition in the form of a Congressional investigation:

> An important result of the announcement of the formation of the Warren Commission was the derailing of a planned independent congressional investigation of the assassination. Johnson told Hoover on November 29 that he wanted to "tell the House and Senate not to go ahead with the investigation."[48]

In addition, there is yet another neutralization of potential political opposition that takes place, exactly according to Luttwalk's parameters, in Texas:

ii) *Neutralization of A Texas Trial and Investigation of Lee Oswald:* Had Lee Harvey Oswald lived, he would have gone to trial, and had a trial taken place, the full resources of the Dallas District Attorney would have been employed, these likely involving the additional and considerable investigative resources of the state of Texas itself. Such investigations could similarly have fueled a political opposition, and thus these had to be neutralized. We know, of course, that Ruby murdered Oswald, and was convicted for the crime, a fact neatly derailing any Texas or Dallas investigation of the alleged assassin and

---

[48] Prouty, *JFK: The CIA, Vietnam, and the Plot to Assassinate John F. Kennedy*, p. 302.

deflecting attention on to Ruby. Then, in a remarkable legal turn of events, on appeal of his case, Ruby's conviction was overturned and he was ordered to stand re-trial outside of Dallas. Ruby died of "convenient cancer" before the second trial ever took place.

3) *Placing the Teams and Seizing the Physical Center of the Voice of Authority:* As has been noted in previous chapters, Lyndon Johnson was sworn in as the 36th President of the United States of America aboard Air Force One in Dallas on the day of the assassination. By evening that night, he was back in the White House in Washington, in physical possession of the one center of "the voice of authority," consolidating his control over the Federal bureaucracy, and coordinating with his close friend J. Edgar Hoover the "investigation" that would create the mythology of Oswald as the assassin.

4) *"Freezing" the Situation:* If one considers the result of that "investigation," subsequently enshrined in the 800-plus pages of the Warren Report, that situation has been more or less frozen since the assassination itself, a fact that would tend to indicate that the interests of the high cabal planning and executing it are to whatever degree still in place.

That these interests are still in place is indicated by an odd though obvious point noted by Prouty, namely, that the Warren Report remains the official government version of the assassination referenced by the Executive department of government ever since:

> That assassination has demonstrated that most of the major events of world significance are masterfully planned and orchestrated by an elite coterie of enormously powerful people who are not of one nation, one ethnic grouping, or one overridingly important business group. They are a power unto themselves for whom these others work. Neither is the power elite of recent origin. Its roots go deep into the past.
>
> Kennedy's assassination has been used as an example of their methodology. Most thinking people of this country, and of the world believe that he was not killed by a lone gunman. Despite that view, the cover story created and thrust upon us by the spokesmen of this High Cabal has existed for three decades. It has come from the lips of every subsequent President and from the pop media representatives and their spokesmen. They are experienced, intelligent people who are aware of the facts. Consider the pressure

216

it must take to require all of them, without exception, to quote the words of that contrived cover story over and over again for nearly three decades.[49]

But in the light of what has been surveyed thus far, it is apparent why these presidents would be made to mouth such a silly story, for in doing so, they tell their masters, and us, that they are willing operants in the magical working, compliant sock puppets willing to state a patent lie in order to hold whatever ephemeral power their office gives them, and willing to follow the orders of the more hidden and more powerful hands that put them there.

C. Concluding Thoughts

Why have I chosen in this chapter the unusual approach of combining the deep occult analysis of Michael Hoffman with that of two analysts, Luttwalk and Prouty, of covert operations and coups d'etat? It is because in the deep alchemy of such operations, the psychology, motivations, and goals of the plotters are the same, whether one call it "alchemy" or "social engineering," the magical result is the same. The JFK assassination combined, as operational strategic objectives, the neutralization of political opposition *for the long term*, and this could only be done by the esoteric alchemical transformation of the American people into the traumatized passivity of sheep. The assassination was both an end in itself, and the means to this wider and deeper end.

The cover-up had to be continued not only to maintain the power of the conspirators, but also the psychological conditioning effected by the Magical Working: the quiescence and passivity of the American sheeple in the face of a murder whose official explanation was self-evident and patent nonsense. That explanation *also* had a magical purpose, for its irrationality was crucial to the inducement of a kind of cultural schizophrenia in the psyche of the American people which in turn only reinforced its shocked docility. As the old adage has it, *divida et impera*. In this case, that which is to be divided and conquered is the mind itself. No longer possessed of a common mind, confronted with a nonsensical "explanation" to a crime that was itself designed to shock it into complete passivity — after all, a president and his alleged assassin had been murdered in cold blood within a mere two days of each other — the

---

[49] Prouty, *JFK: The CIA, Vietnam, and the Plot to Assassinate John F. Kennedy*, p. 334.

"meme" was planted: "You are powerless to resist; you are powerless to know the truth."

That division and conquest — that schizophrenia within the group "over-soul" — occurs even within the JFK assassination research community itself, as evidenced by the fact that some researchers advocate this, and some researchers advocate that, group as being the ultimate culprit.

This also serves to point out that the deepest players are far beyond the covert planners at the CIA, FBI, or any other government agency, and beyond that of even the ordinary and often-suggested corporate and banking interests that had a stake in the assassination. The combination of the ritual elements in the assassination with those of a coup d'état strongly suggest that the deepest players had profound insight and knowledge of occult processes and doctrines, of the principles and procedures of deep psychological warfare, and acted upon them in their planning of the crime. The only ones, in the groups enumerated in this book, with possible access to, and the knowledge and experience in such occult doctrines and practices, would be those with deep connections to fraternal societies — American intelligence with its known connection to quasi-Masonic groups such as Yale's infamous Skull and Bones society, and, of course, the Nazis.

If there were deeply occulted motivations to the assassination, if — as Hoffman alleges — the goal of such conspirators was to return mankind to a "Tower of Babel" moment of history and to reinvoke the presence of "the old gods" on the stage of human history, then a glance at the other abyss, that of deep space, will show why the space race, with its own magical and ritual workings, may have been the deepest motivation behind the president's murder.

6

DEEP POLITICS, DEEP SPACE, DEEP PHYSICS, AND DEEP MAGIC:
THE THIRD ALCHEMICAL WORKING AND THE JFK ASSASSINATION

" The American political and economic machine ...by supporting Nazism (was) allowing a deep moral evil to enter the country at the highest levels of power: the CIA, NASA, the USAF, etc., and eventually US corporations, such as Bell Aerospace, ITT, etc. "
Peter Levenda[1]

Apollo 11, the first manned spaceflight to the Moon, touched down on the lunar surface on July 20, 1969, exactly twenty-five years from the day of the unsuccessful attempt of German General Staff officers to blow up Adolf Hitler and his command staff at his East Prussia headquarters in Rastenburg. Some might be tempted to quickly dismiss this inconvenient anniversary as a mere coincidence, but the fact is that there are numerous symbols within America's space program that point to profoundly occulted covert agendas, some of them with deep connections to the JFK assassination. Indeed, we saw in chapter four that one assassination document, the celebrated "Nomenclature of an Assassination Cabal" by "William Torbitt," specifically mentioned NASA and its Nazis, represented by Dr. Wehrner Von Braun, as being involved in the assassination.[2] But a full exploration of the symbolic and ritual aspects of the space program reveals other players, with deep motivations, and playing for the very high stakes of

---

[1] Peter Levenda, *Sinister Forces: A Grimoire of American Political Witchcraft*, Book Three: *The Manson Secret* (Walterville, Oregon: Trine Day, 2006), pp. 433-434.

[2] It should be pointed out that researcher Jim Keith, prior to his own untimely death during a routine minor outpatient surgical procedure, identified the author of the Torbitt Document as being south Texas lawyer David Copeland. "He had been a close supporter of the Lyndon Johnson/Lloyd Bentsen political steamroller in Texas until 1963, when he severed his ties with the group..." (Jim Keith, *Mind Control, World Control: The Encyclopedia of Mind Control* [Adventures Unlimited Press, 1997], p. 139. Copeland severed his ties with the Johnson-Bentsen political machine because of the ties between it and the other groups implicated in President Kennedy's murder.

219

the high ground of space, and the hegemony conferred by the advanced technologies by which it hoped to explore it, and the technologies it hoped to recover there, and to to keep them secret. As we shall see in this chapter, each of these would have had the means, motive, and opportunity to murder the President. Indeed, beyond the deep politics of the occult workings of his murder, there are occult and magical workings at work in the space program, workings which were playing for the highest stakes of all, and which, once again, President Kennedy had threatened.

A. The First Alchemical Work and Its Symbolic Fulfillment

In the previous chapter we saw that there were three great magical workings: the bringing of primordial matter from heaven to earth, its creation and destruction, and the sacrifice of the king. The last two were symbolically and actually fulfilled in the first explosion of the atomic bomb, and in the assassination itself. But what of the first, the bringing of primordial matter from heaven to earth?

This, says Hoffman, was fulfilled in the Apollo missions themselves, with the bringing of "primordial matter," the incomparably old rocks of the Moon, from "heaven" to Earth in the Apollo Moon landings:

> The third objective of alchemy, the bringing of Prima Materia to prima Terra was accomplished in the 1969 Apollo moon flights and the returning to earth of the moon rocks. Some of these rocks have been "stolen" for use in occult rituals of no mean significance (what astounding masonic (sic) "ashlars" these make).
>
> The "Phoenix" lunar landing module, after its return to the orbiting mother ship piloted by Michael Collins, was jettisoned directly into the sun in fulfillment of one of the most persistent themes of alchemical lore and Rosicrucian poetry: the "sexual marriage" of the sun and the moon.[3]

While Hoffman offers no substantiating evidence for his assertion that some of the Moon rocks were used in the performance of occult rituals, his reference to "masonic 'ashlars'" is worth pursuing a bit further.

According to Albert Pike, author of the Scottish Rite's "Bible" of Freemasonry, *Morals and Dogma*, an ashlar is a symbol of the whole philosophy of the Masonic Craft:

---

[3] Hoffman, *Secret Societies and Psychological Warfare*, p. 90.

You will hear shortly of the *Rough* ASHLAR and the *Perfect* ASHLAR, as part of the jewels of the Lodge. The rough Ashlar is said to be "a stone, as taken from the quarry, in its rude and natural state." The perfect Ashlar is said to be "a stone made ready by the hands of the workmen, to be adjusted by the working-tools of the Fellow-Craft."... They are declared to allude to the self-improvement of the individual craftsman, - a continuation of the same superficial interpretation.

The rough Ashlar is the PEOPLE, as a mass, rude and unorganized. The perfect Ashlar, or cubical stone, symbol of perfection, is the STATE, **the rulers deriving their powers from the consent of the governed**; the constitution and laws speaking the will of the people; the government harmonious, symmetrical, efficient, - its powers properly distributed and duly adjusted in equilibrium.[4]

It is to be noted that the context of this piece of Masonic ritual is understood to be a symbol of *people*, both in an unorganized condition — the "rough ashlar" — and in an organized, that is to say, a *socially engineered* condition — the "perfect ashlar." This will be an important interpretive context in a moment.

The second thing to be noted about the quotation is the double-edged sense in which many of its statements - particularly that about "the rulers deriving their powers from the consent of the governed" - can be interpreted. There is obviously the prosaic sense, namely, that Pike simply means to indicate the nature of the republican form of American government, and is mouthing pious patriotic platitudes. But there is the deeper sense explored in the previous chapter, that of the consent of the people to an obviously criminal act, and even more criminal "explanation" and cover-up, an act of consent which increases the powers of the occult rulers performing the ritual.

The deep connection between this "alchemical" social engineering and Masonic ritual is made clear by another reference to the "ashlar" occurring much later in Pike's tome in reference to citations from the ritual of initiating a Knight of the Sun, or Prince Adept, the twenty-eighth degree of the thirty-three degrees of Scottish Rite Freemasonry:

A rough Ashlar is the shapeless stone which is to be prepared in order to commence the philosophical work; and to be developed, in order to change its form from triangular to cubic, after the separation from it of its Salt, Sulphur, and Merecury, **by the aid of the Square, Level,**

---

[4] Albert Pike, *Morals and Dogma of the Ancient and Accepted Scottish Rite of Freemasonry* (Charleston, S.C.: 1871), p. 5, italicized and capitalized emphasis original, bold face emphasis added.

Plumb, and Balance, and all the other Masonic implements *which we use symbolically.*

Here we put them to philosophical use, to constitute a well-proportioned edifice, analogous to a candidate commencing his initiation into our Mysteries. **When we build we must observe all the rules and proportions: for otherwise the Spirit of Life cannot lodge therein. So you will build the great tower, in which is to burn the fire of the Sages, or, in other words, the fire of Heaven; as also the Sea of the Sages, in which the Sun and the Moon are to bathe.** That is the basin of Purification, in which will be the water of Celestial Grace, water that doth not soil the hands, but purifies all leprous bodies.[5]

This quotation requires careful attention and care in unpacking its carefully coded language.

The "philosophical work" referred to is precisely the alchemical operation of confecting the Philosophers' Stone, the transformation of matter, the bringing down of the *materia prima* into earthly form. But there is also an esoteric operation, that of the transmutation of base metals into gold, in this case, the base metal of unenlightened humanity into the pure gold of an illuminated consciousness. The "philosophical work" is thus a code for these two types of operation.[6]

But our real interest in this passage lies in the bold face passages. Note the use of "Masonic implements," the square, level, plumb and balance. If one did not know that this was a nineteenth century Masonic text, one might conclude one was reading a bizarre description of the torsion physics experiments of Russian astrophysicist Nikolai Kozyrev.[7] The passage hints, obliquely, that it is talking about an encoded physics, an encoded physics probably unknown even to a Masonic adept like Albert Pike.

This is darkly hinted at in the second paragraph. Masonry is an alchemical craft, for in the metaphor of constructing buildings according to the sacred geometry of Masonic "architecture" the real goal is to embody "the Spirit of Life" in those buildings. That one is dealing with a physics here is evidenced by the next part of the passage, referring to

---

[5] Pike, *Morals and Dogma*, p. 787, italicized emphasis original, boldface emphasis added.

[6] For a further discussion of these two types of alchemy, see my *The Philosophers' Stone: Alchemy and the Secret Research for Exotic Matter* (Feral House, 2009), pp. 31-36.

[7] For a fuller discussion of Koyrev's work, see my *The Philosophers' Stone*, pp. 151-192.

"the fire of the Sages" which is "the fire of heaven," the *energy of the sea of space-time itself*, the "zero point" energy of the vacuum.

That this is so is further reinforced by the use of a standard code often found in ancient texts for this physical medium of space-time, for in those texts deep space is referred to as "the abyss," the "primeval waters or primeval ocean," and this is what we see in this Masonic text where the sun and moon are said to "bathe" in this sea.

Finally, note the reference to building "the great tower." While this could be construed to mean the Masonic principle of embodying "rule and proportion" into physical buildings and thus embodying "the Spirit of Life," there is a deeper meaning. Recall that Hoffman stated one long term goal of such alchemical workings was to reinvoke the gods of old. The reference, in other words, is an ancient one, and at this level of meaning the "great tower" is the Tower of Babel itself, a tower which, according to the biblical story, would reach to heaven and allow men "to do whatever they imagined to do." I have argued elsewhere that the real purpose of this tower — and of all pyramidal structures in one form or another — was to access this energy of heaven, this energy of the vacuum, of space-time itself.[8]

On this reading of the passage, we are indeed dealing with a very ancient agenda, the agenda of turning the "rough ashlars" of stone into the "perfect ashlars" of structures able to summon the fire of heaven itself. We are dealing, in other words, with an encoded physics.

Such considerations were, of course, unknown to, or at least not mentioned by, Hoffman, when he asked the following questions:

> But could it be that our government and NASA scientists are as superstitious as a Zuni Indian? Were they compelled by a concept in Hermetic doctrine to perform some kind of ceremonial redressment for the astronauts having left their boot-tracks and techno-junk on the moon?[9]

Could such an ancient agenda have really been part of the space program, with all its attendant implied "superstition," a superstition which, as we have seen, implies a deep physics? And might all of this have been, as the Torbitt Document alleges, a motivation in deep space itself for the murder of President Kennedy and Von Braun's alleged role in it?

---

[8] See my *The Cosmic War: Interplanetary Warfare, Modern Physics, and Ancient Texts* (Adventures Unlimited Press, pp. 204-212.

[9] Hoffman, *Secret Societies and Psychological Warfare*, p. 91.

The answer, according to authors Richard C. Hoagland and Mike Bara, is a resounding yes.

B. The Purpose of NASA and Hoagland and Bara's Basic Theses

Judging by the amount of debunking articles about him, space anomalies researcher Richard C. Hoagland has definitely touched an exposed nerve in the space science community. Since the early 1980s he and a small team of other independent researchers have been studying, analyzing, and collating information culled from NASA, and more recently, the European Space Agency and the Russian space program, information that documents the presence in ancient times within our solar system of an advanced interplanetary civilization. But according to Hoagland and Bara in their New York Times bestselling book *Dark Mission: The Secret History of NASA*, this information has been doctored and suppressed. The question is, why? And what has it to do with the murder of President Kennedy?

Part of the answer to those questions lies in the broad context of the space agency itself, and the real purposes, as Hoagland and Bara see them, for the Apollo Moon landings; and part of the answer to those questions lies in the narrower context of President Kennedy's "grand space plan" and the vested interests it threatened. We will look at each of these in order to construct a speculative and argued case that deep space, and the treasures it potentially contained, were motivations for the murder. In doing so, we will provide a rationalization for the allegations of the Torbitt Document that NASA was involved in the planning and execution of the crime, via its most eminent Nazi rocket scientist, Wehrner Von Braun.

Hoagland and Bara begin their book by noting that NASA, contrary to the popular image it likes to project of being a completely civilian agency, was in fact established in federal law as a "direct adjunct to the Department of Defense," and they then cite section 305(i) of the NASA charter itself: "The (National Aeronautics and Space) Administration shall be considered *a defense agency of the United States* for the purpose of Chapter 7, Title 35 of the United States Code..."[10] It is within this context that Hoagland and Bara construct their complex thesis, of which there are five crucial components:

---

[10] Richard C. Hoagland and Mike Bara, *Dark Mission: The Secret History of NASA* (Feral House, 2007), p. ii, emphasis added by Hoagland and Bara.

1) Thesis One: Advanced technology on celestial bodies in the Solar System was confirmed by early robotic space probes;[11]
2) Thesis Two: There existed in ancient times a Very High Civilization whose traces are detectable in off-world artifacts as indicated by photographs of our nearby planetary neighbors; Hoagland and Bara state this eloquently: "There *had* been a powerful, enormously encompassing, extraordinary solar-system-wide civilization that had simply disappeared, only to be rediscovered by NASA's primitive initial probes. A civilization that, it would turn out later, had been wiped out through a series of all-encompassing, solar-system-wide cataclysms."[12]
3) Thesis Three: The covert purpose of the Apollo Moon landings was to reconnoiter and recover some of this technology from the Moon and return it to Earth;[13]
4) Thesis Four: The real reason the Apollo program was abruptly terminated was that it had accomplished its mission of recovering this technology;[14] and,
5) Thesis Five: within NASA at the time of the Apollo Moon landings there were three factions vying for power and influence within the agency, each with its own roots deep in occultism and esotericism: the Magicians, the Masons, and the Nazis; and that by the time of the Apollo Moon landings, the Nazis and the Masons are in the most influential position.[15]

Into this carefully planned long-term agenda, stepped President John F. Kennedy, with an agenda of his own...

C. JFK's Grand Space Plan and Vision

Hoagland and Bara begin their analysis of Kennedy's grand space plan by citing a little known speech that the President gave shortly after taking office, on April 27, 1961. Consider these words carefully, in the light of all that has been discussed in this and the previous chapter, and consider carefully that it is a modern American President, not George Washington writing about the covert activities of the Bavarian Illuminati,

---

[11] Hoagland and Bara, *Dark Mission: The Secret History of NASA*, p. iii.
[12] Ibid, p. ix.
[13] Ibid, p. v.
[14] Ibid, p. vii.
[15] Ibid, p. vi.

speaking them to the American Newspaper Publishers Association, meeting at the Waldorf-Astoria in New York City:

> The very word "secrecy" is repugnant in a free and open society; and we are as a people inherently and historically opposed to secret societies, to secret oaths and to secret proceedings. We decided long ago that the dangers of excessive and unwarranted concealment of pertinent facts far outweighed the dangers which are cited to justify it.[16]

Hoagland and Bara observe that the historical context of this speech is even more darkly revealing, for on April 18, 1961, NASA had delivered to Congress its "Brookings Report," a report prepared under NASA auspices about what the government's response should be if, during its space exploration, it should come into contact with extraterrestrial life, *or its artifacts.* The report, predictably enough, recommended that any such discovery be kept secret.

For Hoagland and Bara, the President's speech was a direct response to NASA's report, and to the three factions — the Magicians, the Masons, and the Nazis, each with their own deeply occult and covert agendas for the space program — which sought to influence the agency's agenda covertly:

> (The President's) opening comments, speaking of "secret societies" and the dangers of "excessive and unwarranted concealment" of things he felt the American people had a right to know, was an unmistakable shot across the bow of these secret societies, and we take it as a direct reference to the recommendations contained in the Brookings Report. It is also very obvious from his statement that he considered these dark forces of "concealment' to be very powerful. Why else would he ask for the press's help in fighting this battle?[17]

Indeed, as we saw in the previous chapter, there are abundant Masonic fingerprints all over the ritual murder of the President in Dallas on November 22, 1963. Now, with these statements from his speech, we see why that group may have been involved with the planning and cover-up, for the President had taken direct aim at them, *in a temporal context that strongly suggested that he was aware of a hidden agenda in the space program.*

---

[16] John F. Kennedy, "The President and the Press," April 27, 1961, cited in Hoagland and Bara, *Dark Mission: The Secret History of NASA*, p. 94.
[17] Ibid, p. 95.

As Hoagland and Bara point out, President Kennedy conceived of the space program, not as a covert program of an agency of the Department of Defense, as per NASA's own charter, but as a broadly nationalistic and "democratized" process. President Kennedy put it with his customary elegant diction:

> ...Those who came before us made certain that this country rode the first waves of the industrial revolution, the first waves of modern invention, and the first wave of nuclear power, and this generation does not intend to founder in the backwash of the coming age of space. We mean to be a part of it — we mean to lead it. For the eyes of the world now look into space, to the Moon and to the planets beyond, and we have vowed that we shall not see it governed by a hostile flag of conquest, but by a banner of freedom and peace. We have vowed that we shall not see space filled with weapons of mass destruction, but with instruments of knowledge and understanding.
>
> Yet the vows of this Nation can only be fulfilled if we in this Nation are first, and, therefore, we intend to be first. In short, our leadership in science and in industry, our hopes for peace and security, our obligations to ourselves as well as others, all require us to make this effort, to solve these mysteries, to solve them for the good of all men, and to become the world's leading spacefaring nation.[18]

But even here President Kennedy was perhaps threatening hidden vested interests, for what "mysteries" was he referring to that needed to be solved "for the good of all men"?

While all of this was going on publicly, President Kennedy was very quietly, and very secretly, extending an olive branch to the Soviet Union's premier, Nikita Khrushchev, at the very height of Cold War tensions between the two countries, tensions which, as we saw in chapter one, someone within the American intelligence community wished to exacerbate, not ameliorate. On May 25, 1961, President Kennedy addressed a joint session of Congress and issued his now-famous call for America to land men on the Moon and return them safely to Earth before the decade was out, thus officially "launching" the long-term public agenda for NASA.

Yet, a mere ten days later, Kennedy was proposing a remarkable thing:

> Soviet premier Nikita Khrushchev's son, Sergei Khrushchev (now a senior fellow at the Watson Institute at Brown University) has stated

---

[18] Hoagland and Bara, *Dark Mission: The Secret History of NASA*, p. 97.

that after the May 25th public call to "go to the Moon," Kennedy then did an extraordinary thing: less than ten days later, he *secretly* proposed to Khrushchev at their Vienna summit that the United States and the Soviet Union merge their space programs to get to the Moon together. Khrushchev turned Kennedy down, in part because he didn't trust the young President after the Bay of Pigs fiasco, and also because he feared that America might learn too many useful technological secrets from the Russians (who were, clearly, still ahead in "heavy lift" launch vehicles — useful in launching nuclear weapons).[19]

Undaunted, Kennedy continued to press the idea.

In August 1963, the President then met with Soviet Ambassador Anatoli Dobrinyin in the Oval Office and one again (secretly) extended the offer. This time, Khrushchev considered it more seriously, but ultimately rejected it."[20] Then, on September 18,1963, according to NASA's own official history, President Kennedy met with NASA director (and Freemason) James Webb. Here is what NASA's history states about this meeting:

> Kennedy told (Webb) that he was thinking of pursuing the topic of cooperation with the Soviets as part of a broader effort to bring the two countries closer together. He asked Webb, "Are you sufficiently in control to prevent my being undercut in NASA if I do that?" As Webb remembered the meeting, "So in a sense he didn't ask me *if* he should do it; he told me he thought he should do it and wanted to do it..." What he sought from Webb was the assurance that there would be no further unsolicited comments from within the space agency. Webb told the president that he could keep things under control.[21]

Then, on September 20, 1963, President Kennedy stunned the world with the following announcement before the General Assembly of the United Nations:

> Finally, in a field where the United States and the Soviet Union have a special capacity — in the field of space — there is room for new cooperation, for further joint efforts in the regulation and exploration of space. I include among these possibilities a joint expedition to the Moon. Space offers no problems of sovereignty; by resolution of this

---

[19] Hoagland and Bara, *Dark Mission: The Secret History of NASA*, p. 96.
[20] Ibid, p. 97.
[21] Ibid, pp. 97-98, citing SP-4209 "The Partnership: A History of the Apollo-Soyuz Test Project," http://history,nasa.,gov/SP-4209/ch2-4.htm

assembly, the members of the United Nations have foresworn any claim to territorial rights in outer space or on celestial bodies, and declared that international law and the United Nations charter will apply. Why, therefore, should man's first flight to the Moon be a matter of national competition? Why should the United States and the Soviet Union, in preparing for such expeditions, become involved in immense duplications of research, construction and expenditure? Surely we should explore whether the scientists and astronauts of our two countries — indeed of all the world — cannot work together in the conquest of space, sending someday in this decade to the Moon not the representatives of a single nation, but the representatives of all of our countries.[22]

Kennedy's offer to Khrushchev was now open and public, not private, and in the context of the U.N., had placed enormous diplomatic pressure on the Soviet leader to act publicly in the interests of peace and to accept the offer.

The result was predictable, at least within the U.S.A., for Republican Senator Barry Goldwater, who by then was clearly making a bid for the presidency, objected strongly. But opposition came from within the President's own party, from Texas Congressman Albert Thomas, a close political ally of Vice President Lyndon Johnson, and who sat on the House Committee with oversight of NASA. So vociferous was Thomas' reaction that Kennedy had to write him to reassure him that America would continue to have an independent space program regardless of the Soviet response.[23] The Soviets remained quiet, offering no response to the President's U.N. speech.

President Kennedy then followed this speech up with clear executive directives, committing America to the international effort. On November 12, 1963, a mere ten days before his murder, President Kennedy

> issued National Security action Memorandum #271. The memo, titled "Cooperation With the USSR on Outer Space Matters," directed NASA Director Webb to personally (and immediately) take the initiative to develop a program of "substantive cooperation" with his Soviet counterparts in accordance with Kennedy's September 20th UN Proposal. It also called for an interim report on the progress being made

---

[22] Hoagland and Bara, *Dark Mission: The Secret History of NASA*, p. 98, citing http:\\www.jfklibrary.org/Historical+Resources/Archives/Reference +Desk/Speeches/JFK003POF03_18thGeneralAssembly09201963.htm.

[23] Ibid, pp. 98-99.

by December 15, 1963, giving Webb a little over a month to get "substantive" cooperation with the Soviets going.

There is a second, even stranger memo which has surfaced, dated the same day. Found by UFO document researchers Dr. Robert M Wood and his son Ryan Wood... the document is titled "Cassification Review of All UFO intelligence Files Affecting National Security" and is considered by them to have a "medium-high"(about 80%) probability of being authentic. The memo directs the director of the CIA to provide CIA files on "the high threat cases" with an eye toward identifying the differences between "bona fide" UFOs and any classified United States craft. He informs the CIA director that he has instructed Webb to begin the cooperative program with the Soviets (confirming the other, authenticated memo) and that he would then like NASA to be fully briefed on the "unknowns" so that they can presumably help with sharing this information with the Russians. The last line of the memo instructs an interim progress report to be completed no later than February 1, 1964.[24]

It is worth taking a closer look at this memo from two vantage points, that it is authentic, and that it is not.

Assuming it to be authentic, the memorandum's actual words are as follows:

draft

TOP SECRET

November 12, 1963

MEMORANDUM FOR
The Director of Counter Intelligence, Central Intelligence Agency
SUBJECT: Classification review of all UFO intelligence files affecting National Security

As I had discussed with you previously, I have initiated (blacked out) and have instructed James Webb to develop a program with the Soviet Union in joint space and lunar exploration. It would be very helpful if you would have the high threat cases reviewed with the purpose of identification of bona fide as opposed to classified CIA and USAF sources. It is important that we make a clear distinction between the knowns and the unknowns in the event the Soviets try to mistake our extended cooperation as a cover for intelligence gathering of their defence (sic) and space programs.

When this data has been sorted out, I would like you to arrange a program of data sharing with NASA where Unknowns are a factor.

---

[24] Hoagland and Bara, *Dark Mission: The Secret History of NASA*, p. 99.

This will help NASA mission directors in their defensive responsibilities.

I would like an interim report on the data review no later than February 1, 1964.

/s/ John F. Kennedy
Response from Col.

Angleton has MJ directive 11/20/63

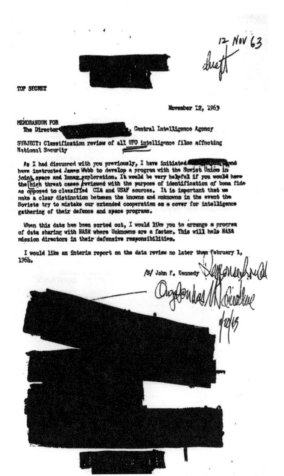

Alleged Kennedy-CIA 1963 UFO Memorandum

This memorandum should be read in the context of another alleged Kennedy UFO memorandum dated June 28, 2961, which is succinctness itself:

THE WHITE HOUSE
WASHINGTOON
DISPATCHED
N.S.C.
JUN 29 3 01 PM'61

TOP SECRET   JUNE 28, 1961
NATIONAL SECURITY MEMORANDUM

TO: The Director, Central Intelligence Agency
SUBJECT: Review of MJ-12 Intelligence Operations as they relate to Cold War Psychological Warfare Plans
I would like a brief summary from you at your earliest convenience.
TOP SECRET

J.F. Kennedy

Alleged 1961 Kennedy-CIA UFO Memorandum

It is important to understand that in the bureaucratic ways of Washington, the 1963 memorandum did not come as a bolt out of the blue to the CIA from the White House, but rather, that it was probably memorializing discussions that had already taken place. Indeed, this is what the memorandum itself actually states at the very beginning of the text: "As I had discussed with you previously..."

We have already indicated that President Kennedy initially and secretly proposed his joint Lunar space program to Premier Khrushchev at their summit in Vienna in 1961. Given that neither man spoke the other's language, there would have been at least two more men in the room with them at the time: their translators. In the ways of power within both countries, inevitably, this would have meant that those in the positions of bureaucratic power would have known of Kennedy's secret initiatives long before Kennedy went public with the proposal at the UN in 1963. This fact, plus the assumption that these two memoranda are authentic, would have spelled but one conclusion to those involved in the potentially high technological stakes represented by UFOs and by space exploration: the President intended to share the data with America's worst enemy! Indeed, elsewhere I have proposed that at least *some* of those UFO secrets represented not advanced extra-terrestrial technology, but advanced *Nazi* technology.[25] By threatening to smash the CIA into a thousand pieces in the wake of the failed Bay of Pigs invasion and combining all this with demands to review UFO classifications, President Kennedy was thus threatening the vested interests of the black projects of the American military-industrial complex, and, by extension, the Nazi interests that had cloaked themselves inside of the American space agency, its intelligence services, and its military, by being willing to share all this with the Soviets. Thus, even if these memoranda are *not* authentic, nothing really changes, for the same threat is still in place. Notably, that threat, whether the memos are authentic or not, emerged shortly into the Kennedy presidency, in 1961, with his threat to the CIA.

One thing emerges, however, from a consideration of these two memos, and that is, if they *are* authentic, then beginning in 1961, as Kennedy is making his first secret overtures to Khrushchev about a joint lunar program, he is also inquiring about UFOs and therefore about the technological potential they represent. If the memoranda are authentic, in other words, the conspirators had yet another motivation and inducement

---

[25] See my *Roswell and the Reich: The Nazi Connection* (Adventures Unlimited Press, 2010), pp. 373-507.

to murder the president, this time, a very powerful one: keeping advanced technology secret.

In any case, Sergei Khrushchev later confirmed that his father had finally decided, early in November 1963, to *accept* President Kennedy's offer of a joint lunar program:

> Sergei Khrushchev, in an interview given in 1997 after his presentation at a NASA conference in Washington, D.C., commemorating the fortieth anniversary of Sputnik, confirmed that while initially ignoring Kennedy's UN offer, his father Nikita changed his mind and decided in early November 1963 to accept it. "My father decided that maybe he should accept (Kennedy's) offer, given the state of the space programs of the two countries (in 1963)," Khrushchev said. He recalled walking with his father as they discussed the matter, and went on to place the timing of his father's decision as about "a week" before Kennedy's assassination in Dallas, which would date it right around November 12-15. Late, in a 1999 PBS interview, he repeated the claim: "I walked with him, sometime in late October or November, and he told me about all these things."[26]

Hoagland and Bara repeatedly suggest throughout their book that this proposal for a joint Lunar mission between the USA and USSR might have been one motivation for the assassination.[27] Viewed against the backdrop of these memoranda, the planning for the assassination and the space motivations behind it, dated from very early in the Kennedy Administration, in early 1961 itself.

Within this context it is worth citing Hoagland and Bara at great length on the strong suggestions of a "space and NASA motivation" behind the president's murder:

> The plans for Kennedy to go to Texas had been made the previous spring, when Vice President Lyndon Johnson stated that Kennedy might visit Dallas in the summertime. It wasn't until September that a letter from Johnson aide Jack Valenti announced the Texas campaign swing. The trip centered around a special testimonial dinner for none other than Congressman Albert Thomas, the man who held the NASA purse strings and who Kennedy, by all accounts, adored. Thomas was dying from terminal cancer, and Kennedy was greatly relieved that he had decided to run for re-election and had avoided having an open seat in Congress to contest. Originally proposed as a one-day trip for

---

[26] Hoagland and Bara, *Dark Mission: The Secret History of NASA*, p. 100.
[27] Ibid, pp. v, 101-108.

November 21, by October Lyndon Johnson had become involved in the planning and a second day was added, November 22.

Kennedy was in a festive mood the evening of the 21st, pointing out Thomas' many contributions to the space program (which he was now about to hand over to the Russians!) and declaring him to be a good friend.

"Next month, when the U.S. fires the world's biggest booster, lifting the heaviest payroll into... that is, payload..." Here the President paused a second and grinned.

"It will be the heaviest payroll, too," he quipped. The crowd roared.

"The firing of that shot will give us the lead in space," the President resumed in a serious vein. "And our leadership could not have been achieved without Congressman Albert Thomas..."

Kennedy departed after his speech, followed soon by Thomas and Vice President Johnson. They both accompanied him to Dallas the next morning on Air Force One.

....

We've all seen the iconic photo, with a somber Johnson, his hand on the Bible, standing next to a dazed Jacqueline Kennedy as various aides looked on. One of the most prominent men in the background is a distinguished, bow-tied gentleman who is watching the proceedings very closely. Of course, it is Congressman Albert Thomas. What most of us have never seen is the next photo, taken immediately after the oath was completed. In it, LBJ has a broad smile as he makes eye contact with Congressman Thomas. Thomas, also smiling, returns the gesture with — of all things — a *wink*. While everyone else remains somber, Thomas and Johnson are the only two people in the picture who are smiling. The unspoken message between the two men could not be more clear: "We got him!"[28]

Of course, a mere wink in a photograph is not enough to prove a conspiracy involving President Johnson, nor is it enough to prove that one of the motivations for it was President Kennedy's attitudes and policies regarding space.

There are, however, "a couple of curious postscripts" to this story, and it is worth citing Hoagland and Bara at length once again to see what they are:

By most accounts, Johnson should have still been President by 1969 when Neil Armstrong and Buzz Aldrin first walked on the Moon. He was constitutionally able to stand for re-election in 1968, but his great

---

[28] Hoagland and Bara, *Dark Mission: The Secret History of NASA*, pp. 106-107.

unpopularity because of his mishandling of Vietnam convinced him to forsake a second elected term and retire from public life. You would have thought, after being the head of the space program for so many years as Vice President and then continuing Kennedy's vision after his death, that Johnson would have been keenly interested in the events of July 20, 1969. But, as reported by presidential historian Doris Kerns Goodwin, Johnson not only didn't watch the Lunar Landing himself, he refused to let anyone at his Texas ranch watch it either, and ordered all the TVs to be turned off.

Perhaps, in the twilight of his life, with ample time to reflect on his own actions, the space program was no longer a source of pride for him, but of shame.

Recently, Saint John Hunt, the surviving eldest son of E. Howard Hunt — an infamous CIA operative actively involved with Watergate and long-rumored to have also been a key player in the Kennedy assassination — released a "deathbed confession tape" from his father. In a story published in *Rolling Stone* magazine, Saint John Hunt stated his father admitted to being one of the famous "three tramps" in photos of Dealy (sic) Plaza taken after the assassination and detailed specific players involved in the Kennedy assassination. The tape contains a remarkable "confirmation" in the light of the completely independent evidence presented here that, above the CIA operatives (and contractors) who actually planned and carried out the plot to kill Kennedy, including E. Howard Hunt himself, they were all directed by one "top man."

Lyndon Baines Johnson.

We are left to contemplate our own accusations here. If men like Johnson and Thomas were willing to go so far as to orchestrate the murder of the President in order to protect the Unites States' own singular (and singularly expensive) space program, then they must have expected to find wonders beyond imagining over the course of their voyages.

The only question for us was what, in fact, *did* they find, and was it worth the price that ... the country (and History) ultimately paid?[29]

All the indicators here and in previous chapters have strongly implied that Johnson was indeed one of the conspirators, a case that will be examined closely in the next section. For now, the we have seen that the implication of Hoagland's and Bara's hypothesis is that very high technological stakes formed a motivation to the assassination.

The question is: what were they?

---

[29] Hoagland and Bara, *Dark Mission: The Secret History of NASA*, p. 108.

Newly sworn-in President Lyndon Baines Johnson turns and looks at Congressman Albert Thomas, winking back at him in the background

> D. *Turning the Esoteric Stream:*
> *What Did NASA Know, When Did It First Know It,*
> *and How Did it Know?*
> 1. *The Sources of Foreknowledge: Ancient and Esoteric Texts,*
> 2. *and Space Probes.*

In answering the question of the space motivation for the President's murder, we have to ask the question "What did NASA know... and *when* did they first know it?"[30] Answering that question will reveal yet again the heavy hand of esotericism and occult workings, of artifacts and all the technological potential they represent, and of deep physics, deeply encoded.

As has already been indicated, Hoagland and Bara maintain that one source for the foreknowledge of ancient artifacts and therefore of potential technology on the Moon would have been early NASA unmanned space probes. This is not the place to summarize Hoagland and Bara's massive research, as it is not directly within the purview of this book. However, it is crucial to note that they present evidence of vast architectural anomalies on the Lunar surface — and above it! — in *Dark Mission.*[31] Many of these anomalies would have been apparent to

---

[30] Hoagland and Bara, *Dark Mission: The Secret History of NASA*, p. 199.
[31] Ibid, pp. 113-198.

photographic analysts pouring over the photographs returned from Lunar orbit and the lunar surface by NASA's unmanned probes, sent to map the surface of the Moon prior to the Apollo landings. This would have been known as early as 1961-62 with the earliest NASA *Ranger* probes.

There is another source for this foreknowledge, one that would have been known to the three occult factions within NASA, the Magicians, the Masons, and the Nazis, and that is ancient texts and esoteric lore. As I have detailed in my book *The Cosmic War,* many of these ancient texts, if properly decoded from the standpoint of physics, clearly pointed to the existence of a very ancient high civilization of an interplanetary nature within our own solar system.[32]

2. Esoteric and Masonic Influences Within NASA Mission Planning and Symbolism: The Moon Landings as Ritual Magic

Is there evidence of occult agendas at work within NASA, as Hoffman himself stated earlier in this chapter?

It is here that Hoagland's and Bara's research enters an extremely controversial but vital area, for the evidence is overwhelmingly "yes."

One need only, they maintain, look at the naming of the first three manned space flight programs — Mercury, Gemini, and Apollo — to see a hidden esoteric agenda at work:

> As far as the mythology goes, Mercuery, the gods' messenger, seems appropriate for the single man capsule and its quick missions. Yet the NASA symbol for Project Mercury is a representation of the *element* mercury, rather than the Greek god Mercury, and is similar to a stylized Egyptian ankh. Alchemists considered mercury as the "first matter" from which all other metals were derived. So was this a dual, *alchemical* meaning for the name "Project Mercury?"
>
> Gemini, which means "the twins" in Latin, could not only refer to the two-man capsule, but also to the rendezvous and docking procedures which were perfected on Project Gemini and which were crucial to the later Apollo missions to the Moon. Gemini is also frequently referenced to the constellation that borders Orion and boasts the twin stars Castor and Pollux as its most prominent features; other myths link Castor and Pollux with the morning and evening stars (the planet Venus).
>
> Certainly, there is an inherent "duality" with all of these associations that well fits the "twins" designation of the NASA Program Two

---

[32] See my *The Cosmic War: Interplanetary Warfare, Modern Physics, and Ancient Texts* (Adventures Unlimited Press, 2007), pp. 139-233.

astronauts... two vehicles redesvousing in space... the twin stars Castor and Pollux.

Then we have Apollo.[33]

Apollo presented very special problems...

... and special questions. The mission patches of the Apollo program were, as Hoagland discovered, loaded with esoteric symbolism and references:

> The Earth and the Moon flank a large stylized letter 'A' against a background of stars. The Constellation Orion, "The Mighty Hunter," is positioned so that its three central stars, known as Orion's belt, form the bar of the letter "A." These stars are Mintaka, Alnilam and Alnitak. The star shown above the Moon is Orion's shoulder, the red star Betelgeuse, and his other shoulder on the right top side of the "A" is the white star Bellatrix. Under the right side of the "A" is Orion's foot, the blue-white star Rigel and under the left side of the "A" is Orion's other foot, the blue-white star Saiph. Rigel is one of the Apollo Astronaut's thirty-seven navigational stars. Between the lines of the "A" is Orion's sword and in the center of the sword is the Orion Nebula.[34]

This led Hoagland and Bara to ask, and then answer, a significant question:

> But, what is a mythological *Egyptian* stellar deity doing representing an official *U.S.governmental* exploration of the Moon? And, in a program known under the designation of a Greek "sun god," Apollo. Why not, for example, "Diana" — the Greek goddess of the Moon?
>
> The initial answer is quite simple: "Apollo" is actually "Horus" — if one examines in detail Greek mythological literature and its derivations from the earlier Egyptian. Horus, like Apollo, is the Egyptian "god of the sun" (and also, curiously, ruled over Mars). Thus, it turns out that the $20 billion NASA Apollo Exploration Program of the Moon was, in fact, nothing less than a disguised "Osiris/Horus Lunar Landing Program"... straight out of ancient *Egypt*.
>
> ...
>
> Indeed, it is distinctly possible (and Hoagland certainly believes it...) that the massive "A" on the program patch does *not* stand for "Apollo" at all, but rather the Greek derivation of Orion/Osiris-
>
> "Asar."

---

[33] Hoagland and Bara, *Dark Mission: The Secret History of NASA*, p. 200.
[34] Ibid.

Perhaps the answer lay in the patch itself, with its many hints and links to a far earlier mythological epoch, the era of Osiris/Asar and his successor, Horus/Apollo. The three belt stars seemed to represent the three astronauts as "sons of Orion/Osiris" — but, as Osiris was a god of "resurrection," it seemed odd that the first attempt by Man to visit the Moon would be associated with a rebirth.

A rebirth of *what?*

It was only after Hoagland noted the name of another space vehicle — the Shuttle Atlantis — that he began to put the pieces together. What if this *wasn't* the first time Man had reached across space to touch the Moon? What if the ancient Egyptian "Zep-Tepi" (Literally, "the first time") Era of Osiris/Horus was not a myth... but a *reality?*[35]

Two of the hidden occult-influenced groups within NASA definitely had their own traditions of precisely such a time, the Masons with their constant references within their ritual to pre-Deluge times and a high civilization that existed then, and the Nazis, with their belief that the Aryan race actually originated off this planet.

Of course, all this was pure speculation however. Was there anything else that showed evidence of a hidden occult agenda playing itself out in the Apollo program in a vast ritual of celestial magic?

Indeed there was.

Hoagland discovered that when the Lunar Excursion Module containing Apollo 11 astronauts Neil Armstrong and Buzz Aldrin set down on the surface of the Moon on the twenty-fifth anniversary of the failed bomb plot against Adolf Hitler — on its own darkly suggestive of hidden agendas — that the star system Sirius hovered "over the Apollo 11 landing site at precisely 19.5 degrees above the lunar horizon."[36] 19.5 degrees is significant, for it is indicative of the deep "tetrahedral physics" that Hoagland and associate Errol Torrun decoded from their celebrated study decoding the ruins of the Cydonia complex on Mars. If one takes a tetrahedron and circumscribes a sphere around it, with one point of the tetrahedron touching the axis of rotation, then divides the surface of that sphere with traditional latitude and longitude coordinates, the other three points of the tetrahedron will touch the surface of the sphere at 19.5 degrees north or south latitude as a universal geometrical law. This, Hoagland discovered, was an important clue to a deep physics taking place within all massive rotating bodies, for across the solar system,

---

[35] Hoagland and Bara, *Dark Mission: The Secret History of NASA*, pp. 204-205, emphasis in the original.

[36] Ibid, p. 212.

energy upwellings within planets would occur at this latitude, from the great Red Spot on Jupiter, to the storm on Neptune, to the average distribution of sunspots on the corona of the Sun. The presence of Sirius at this latitude "suggested that as far back as 1969, NASA was *fully aware* of the significance of the Cydonia "*tetrahedral geometry*" — and perhaps the physics behind it — even though this was more than half a decade before the first images of that crucial Martian region would be taken."[37]

Additionally, astronaut and Freemason Buzz Aldrin, at exactly 33 minutes after the landing, held a special Masonic "communion" ceremony to commemorate the Egyptian god Osiris.[38] As if that were not enough, in a mission where every last ounce of weight had to be pre-planned and precisely calculated, Aldrin had brought with him the flag of the Supreme Council of the Southern Jurisdiction of the Scottish Rite of Freemasonry![39]

This led Hoagland to press the questions home:

As far as (he) was concerned, there could no longer be any question that this *entire* sequence of events was meticulously planned and executed flawlessly — by *someone*. But "who" within NASA would have had such power — and the desire — to literally hijack the First Lunar Landing... and in such an arcane fashion?

He soon had his answer.

In looking at just who officially picked the Apollo Landing Sites, he discovered yet *another* "Egyptian connection."

Dr. Farouk El-Baz is an Egyptian geologist who tutored the Apollo astronauts in the developing science of "lunar planetology." Born in Cairo and educated in the United States, El-Baz taught in Germany and the U.S. before becoming involved in the U.S. space program in 1967. In that year, he applied to "Bellcom" (a subsidiary of AT&T) — which up to that point had been (as you would expect) handling communications for the Apollo Program.[40]

It was, in fact, El-Baz who was the Secretary of the Landing Site Committee.[41] Investigating further, Hoagland discovered that El-Baz's father was an expert in the religion of ancient Egypt.[42]

---

[37] Hoagland and Bara, *Dark Mission: The Secret History of NASA*, p. 212.
[38] Ibid, pp. 207-208.
[39] Ibid, pp. 225, 273.
[40] Ibid, p. 215.
[41] Ibid, p. 216.
[42] Ibid.

One must pause to consider precisely what this means, lest its significance be lost. The significance is revealed in the simple physical mechanics of missions planning, of launching an interplanetary expedition of 250,000 miles one-way journey over several days, to land at a pre-determined site where certain stars are in certain alignments at certain times, and on a precise day which is itself an ominous anniversary, in order to conduct a "communion ceremony" at a certain (Masonic) time, for this means that it was *these* considerations that *had* to have had "the highest priority, over all *other* publicly stated goals of the Apollo landing program. They would have to be given top priority over all other objectives, be they political, general mission science, specific lunar geological sampling and even crew safety."[43] The simple celestial mechanics involved means, quite simply, that the landing at this site, at this time, with the stars in these alignments, on that anniversary, was *not* coincidence, since mission planning was a matter of precise detail, and done months in advance.[44]

Hoagland summarizes the occult influences at work in this vast scenario with frightening clarity:

> Once they had established themselves in all the key positions throughout the new Space Agency — Von Braun (the Nazi, ed), Webb (the Freemason, ed.), Von Karman (the Magician, ed.), El-Baz (the Egyptian religion expert, ed.) and all the rest were then able to proceed with plans they had apparently been incubating quietly for many years "pre-NASA." With "Brookings" as a specifically-designed political excuse for keeping key future NASA discoveries secret, the elite leadership of this clandestine occult hierarchy were able to set in motion an "inner program" — carefully hidden from the general public and the "honest" side of NASA — which appears to have been no less than a massive technological effort to confirm their shared *religious visions...on the surface of the Moon and beyond...* to which they... *and they alone...* deserved *sole* access.[45]

By the time of Apollo 16's landing on the Moon on April 20, 1972, the symbolism had become blatant, for the Lunar Module was *named* Orion, and the date of the landing was Adolf Hitler's birthday.

---

[43] Hoagland and Bara, *Dark Mission: The Secret History of NASA*, p. 214.

[44] As Hoagland also points out, the anagram N.A.S.A. might also be taken in a dual manner, with each letter having its own Egyptian significance, standing for the gods Nephtys, Ausir (Osiris), Set, and Aset (Isis). (p. 252)

[45] Ibid, p. 247, emphasis in the original.

This was the third such lunar landing on a significant "Nazi" anniversary — Apollo 11 being the first, on the 25th anniversary of the failed bomb plot against Hitler on July 20, 1944 — and Hoagland and Bara mince no words on what they believe the significance to be:

> This new "ritual coincidence," a second NASA mission *deliberately* landed on the day of Hitler's birth,

(with a Lunar module named after Orion/Osiris, Egyptian god of rebirth and resurrection, let it be noted)

> finally brought the astonishing set of alignments into crystal clear, sharp focus. For, by these repeated "ritual coincidences" — commemorating the infamous leader of the Third Reich — the key players behind this entire NASA lunar ritual were now overwhelmingly identified as none other than the NASA members of the former Reich. NASA — at the highest levels — had effectively been "taken over" from the Masons by Von Braun.
>
> Further, it was now clear from the "ritual timing" of Kennedy's critical address to that joint Congressional session (May 25, 1961), that the Nazis had carefully setup the President on what the *real* objectives of Apollo would become, including the insitu reconnaissance and return to Earth of artifacts from the ancient ruins that the Nazis somehow knew about and clearly viewed as being left —
> *By their own ancestors!*
> No wonder Kennedy was murdered, immediately after his repeated offer to share this priceless "Nazi heritage" with their worst enemies, the Russians, was finally accepted.[46]

If this seems far-fetched, one need only recall a fact that I document in my previous book *Roswell and The Reich: The Nazi Connection*, namely, that Von Braun and company had successfully duplicated within NASA the *exact* command structure that they and their Nazi colleagues held within Hitler's Third Reich's secret rocket program.[47]

---

[46] Hoagland and Bara, *Dark Mission: The Secret History of NASA*, p. 254.

[47] See my *Roswell and The Reich: The Nazi Connection* (Adventures Unlimited Press, 2010), pp. 350-358. Hoagland and Bara comment on this q.v. *Dark Mission: The Secret History of NASA*, p. 246.

E. Deep Space, Deep Politics, Deep Physics, Deep Magic, and The
Murder of JFK
1. A Hidden Physics and Technology in Play During the
Apollo Program?

There possibly was another deep magic in play as well during the Apollo missions: a deep physics, the deep magic of a hidden technology, that got us to the Moon, and more importantly, *off* of it once we landed on it, a deep physics brought into play and shared with NASA for the potential prize of bringing back potentially even more precise knowledge and even more advanced technology.

In several of my previous books I have outlined a case that concerns the existence of an alternative physics and technology having deep roots in the secret weapons projects of the Third Reich, a case that is a crucial context here for a proper understanding of the issues in play with respect to space science and technology matters on the one hand, and the JFK assassination on the other. Briefly stated, that case and context is as follows:

1) Nazi Germany had started a project, the so-called Nazi "Bell" project, to lead to a gateway technology designed to manipulate gravitational torsion fields within space-time[48] to give them access to three different things:
   a) a technology to tap into the virtually limitless energy supplies of the "zero point energy" or the energy of the physical medium itself;[49]
   b) a technology to lead to a practical "antigravity" field propulsion decades in advance of anything the Allies or Soviets were conceiving;[50] and,
   c) a technology that, tapping into the virtually limitless energy of the physical medium, could be weaponized in the ultimate

---

[48] Joseph P Farrell, *Secrets of the Unified Field: The Philadelphia Experiment, the Nazi Bell, and the Discarded Theory* (Adventures Unlimited Press, 2008), pp. 1-42, 262-288.

[49] Joseph P Farrell, *The Nazi International: The Nazis' Postwar Plan to Control Finance, Conflict, Physics and Space* (Adventures Unlimited Press, 2009), pp. 313-350.

[50] Joseph P Farrell, *The SS Brotherhood of the Bell: NASA's Nazis, JFK, and Majic-12* (Adventures Unlimited Press, 2006). pp. 141-308.

weapon that would make the power of a hydrogen bomb look like a firecracker;[51]

2) At the war's end, the Nazis had 60 of their own scientists working on the project murdered to prevent detailed knowledge of it from falling into Soviet or Allied hands;[52]

3) At least one of the Bell project scientists, Dr. Ronald Richter, ended up in Argentina where he continued post-war independent Nazi research into aspects of the project,[53] while another top Bell project scientist, Dr. Kurt Debus, ended up in this country with Von Braun's rocket team;

4) Dr. Debus ended up at Cape Canaveral where he was a senior flight administrator during the Apollo program, duplicating exactly the position he held within the chain of command in Nazi Germany within Von Braun's rocket program there.[54] Debus thus has his feet firmly planted in *two* secret "space" programs within Nazi Germany, the "public" program raining rockets down on London, and the much more exotic and secret program call the Bell;[55]

5) Von Braun discovered possibly as early as the mid-1950s that gravitational calculations using standard Newtonian calculations were incorrect, and that there was an unknown torsion effect taking place in outer space with space probes.[56] Additionally, there is a strong circumstantial case to be made that an alternative technology was in play that made the Moon landings possible, a possibility suggested by Debus' presence in his position within NASA, a torsion technology stemming from the Nazi Bell project and perhaps shared with the U.S.A., in return

---

[51] Farrell, *The SS Brotherhood of the Bell*, pp. 141-308.

[52] Ibid, p. 149.

[53] Farrell, *The Nazi Internationa*, pp. 249-350.

[54] Joseph P Farrell, *Roswell and The Reich: The Nazi Connection* (Adventures Unlimited Press, 2010), pp. 356-357.

[55] Farrell, *The SS Brotherhood of the Bell*, pp. 155-157; and Farrell, *Roswell and The Reich*, pp. 350-358; 426-435.

[56] Richard C. Hoagland, "Von Braun's 50-Year Old Secret," Pts 1 and 2, http://www.enterprisemission.com/Von_Braun.htm and http://www.enterprisemission.com/Von_Braun2.htm

for access to whatever secrets were learned during the Apollo mission.[57]

6) That an alternative technology to get us off the Moon once we were on it is indicated by three significant things:

a) Dr. Von Braun let slip to *Time* magazine shortly after the first Apollo Moon landing — Apollo 11 — that the neutral point of gravity was some 43,500 miles from the surface of the Moon, much further out than the 23,500 miles calculated for that position using standard Newtonian mechanics. This would suggest a much more massive Moon than has been publicly acknowledged, and this in turn means that the small rocket aboard the Lunar Excursion Module(LEM) may not have been sufficient on its own to return astronauts Armstrong and Aldrin to the Command Module in lunar orbit above. Some other technology was therefore in play;[58]

b) The signature of a rocket's acceleration is geometric, i.e., a rocket-propelled craft, when beginning acceleration, will travel a little further per unit of time. But the television footage of the Lunar Excursion Modules taking off from the Moon shows something very different: the LEM simply "pops up" at a more or less *uniform* rate of speed and flies away. In other words, the video footage does not suggest that a rocket is the only means of propulsion being utilized;

c) The presence of Nazi scientist Dr. Kurt Debus, himself a scientist who worked on the Nazi Bell project, a project heavily investigating torsion field phenomena, as a senior flight administrator at Cape Canaveral during the Apollo Moon landings suggests that this was precisely the type of technology in play, and that someone with experience with it was needed in that position.

Points 5 and 6 deserve a little closer scrutiny.

The Bell device stood approximately 15 to 18 feet tall, was obviously bell-shaped. The outer covering of the device was of some ceramic type of material, and around it there were ports for heavy-duty electrical cabling. The device used two types of electrical potentials, AC

---

[57] Farrell, *The Giza Death Star: The Paleophysics of the Great Pyramid and the Military Compound at Giza* (Adventures Unlimited Press, 2002), pp. 219-220, and Farrell, *The SS Brotherhood of the Bell*, pp. 124-128.

[58] See the discussion in my *The SS Brotherhood of the Bell*, pp. 124-128.

and DC. Inside the device there were two counter-rotating cylinders that rotated at great speeds around a central axis. They were stacked one on top of the other. These cylinders, and the center of the device, were electrically polarized. Into these cylinders was placed a compound code-named "IRR Xerum 525," a compound of mercury and thorium oxide.[59] Once the compound was placed into the device and the device was spun up, the compound was electrically pulsed with massive DC voltage, creating a plasma, de-exciting the thorium, and releasing massive bursts of gamma-ray energy. The net result of all of this was that the device created a small space-time "bubble" around itself via a massive "torsion sheer" effect, and it levitated.[60]

One may understand "torsion" by a simple analogy. Imagine emptying an aluminum soda can, and then wringing it like a dishrag with both hands. The can spirals, folds, and pleats, and this spiraling, folding and pleating represents what torsion does to the fabric of space-time. As the spiraling occurs, the ends of the can draw closer together. In other words, an extreme torsion sheer will massively warp and distort the fabric of space-time and anything within its field.

So is there any evidence that NASA was itself quietly investigating the use of torsion fields as a means of enhancing space flight capabilities in an exotic propulsion technology *after* the period of this hypothesized sharing by the Nazis of torsion-based technology with the American program?

Indeed there is. Engineer Paul Murrad, of the Space Technology and Applications International Forum, a forum sponsored by the University of New Mexico, indicated that torsion fields were being seriously investigated as a means of efficient space field propulsion:

> ... The only field that (can)_ support faster than light phenomenon (sic et passim) according to some Russian physicists (is) the spin or torsion field. Torsion is different from these other three fields (electrostatics, magnetics, and gravitics) that (have) spherical geometry. Torsion (can) be right-handed of left-handed and is based upon a cylindrical field and can be created by *large accumulations of electricity and rotation of a body* that if, above a certain speed, (will) enhance the torsion field.

---

[59] Joseph P Farrell, *The Philosophers' Stone: Alchemy and the Secret Research for Exotic Matter* (Feral House, 2009), pp. 277-305.

[60] For a much fuller discussion and rationalization of the construction of the Bell device and the physics behind it, see my *SS Brotherhood of the Bell,* pp. 171-308; my *Secrets of the Unified Field,* pp. 262-288, and my *The Philosophers' Stone,* pp. 277-305.

> Torsion can lead to other phenomenon to include frame dragging. Here in a vacuum, frame dragging occurs when a r*od is inserted concentrically inside of a cylinder and has no physical contact with that body.* If the rod is suddenly removed, the cylinder will also move or is dragged along with the rod.[61]

Notably, there are three features Murrad mentions here, emphasized in the above quotation, that are principles in evidence in the construction of the Nazi Bell device, namely, (1) the use of high voltage electrostatics, (2) the rotation of the body (in the Bell's counter-rotating metal drums around a central axis), and (3) the Bell likewise had a central core that may not have been in physical contact with the rotating drums.

In my view, these resemblances are probably not coincidental, given the presence of Dr. Debus within the Apollo program, and the indications of the use of a torsion-based alternative technology within the Lunar Excursion Module to get us off the Moon.

2. Deep Physics, Deep Magic, and the Murder of JFK

There are thus two powerful technological motivations behind the murder of JFK and the desire of the conspirators to keep them secret:

1) The implied physics and technology that *got* us to the Moon and more importantly, *off* of it; and,
2) The implied physics and technological potential of whatever was *found* there.

It is to be noted that this technology would definitely have been something that petroleum interests such as H.L. Hunt and Clint Murchison would have wanted to see suppressed, since it did an end run around petroleum as an energy source. Kennedy's plan for a joint space program with the Soviets would not only have threatened to expose these technologies, it potentially would have ended the petroleum "monopoly" over world energy supplies. It is also to be noted that Kennedy's proposed joint space program would have also threatened the Nazis, who evidently made *some* of their advanced technology available to the Apollo program, because the implication of Kennedy's proposal might have made that technology available to their hated enemies, the Soviets. Finally, such a joint space venture threatened the charter of NASA itself,

---

[61] Hoagland and Bara, *Dark Mission: The Secret History of NASA*, p. 59, emphasis added.

allowing the Soviets a camel's nose into the tent of the America military-industrial complex, for after all, NASA was an agency of the Department of Defense.

In the last two chapters we have discovered the clear and unmistakable fingerprints of an occult agenda, indeed, a Masonic agenda, all over the murder of President Kennedy, as well as all over the program he officially helped to establish, the Apollo manned lunar landing program.

The questions of all the previous chapters have now piled up. Who had connections to NASA's Nazis via Von Braun? Who numbered high ranking Freemasons among his circle of political intimates and associates, including J. Edgar Hoover and Chief Justice Earl Warren? Who had personal connections with, and indeed, was even implicated in the shady dealings of, organized crime? Who had known political connections in Texas, connections that numbered Texas "big oil" in his portfolio? Who had a deep hand in the formation of American space policy? Who reversed Kennedy's Vietnam and fiscal policies? Who helped to plan the details of the Texas trip that resulted in the murder of the president? Who personally headed off any Texas state or Federal investigation of the crime by establishing the Warren Commission, and who personally selected its members? Who had control of Air Force One in the crucial hours after the assassination, and who took physical possession of the "voice of authority" in the White House? Who would have had the authority to order the alteration of forensic evidence that indicated other shooters involved on that day?

The answer is obvious:

Lyndon Baines Johnson.

To him we now turn a closer eye.

PART TWO:
LYNDON BAINES JOHNSON AND THE ARCHITECTURE OF THE CONSPIRACY:
ARCHITECT, OR BUILDER?

"If one combines the admissions and strange facts of Lyndon B. Johnson with the statements of Jack Ruby it becomes crystal clear that Johnson was aware that Kennedy was going to be murdered."
Craig I. Zirbel,
The Texas Connection, p. 223.

251

7
LBJ:
A STUDY IN CHARACTER, CONNECTIONS, AND CABALS

"It was subsequently leaked that the close members of the Kennedy camp on the plane were 'holding Johnson responsible for the assassination.'"
Craig I Zirbel[1]

Lyndon Baines Johnson held the office of the presidency by dint of the timely assassination of John F. Kennedy, and it *was* timely, for by succeeding to the presidency, he forestalled investigations into scandals that broke around him shortly before, scandals that could have ended his political career, and with it, his burning desire to be president. Those scandals would also have ended the career of a very powerful man who represented the deep parapolitical power structures of America.

But can Johnson's involvement in the assassination honestly be advanced as a credible case? And if so, how was he involved? What does his involvement say about the putative architecture of the conspiracy, and more importantly, what does it say about the nature of the parapolitical powers and structures of American politics and culture? Answering the first question — advancing Johnson's involvement as a credible case — is not as difficult as it might seem, provided one understands some basics of criminal investigation, and how deeply the Warren Commission failed in this respect:

> After a crime has been committed, the first principle in any criminal investigation is to evaluate the crime scene for clues. Once this has been accomplished the next phase of every criminal investigation focuses upon the persons who may have committed the crime. This not only involves attempting to physically link the evidence to particular suspects, but it is also strongly based upon logical deduction... Logical deduction in a criminal case requires an examination of each criminal suspect in relation to three factors of the crime: character, motive, and opportunity. A proper evaluation of each criminal suspect then results in a separation of the suspects into one of two categories known as "Prime Suspects" and "suspects." As more evidence is acquired and as additional deduction occurs, the suspects are then moved from one

---

[1] Craig I. Zirbel, *The Texas Connection* (New York: Time-Warner, 2001), p. 253.

253

[handwritten marginalia: utter failure of the Warren Commission]

category to the other. Hopefully, this eventually results in one prime suspect who is deemed to be the probable culprit and is then normally charged with the crime.

In this case, so far as is known and publicly reported, the Warren Commission only performed its criminal investigation as to one suspect, Lee Harvey Oswald. It failed to examine the criminal potential of any other suspects. By investigating only one suspect, the Commission failed to fully investigate the assassination of a world leader.[2]

But as has been seen in previous pages, the Warren *Report* is to be distinguished from the *evidence* presented in the 26 volumes of the Warren Commission, evidence that, as Hoffman observed, clearly pointed the finger of culpability not to Oswald, but to the circle of power and interests surrounding President Johnson, and moreover, interests represented on the Warren Commission itself.

Researcher Jim Marrs notes one thing about the immediate post-assassination discussion in Texas, as news was quickly flashed and the speculations over anxious dinner tables began:

> In Dallas on the day Kennedy died there were those people iconoclastic enough to suggest that Vice President Johnson was behind the assassination. These were mostly long-time Texas residents who had heard vicious stories about Johnson for years and who figured the Texas politician had more to gain from Kennedy's death than just about anyone. Even today, many serious students of the assassination cannot discount the idea that Johnson, in some way, played a role in the Dallas tragedy.[3]

The question is, what were those "vicious stories" about Johnson? Did the Vice President possess the character and the connections to have made him a prime suspect?

A. An Overview of LBJ's Character, and Connections

The alliance between Kennedy and Johnson was purely a matter of power politics, for there was no love lost between the two men. Indeed, they quarreled in Kennedy's motel room on the eve of the assassination

---

[2] Zirbel, *The Texas Connection*, p. 81.
[3] Jim Marrs, *Crossfire:The Plot that Killed Kenned*, p. 289.

itself.[4] As for Johnson, he never lacked for people who had negative things to say about him.

> As an initial overview of Lyndon Johnson's character, it can be said that some people viewed Johnson as "a man who would stoop to commit any type of act and who managed to combine the worst elements of mankind's traits into his personality." Others who reported on his political career considered him to be a "total opportunist, devoted only to profit and personal gain." And still others, including a fellow U.S. Senator, felt that Johnson was the "phoniest individual who ever came around." These opinion statements could be considered as only jealous comments by a few enemies if they had not been regularly repeated by hundreds of different people throughout Johnson's career. In fact, Lyndon Johnson's grandmother pulled no punches about her own negative feelings for him. Repeatedly she declared that LBJ was going to wind up in jail — "just mark my words." Even though Johnson missed the penitentiary for the presidency his grandmother's prophecy still came very close to the mark. While he was never indicted nor convicted of a crime, Johnson led a political life that was constantly embroiled in scandals and a number of his cohorts, who were less politically connected, ended up being convicted of crimes and jailed.[5]

This is putting it mildly, for Johnson adopted a public persona utterly and diametrically opposed to the crudeness and hypocrisy he exhibited in private, and every public persona was adopted with a view to enhancing his own political power.

In this respect, Johnson was perhaps the first major national politician to make a point of "pimping God" to advance his power, a practice now commonplace, for his views on religion were strictly utilitarian, as were, it turns out, his views on government property; indeed, the following might be considered "classic LBJ behavior":

> In Lyndon Johnson's case it can be positively stated that he went to church. In fact, on any given Sunday Johnson was often seen in more than one church. But, this is the only positive thing that can be said about his religious practices. From boyhood on Johnson refused to take to Christianity and in the words of a friend "LBJ never had a religion." Johnson went to church and attended multiple church services because that was where the voters were on Sunday. One Washington religious leader publicly proclaimed that LBJ was a man "whose public house was splendid in appearance... but whose entire foundation was rotted by

---

[4] Zirbel, *The Texas Connection*, p. 7.
[5] Zirbel, *The Texas Connection*, pp. 86-87.

termites." While others stayed for post-service coffee, Johnson would race away at high speed to another church full of voters. And, while Johnson's press agents attempted to impress the public by disclosing Johnson's religious generosity, such as his "gift" of an automobile to a poor minister, they couldn't hide the truth forever. It later was discovered that his wonderful "gift" of an automobile was actually a gift of U.S. government property![6]

So much for "thou shalt not steal."

Johnson's theft of government property was not the only thing his thievery was limited to, for stealing elections was a Johnson specialty. In fact, Johnson even liked to joke about his stealing of elections, for he would often joke about the poor Mexican-American boy whose father had returned from the dead. How did the boy know this? Because his father had voted for Johnson![7] The pattern apparently was not limited to the dead voting for him either, for Johnson stole his first election in college when several people voted for him more than once.[8]

But by far the most infamous example of an LBJ election fix was the election that propelled him into the United States Senate into the position where he would eventually become the powerful U.S. Senate Majority leader, a contested election that was contested until long after Johnson was dead:

> Johnson entered a race for the Senate in 1948. It was a close race between Johnson, still identified with Roosevelt and the New Deal, and conservative Texas governor Coke Stevenson, who managed to defeat Johnson in the Democratic primary. However, Stevenson didn't have a clear majority, so a run-off election was called for August 28.
>
> Due to slow communications and manual voting procedures, the election outcome was in doubt for several days. Finally on September 2, Johnson went on radio with a "victory speech," which shocked the confident Stevenson forces.[9]

The voting results of Precinct 13 in Texas had been changed, with an added 202 votes for LBJ, which gave him a squeeky margin of only 87 votes statewide over Stevenson, earning him the sobriquet of "landslide Lyndon," and beginning one of the "longest legal feuds in Texas history":

---

[6] Zirbel, *The Texas Connection*, pp. 88-89.
[7] Ibid, pp. 93-94.
[8] Ibid, p. 94.
[9] Marrs, *Crossfire: The Plot That Killed Kennedy*, p. 291.

Johnson's opponents claimed the 87-vote "correction" in the 1948 election came only after frantic phone calls between Johnson and George Parr, a powerful south Texas political boss known as the "Duke of Duval County."

The controversy continued into 1977, when Luis Salas, the local election judge, admitted to the *Dallas Morning News* (that) he had certified fictitious ballots for Johnson on orders from Parr, who committed suicide in 1975. Salas told newsmen, "Johnson did not win that election; it was stolen for him."[10]

And Parr was not the only man around LBJ to die conveniently, as we shall see.

There is a great deal of evidence to suggest that LBJ's "unique skills" were put to their severest test in the hotly contested 1960 election between then-Massachusetts Senator John F. Kennedy and then-Vice President Richard M. Nixon. It is now well known, of course, that Chicago Mayor Richard Daley helped to secure the Cook County vote in Illinois for JFK by having ballot boxes with votes cast for Republican Nixon dumped into the Chicago river, where they were subsequently found.[11] But the real scene of voting fraud activity was not taking place in Cook County, Illinois, for predictably enough, the most voter fraud occurred in Texas, where Johnson's well-known "connections" secured the crucial southern state.[12]

Perhaps the most telling feature of LBJ's personality — and his potential motivation for participation in an assassination plot — comes from his life-long obsession to become President of the United States. When he was still a school teacher, Johnson was mocked by his students. His response was to "scold them" and to say that they "were looking at the 'future President of the United States.'"[13] That burning desire continued after the hotly contested 1960 election, for

(when) Kennedy took office he was immediately met with Johnson's first unreasonable request. Vice President Johnson proposed to President Kennedy that he should be allowed to move into the White House to share the presidential power with President Kennedy under a two person presidential system. At first Kennedy thought Johnson was

---

[10] Marrs, *Crossfire: The Plot That Killed Kennedy*, p. 292.
[11] Zirbel, *The Texas Connection*, p. 97.
[12] Ibid.
[13] Ibid, p. 114.

joking, but when the Vice President persisted, President Kennedy flatly refused to create a new governing duet for America.[14]

Weirder still was LBJ's subsequent behavior after Kennedy had refused his "offer" to share power, for Johnson would have himself driven to the White House each day where he would make a point to roam the halls, passing each day by the Oval Office, then walk out the back doors, through the White House grounds, and across the street to the Old Executive Office Building where his offices were actually located, a practice that "has never been followed by any other Vice President in history!"[15]

There is even some suggestion of devious and almost Byzantine maneuvering on LBJ's part to get him the vice presidential nomination on the 1960 Kennedy presidential ticket, a fact made the more peculiar because Johnson, during the Democratic primary races, had gone out of his way to attack and vilify Kennedy. One version of the story — that recounted by several witnesses present at the 1960 Democratic Party National Convention — is worth noting. After the bitter political contest between the two men for the nomination, JFK knew that he would have to cement party unity if the Democrats were to have any chance of success against incumbent Vice President Richard Nixon.

> To accomplish this task, Kennedy strategists thought that unity could be accomplished if Kennedy offered the second position on his ticket to Johnson which would appease fractionating Democratic groups and also placate LBJ. It was expected that Johnson would turn down the offer and would then return to the Senate as its powerful majority leader. The offer was only to be a token gesture and everyone knew it. In fact, until only hours before Kennedy's actual offer Johnson had publicly told reporters that he would never accept a position on the Kennedy ticket. Whether LBJ was so cunning that he actually baited Kennedy into making a public offer to him which he then would publicly accept, or just changed his mind, will never be known. What is known is that no matter what version is accepted as true, once Kennedy offered the job to Johnson, rather than decline it, to the surprise of everyone, he accepted it. This created shock waves at the convention.[16]

---

[14] Ibid, pp. 115-116.

[15] Zirbel, *The Texas Connection*, p. 116.

[16] Ibid, p. 128.

That isn't the end of the story, however. One of LBJ's subordinates who was present in LBJ's hotel suite the evening Johnson lost the party's nomination to Kennedy maintained that LBJ actually demanded the number two position, *before* he made a public statement to the effect that if offered it, he would not accept it. LBJ was overheard stating that he deserved the Vice Presidency and intended to get it.[17]

Then, of course, came LBJ's public statement to a reporter that, if offered the position, he would not accept. Yet, mere hours later, he had been offered, and had accepted, the position. When questioned about this by the very same reporter to whom he had stated mere hours earlier that he would not accept, Johnson said something darkly revealing: "...I have now learned that one out of every four Presidents dies in office... and I am a gambling man!"[18]

Ponder that statement carefully, for it means that Johnson was of such low character as to be able and willing to go on public record that his hope was that Kennedy would die in office...

Mention must also be made of Johnson's now well-known and numerous affairs, as one of them sheds further light on his character, and another of them will become a crucial source of information. While Johnson was climbing the ladder of political power, he carried on a number of illicit affairs, allegedly including one with Madeline Brown for 20 years, and with whom he may have sired an illegitimate son.[19] We will have occasion to return to Madeline Brown in the next chapter. One of the affairs was with the wife of one of his powerful political backers.[20]

What emerges from all of this is a picture of a man with a lust for power and a character that drove him to do almost anything to acquire it, including fraud on a massive scale, a taste for flirting with danger with the wives of his very own backers, and a publicly-stated admission that he accepted the Vice Presidential nomination hoping that Kennedy would die in office. This author concurs with researcher Craig Zirbel's assessment of LBJ, his character, and standard methods of operation:

> Johnson was a political schemer. His standard practice was to make bold illicit moves to his advantage and then rely upon his power to cover up the resulting problems. He did this time and time again. Lyndon Johnson had the character, temperament, and immoral nature to eliminate anything obstructing his path to power — including

---

[17] Zirbel, *The Texas Connection*, pp. 128-129.
[18] Ibid, p. 129.
[19] Ibid, pp. 89-90.
[20] Ibid.

possessing the intellect, the capacity, and the creativity to successfully kill![21]

We have seen in previous chapters that Johnson's political connections ran very far, and very deeply, into most if not all of the groups whose interests coalesced around the removal of President Kennedy. He thus would have had powerful pressures on him to participate, if not in the conspiracy to commit the crime, then at least in the cover-up that sustained him in office.

But the question is, did he have powerful motivations to do either? Did Lyndon Johnson have the standard prerequisites to qualify as a prime suspect in the criminal investigation that *should* have been performed in the wake of Kennedy's murder? We have seen that with his powerful connections, and later the power of the Presidency itself, he certainly had the *means*. In later chapters, we will address the problem of opportunity. But for now, we must ask, did he have powerful personal *motive* to participate in a conspiracy to commit the crime? Should a President of the United States actually be considered a prime suspect in the political crime of the last century?

B. LBJ's Scandals and Modus Operandi: Motives Revealed

There is no doubt that Johnson was in a compromised position at least with respect to two of the groups involved with interests in eliminating Kennedy, big oil, and the Mafia, for he accepted large cash kickback payments from both, including allegedly a $100,000 payoff from Teamster Union boss and mobster Jimmy Hoffa, and a known bribe of $50,000 personally delivered to him by a Gulf Oil executive.[22] Jim Marrs notes that LBJ had received cash contributions from top mobsters connection to New Orleans crime boss Carlos Marcello, and that over a period of ten years during his career in the U.S. Senate he had received more than half a million dollars in pay-offs to kill or water-down anti-crime legislation.[23]

Johnson in turn used such funds in typical fashion to further extend his network of powerful connections and enhance his own power in the process:

---

[21] Ibid, p. 107.
[22] Zirbel, *The Texas Connection*, p. 102.
[23] Marrs, *Crossfire: The Plot That Killed Kennedy*, p. 293.

Johnson's rise to national power, however, came from his ability to dole out the money to other politicians. Early on wealthy Texans quickly realized that national influence for their Texas businesses could not be based on only their two U.S. Senators. They shrewdly determined that if they could get other U.S. Senators in the "hip pocket" of one of their senators it would result in strong political clout for him and them.

And of course, they selected Johnson to be the "bag man" probably based on their analysis of his character. Johnson became a master at doling out money in exchange for favors. LBJ's money bag was nonpartisan and he became so savvy that he only contributed to politicians who were certain to win, contributing heavily to those who were "shoe-ins" and giving little or nothing to those who might lose. This allowed Johnson and his Texas cronies to create a Congress that was stacked only with victors who owed Johnson favors. The money bag allowed LBJ to buy respect on Capital Hill and eventually seize the position of majority leader in the Senate, the second most powerful position in government.[24]

Such power does not exist in a vacuum nor avoid public scrutiny, and in fact Johnson was faced with three major scandals during his vice presidency. These three scandals, the Billy Sol Estes Affair, the TFX fighter scandal, and the Bobby Baker affair "came closer to directly centering on Lyndon Johnson," that is, until Kennedy was assassinated.[25]

1. The Billy Sol Estes Affair and the Marshal Investigation

The first of these scandals contains *prima facie* evidence from one of the principals that Johnson was, indeed, capable of murder to maintain his power and position:

Soon after Johnson became vice president, yet another investigation into his financial dealings got underway. This time it involved a big-time Texas wheeler-dealer named Billie Sol Estes. Henry Marshall, a Department of Agriculture official, was looking into Estes' habit of acquiring millions in federal cotton allotment payments on land which was under water or actually owned by the government. Marshall was particularly interested in Estes' connections with his long-time friend, Lyndon Johnson. However, before any official action could be taken, Marhsall was found dead in a remote section of his farm near Franklin, Texas. He had been shot five times in the abdomen. Nearby lay a bolt-action .22-caliber rifle.

---

[24] Zirbel, *The Texas Connection*, pp. 102-103.
[25] Ibid, p. 136.

Five days later, without the benefit of an autopsy, a local peace justice ruled Marshall's death a suicide.

(In 1985 Estes, after being granted immunity from prosecution, told Texas media that Johnson had ordered Marshall's death to prevent his connections with Estes from being exposed....)

At least three other men connected with the Estes case died in unusual circumstances.[26]

Johnson himself fired the flames of the investigation to begin with, for as Department of Agriculture suspicions began to focus on the Texans, Vice President Johnson wrote a letter to the Secretary of Agriculture supporting Estes' dubious practices at the end of January, 1961.[27]

This only made the investigation focus on both men, and Marshall was assigned to investigate the tangled records of Estes' land holdings, issuing his report to the Department of Agriculture later that spring.[28] When Estes was finally arrested as a result of the dead Marshall's investigation, three unusual things happened:

- LBJ's personal legal counsel showed up as Estes' principal attorney;
- Billy Sol Estes refused to talk; and
- Billy Sol Estes' accountant (who was the only other man besides the dead Henry Marshall who could unravel the fraud) was found dead in his car.[29]

Granted immunity and stating that Johnson was involved would constitute *prima facie* evidence for any grand jury, and would most likely constitute enough evidence to lead to an indictment. Lyndon Johnson, according to his long time friend Billy Sol Estes, was capable, and actually did, commit murder to protect his power.

2. The TFX Fighter Scandal

The second major scandal that rocked Johnson's vice presidency was the TFX fighter scandal.[30] Two companies, Washington state-based Boeing, and Texas-based General Dynamics, were vying for the huge

---

[26] Marrs, *Crossfire: The Plot That Killed Kennedy*, p. 295.

[27] Zirbel, *The Texas Connection*, p. 137.

[28] Ibid.

[29] Ibid, p. 139.

[30] The TFX would eventually become the swing-wing F-111 fighter-bomber.

multi-million dollar Federal contract to build the new carrier-born fighter for the Navy. Johnson, who had been unsuccessful in his bid to move into the White House and essentially become a "co-president" with Kennedy, did manage to extract from JFK the power to make a few appointments within the federal bureaucracy, and one of those he was allowed to make was the Secretary of the Navy, a "politically insignificant" position but one carrying "economic clout in the billions of dollars for those businesses who compete in providing military hardware to the Navy."[31] Johnson chose his old-time Texas buddy, and past presidential campaign manager...

...John Connally.[32]

Before the contract was awarded to General Dynamics, however, Connally resigned as Secretary of the Navy to run for Governor of Texas. Undaunted, Johnson replaced him with yet another Texas crony, Fred Korth. Once in office, Korth awarded the contract, predictably enough, to the Fort Worth-based General Dynamics, in spite of the fact that it appears that the corporation had falsified its test data.[33] The result of all this was that "a 'minor' scandal arose in Washington, D.C., where it was rumored that not only had Johnson put the 'fix' in to get the plane for General Dynamics, but that he was personally rewarded for his efforts with satchels full of cash."[34] Korth was charged with conflicts of interest, and the case began to be investigated, but, like Billy Sol Estes before him, he kept his mouth shut.[35]

The effect of these two scandals on the Kennedy Administration was palpable:

> Even though the Billy Sol Estes and the TFX scandals did not politically destroy Johnson, it may have been only because Estes and Korth refused to cooperate and this kept the investigators from tying Johnson in. And, while the bulk of the publicity from each of the scandals ended before Kennedy's death, the political repercussions continued and President Kennedy knew, and the public suspected, that his administration had a "bad apple" occupying the right hand man

---

[31] Zirbel, *The Texas Connection*, p. 141.

[32] Ibid, p. 142. LBJ another ally in Fort Worth congressman Jim Wright, later House Majority Leader and successor to Tip O'Neill as Speaker of the House in the early 1990s.

[33] Ibid.

[34] Ibid.

[35] Ibid, p. 143.

position in the White House. It had become clear to everyone that Johnson and his friends were tainting the Kennedy presidency.

In fact, on the day of the President's death the reason Kennedy flew the few miles from Fort Worth to Dallas rather than drive, was because his advisors realized that any drive between the two cities would require the President to travel right past the front door of General Dynamics' plant. Kennedy flew because he did not want to be reminded nor did he want the public to remember anything about the fiasco.[36]

In other words, the effect of the two scandals was to drastically diminish LBJ's political value to the Kennedy White House, and Kennedy began to toy with the idea of dropping his vice president from the ticket in the 1964 general election, a decision cemented by the next scandal...

3. The Bobby Baker Affair

No scandal came so close to ending Lyndon Baines Johnson's political career and cachet than did the Bobby Baker affair "that blew onto the scene just months before Kennedy's death,"[37] for the simple reason that Baker was so tightly connected to Johnson. Just how close the two men were was explicitly spelled out by researcher Craig Zirbel:

> It was Johnson who publicly proclaimed in front of the entire U.S. Senate that Baker was his most trusted, most loyal, and most competent friend. In fact, Johnson told the whole world that if he had a son, Bobby Baker would be him. And it was Johnson who had proudly told the American people about "Lyndon's boy"... and proclaimed:
> "Bobby is my strong right arm. He is the last person I see at night and the first person I see in the morning."
> It was for these reasons that when the Senate and later the media began investigating Bobby Baker, the connection to Lyndon Johnson was too close for comfort. And, until President Kennedy was killed, the scandal was so closely tied to Johnson that it appeared impossible for him to escape.[38]

President Kennedy and his advisors sat up and took notice.

The scandal began in September 1963 when it was learned that Baker was being sued for $300,000 by one Ralph Hill, who charged in the suit that he was trying to recover monies paid to Baker for peddling

---

[36] Zirbel, *The Texas Connection,* p. 143.

[37] Ibid, p. 144.

[38] Ibid, pp. 144-145.

influence to keep Hill's vending machines in government buildings. Baker had influenced the government alright, but influenced it to replace Hill's machines with ones Baker owned.[39] Baker's company, it was learned, held federal vending machine contracts worth over three and a half million dollars in California alone.[40] What made matters very much worse for Johnson — and for the Kennedy White House — was that between them, Baker and Johnson controlled the campaign checkbook for the Democratic Party senatorial campaigns, in addition to the fact that Baker was the Secretary to the Majority leader.[41] When the Senate decided to investigate, Johnson hurried back to the country from a foreign tour and attempted to quash the investigation, to no avail, because President Kennedy himself had given the Senate the go ahead "to allow all investigations to continue to their final conclusion."[42]

Finally, on Oct 7, 1963, Baker resigned as secretary to the Senate Majority Leader, and Johnson fled Washington, D.C. to his Texas ranch where he remained more or less in seclusion. Adding to Johnson's fears was the fact that President Kennedy "flatly told the press that when the Baker investigation concluded others would also be fully investigated. By this Jack Kennedy gave clear warning that he had no intent to stop any investigation prematurely to protect LBJ."[43] There were even strong indicators that Kennedy intended to drop LBJ from the 1964 ticket, and that his statements to the press were laying the foundation for that move in public opinion.

Of course, all that came to an end on November 22, 1963 in Dallas, for once in office, Johnson had the investigation into the Bobby Baker affair temporarily stopped and deferred until after the November 1964 presidential election. Johnson even went so far as to threaten the Republicans in the 1964 election to stay away from the Bobby Baker affair, "because he had the goods on them."[44] It was a "sudden" but definitely convenient reversal of fortunes:

> How Johnson stopped the press from continuing their investigation is unknown, except the facts demonstrate that this did occur. What is known in retrospect is that Johnson's order was obeyed by all.

---

[39] Zirbel, *The Texas Connection*, p. 145.
[40] Ibid, p. 146.
[41] Ibid.
[42] Ibid, p. 147.
[43] Ibid.
[44] Ibid, p. 148.

> If Jack Kennedy had not been murdered the Baker investigation would not have ended. If Jack Kennedy had not been murdered the Baker scandal would have either destroyed or tarnished Johnson's image so completely that he would not have been on the 1964 ticket. If the President had not been slain, the truth about LBJ may have put him in prison, as his grandma predicted, rather than into the White House.[45]

That, in any grand jury's or criminal investigation's estimation, would in itself qualify Johnson for an indictment and as a prime suspect in the crime itself.

C. Swastikas and Masons in the Oily Footprints

We have noted in the previous part of this book LBJ's many connections to NASA, to Hoover, to the mafia, to intelligence, to Texas big oil, a tapestry of connections that researcher Craig Zirbel summarizes in the following fashion:

> ...
> - Johnson was one of the main figures involved in urging the President to make the trip;
> - On the day before the assassination, Johnson and the President got into a fight over switching seating positions in the vehicles for the upcoming motorcade. Johnson wanted Connally out of JFK's car and his enemy Senator (Ralph) Yarborough to sit in Connally's seat.[46]

It is necessary to pause for a moment and consider this well-known fact from a slightly different perspective, that of Johnson political crony John Connally.

As the reports of gunfire began to be heard that day in Dealey Plaza, Governor Connally, as is now well-known, screamed "My God, they're going to kill us all," a statement many have assumed was made in the panic of the moment. But what if it was not? What if it was the statement of "someone in the know" about the assassination, a statement made in the sudden and horrifying realization that he might, too, have been a target? While we will never know, it is perhaps significant that Johnson's fight with Kennedy on the night before the assassination is surely suggestive of someone trying to protect a friend. In any case, to

---

[45] Zirbel, *The Texas Connection,* pp. 148-149.
[46] Ibid, pp. 156-157.

continue with Zirbel's summary of the connections we have outlined in part one:

- Johnson's strongest supporters for his Presidency lived in Dallas;
- Some of Johnson's strongest supporters in Dallas made threatening remarks against the life of President Kennedy;[47]
- Johnson's appointees as Secretary of the Navy each had preassassination contact with the Oswald family, and one appointee even had contact with Oswald less than 2 months before the assassination;[48]
- One of Johnson's strongest supporters in Dallas was visited by Oswald's murderer (Jack Ruby), the day before the assassination;
- Oswald's murderer (Ruby) was found to possess evidence directly linking him with one of Johnson's strongest supporters in Dallas;
- Johnson's friends had contact with Ruby's trial court judge (who committed reversible error) and gave him a California resort trip and book contract; and
- Johnson created the Warren Commission which seized the evidence, investigated the murder, and only reported to him.[49]

It would be difficult, says researcher Zirbel, "for any reasonable person to conclude that such connections were merely coincidental."[50]

Indeed, such connections defy statistical probabilities and are yet more indications that the normal procedures of criminal investigations were simply ignored in the case of President Kennedy's murder.

While such connections are known to standard assassination research, we have in the previous chapters also indicated three connections or groups not normally considered:

1) International Fascism, i.e., the post-war Nazi International and all its attendant fronts, including West German intelligence (the Gehlen Organization), with its own connections to Texas

---

[47] We have seen that Johnson was connected to the mob boss Carlos Marcello via the latter's gambling operations in Texas, and Marcello certainly made threatening remarks against the President's life. As we also saw in part one, it was a member of the Hunt family that took out the "Wanted for Treason" ads in the Dallas papers against Kennedy on the day of the assassination.
[48] There were, of course, John Connally and Fred Korth. It was Connally to whom Oswald wrote, asking for his help as governor in getting his Marine dishonorable discharge upgraded to an honorable discharge.
[49] Zirbel, *The Texas Connection*, pp. 156-158.
[50] Ibid, p. 156.

petroleum interests, and symbolized by the Mauser and Mannlicher-Carcano rifles allegedly used by Oswald;

2) NASA, both via its heavy Nazi presence, and for the implication that there were powerful technological motivations possibly in play behind the President's murder; and,

3) A deep occult, "Masonic" agenda, epitomized by the heavy symbolism in play at Dealey Plaza.

Johnson, of course, had deep contacts to the third element, being a personal friend of J. Edgar Hoover and Chief Justice Earl Warren, both high-ranking Freemasons, and both heading up aspects of the post-assassination "investigation" and cover-up.

Additionally, Johnson was a personal friend of Nazi rocket scientist Dr. Wernher Von Braun, since the latter had sought out Johnson upon his arrival to the United States when Johnson was a rising power in the U.S. Senate. As has been noted in previous pages, the "Torbitt Document" by Texas lawyer David Copeland — a former member of the Johnson political machine in Texas — implicated both men in the planning of the assassination.

But what of the first element, the Nazis themselves? Is there anything more linking Johnson to them other than his close association with Von Braun?

There is, and it is that connection between Johnson and Texas oil tycoon H.L. Hunt, his major Dallas political backer, and the latter's connection to West German intelligence outlined in chapter one, for that apparatus was nothing but a front for a house of Nazi spies.[51]

*Johnson, in short, was the **one** man where all the coalescing interests in the assassination coalesce.*

And that raises a question: at which of the three levels was he involved?

We know that at the minimum Johnson participated in the crime at least as an accessory after the fact, by ordering the formation of the Warren Commission to forestall Texas state and Congressional federal investigations. That is, we know he was involved in the third stage of the cover-up itself.

But could he have been involved in the first stage, the actual planning of the crime itself, as the Torbitt Document first openly dared to allege?

The answer to that question is even more disturbing.

---

[51] See chapter one, pp. 51ff.

8
LBJ AND THE PLANNING OF THE TEXAS TRIP:
THE *PRIMA FACIE* CASE FOR LBJ'S INVOLVEMENT IN THE CONSPIRACY

"I have always believed, and argued, that a true understanding of the Kennedy assassination will lead, not to 'a few bad people,' but to the institutional and parapolitical arrangements which constitute the way we are systematically governed."
Peter Dale Scott[1]

Though few people have noticed it, in yet another of those many "odd coincidences" that keep stacking up with respect to the Kennedy assassination, when Lee Harvey Oswald was being transferred by the Dallas Police Department to the sheriff, there was *already* an ambulance in the basement garage ready to whisk him away. Of course, such a fact can be, and was, explained away as a simple precautionary matter in case "something happened."[2] Indeed, "something" did "happen," as Jack Ruby, on national television, stepped forward, jabbed a pistol into Oswald's stomach as he shouted "Oswald!" and pulled the trigger. So of course, there may also be *another* explanation as to why an ambulance was present, for perhaps it was not to "take care" of Oswald should "something happen," but perhaps it was to take *care* of him, to finish the job via medical ineptitude should the bullets not prove sufficient.

A. The Necessary Context in which to View the Planning of the Texas Trip:
1. Oswald, the Architecture of the Conspiracy, and The Implied Connections

Such planning would be commensurate with a conspiracy to murder the President and was present from the start. Consider only the detailed planning necessary to such a conspiracy, and the *architecture that it suggests*:

---

[1] Peter Dale Scott, *Deep Politics and the Death of JFK,* p. 11.
[2] Zirbel, *The Texas Connection,* p. 192.

269

1) to "run" Oswald to the Soviet Union as a "defector" just in time to sabotage Powers' U-2 flight and ruin the Eisenhower-Khrushchev summit;

2) to "run" Oswald *back* to the United States with the daughter of a Soviet military intelligence colonel in tow;

3) to "place" one or more Oswalds in New Orleans in both pro- and anti-Castro camps;

4) to place one or more "Oswalds" in the Soviet Embassy in Mexico City;

5) to place Oswald, and possibly Oswald look-alike Billy Lovelady, at the Texas School Book Depository on the day and scene of the crime;

6) to incriminate Oswald with two different rifles each with their own dark symbolic significance — a German Mauser and an Italian Mannlicher-Carcano — and then to remove the one, and plant Oswald's palm print on the other;

7) to plant the "Magic Bullet" on a stretcher in Dallas;

8) to have the power to force Ruby to shoot Oswald on national television; and finally,

9) Oswald himself, in the tapestry of his relationships to the groups involved in the assassination, from Nazis, to intelligence, to anti-Castro Cubans, to the NASA space agency, to the FBI and to the Mafia, becomes from the occult point of view, the necessary counter-balancing ritual "blood-offering" atonement for the murder of the president performed in behalf of those very same interests.[3]

---

[3] This highlights the occult significance of the Oswald "doubles" or *Doppelgängers*, for such doubles function, within esoteric doctrine, as "stand-ins" or substitutes for the real person. Thus, from the esoteric point of view, it is not important that the *real* Oswald was implicated with all these groups, just so long as his doubles were, and thus tying Oswald in with them *magically* in the public consciousness and act of consent to that perceived relationship via the funcitionality of the corporate person "Oswald", formed by the real one and the doubles, the carefully engineered "Oswald persona" of public perception. In esoteric doctrine, any such actions taken by them in Oswald's behalf are imputed to the real Oswald. Such "substitutionary atonement" thinking does form a component of the deepest black arts, and indicates a profound psychosis operative at a very deep level within the western cultural consciousness. But that is a subject for a whole other book.

With respect to the first six points, we have drawn the conclusion that *only* those with deep connections to intelligence could have pulled off these feats, and moreover, given the known historical circumstance of the "deal" between OSS Zurich Station chief and later CIA director Allen Dulles, and Nazi General Reinhard Gehlen, head of Nazi military intelligence in the Soviet Union during the Second World War, we know now that any intelligence contact with Oswald prior to and during his stay in the USSR *most probably would have come from Gehlen's organization acting in behalf of the CIA prior to and during Oswald's Soviet period, and possibly **without** the CIA after it.*[4] Moreover, we now know that Texas oilman H.L. Hunt, who had known contact with Oswald,[5] had managed to buy influence within this very same intelligence agency. In short, *Texas oil interests had the power and influence to run and implicate Oswald with or without the CIA's direct assistance.* We have already suggested that DeMohrenschildt, as Oswald's Dallas handler, was in direct contact with the Texas oilmen, and, given his murky World War Two background in Nazi intelligence, was probably their liaison to Gehlen's organization.[6]

2. The Assassination and the Removal of Normal Security Protocols: The Implied Connection

---

[4] This raises a disturbing question, one that I do not believe has ever been seriously entertained, much less suggested. It is now well-known that CIA counter-intelligence guru James Jesus Angleton was convinced – nay, obsessed – with the idea that there was a Soviet mole inside the CIA, to such an extent that the entire end of his career was spent unsuccessfully looking for that mole. But what if it was not a *Soviet* mole at all, but rather, a *Nazi* one? What if all the inexplicable intelligence failures of the CIA were not the result of the unthinkable, of a highly placed Soviet mole inside the organization passing along secrets to Moscow center, but of the even more unthinkable results and implications of the Faustian deal struck by Allen Dulles himself and General Reinhard Gehlen? And there is another possibility: if there was a Soviet mole, what if the mole was not inside the CIA, but inside of Gehlen's organization? Worse yet, what if Gehlen actually knew who it was, and continued to use him for his own purposes. In this respect, the German Felfe affair is worth another look, for there is something unconvincing about Gehlen's explanations of it.

[5] q.v. chapter one, p. 48.

[6] The alternative scenario is that Oswald was being run both by the CIA and the BND, in addition to his known FBI contacts once he was back in this country.

A very different set of groups and connections is implicated in the removal of the normal presidential security protocols on November 22, 1963. As was seen in chapter five, these involved the following major lapses of security:

1) Windows in high rise buildings were left open over Dealey Plaza;
2) No Secret Service agents were stationed on the roofs of these buildings;
3) The route chosen involved the motorcade slowing below the established 40mph speeds optimal for motorcade;
4) Military counter-intelligence units that should have been activated and present in Dallas on the day of the assassination were ordered to "stand down";

Additionally, we saw in chapter two that elements within the U.S. military and the Secret Service were implicated in the suppression or tampering with evidence.

In order for such lapses to occur, and in order for any agency of the government to have been involved in the alteration or suppression of evidence, someone in a position of authority would have had to be involved to issue such orders.

It is within the above two contexts that one should examine closely the role of Lyndon Johnson in the actual planning of Kennedy's Texas trip.

B. LBJ and the Planning of the Texas Trip
1. The Meeting between JFK, LBJ, and John Connally

Planning of the Texas trip was underway for at least a year previous to the actual event. By April 23, 1963, Vice President Johnson announced the fact that the President would make a tour of Texas. These plans were initially finalized at a meeting between President Kennedy, Vice President Johnson, and Texas Governor John Connally at the Cortez Hotel in El Paso.[7] It was Governor Connally who initially suggested a motorcade through downtown Dallas and put into motion the planning for it and arranged the place for the luncheon.[8]

In this regard it is important to note that once he was President, Lyndon Johnson always denied any involvement in the actual planning

---

[7] Zirbel, *The Texas Connection*, p. 5.
[8] Ibid, p. 6.

of the trip.[9] Zirbel makes a number of crucial observations with respect to this fact:

> These denials and minimizations were grossly untrue since Johnson was a major participant in urging and planning the trip.
>
> *The post-assassination denials by Johnson are important to show that Johnson knew his involvement with planning the trip was important from a criminal investigation standpoint. It demonstrated an opportunity to commit the crime.*
>
> It is uncontroverted that Johnson had substantial control over Kennedy's Texas trip and his itinerary. Kennedy placed the trip in Johnson and his friends (sic) hands since Texas was their home state. The trip had been under consideration for almost a year when, on April 23, 1963, Johnson announced that the President would visit Texas in the near future. Less than 45 days after this announcement the basic outline for a November trip to Texas was agreed upon in a private meeting between Kennedy, Johnson and Connally at the Cortez Hotel in Texas. The Secret Service, the bulk of the White House Staff, and the public, however, were not informed about the details of the trip until just weeks before it occurred. *From the outset, only the three knew the details.*[10]

From the standpoint of the normal architecture of conspiracies, there are two logical possibilities that must be considered:

1) LBJ, while intimately involved in the actual planning of the trip, may not have been involved in the actual planning of the *crime* itself. He, or Connally, may have let details of the trip slip to their contacts in Texas. Such lapses, while careless and clearly violations of normal security procedures, would nonetheless not implicate them in planning the murder; or,
2) Either LBJ or John Connally, or both, were planning the trip in full foreknowledge that it was a necessary component in an elaborate plan to murder the president and install Johnson in the White House. As such, any information as he or Connally leaked to their Texas contacts were deliberate leaks, made in order to place the patsy, Oswald, and the actual shooting teams, at Dealey Plaza.

---

[9] Ibid, p. 161.

[10] Zirbel, *The Texas Conenction,* p. 161, emphasis added.

With these two possibilities in mind, a further look at the evidence will enable us to decide which one is the more probable.

2. The Damning Details
a. Of the Trip Planning Committee

When the motorcade route was originally planned, the route proceeded directly on the standard downtown Dallas parade route, down Main Street — the center street in "Poseidon's trident" of streets that form the unusual feature of Dealey Plaza — and from there, directly on to the Stemmons freeway. The route eventually selected and approved, however, required the now infamous turn on to Houston, and then onto Elm in front of the Texas School Book Depository.[11]

The reason for the selection of this unusual route, a route that completely violated normal security protocols, the more so since a straight route was available, could have been for one reason and one reason only: to place the presidential limousine in a "kill" zone of triangulated crossfire, and at a distance from the target that sharpshooters could manage. Firing at a quick moving target on Main Street — the center street — from covered positions that were only available on the side streets, would have jeopardized operational success.

Needless to say, White House staffers were not oblivious to the dangers of this route, once the details were known to them. At this juncture, Kennedy sent his personal representative, Jerry Bruno, to Dallas to review the route and to meet with Governor John Connally.

> Over a month before the trip, Bruno demanded that the Texas planners' motorcade route not be taken. Bruno felt that the Texas planners' route created unnecessary risks for the President by making him a slow moving target in an open area. In late October, Bruno flew to Dallas to specifically meet with Connally to discuss more details of the President's trip. Before Bruno met with Connally, he talked with U.S. Senator Ralph Yarborough of Texas. Their discussion ended with Yarborough *warning Bruno that Johnson and Connally would be "...after John Kennedy in a minute if they thought they could get away with it politically."* Bruno then left Yarborough and went to see Connally as planned.

---

[11] Zirbel, *The Texas Connection*, p. 162. It should also be pointed out that Dallas Mayor Cabell, brother of the CIA's General Cabell whom Kennedy fired for his role in the Bay of Pigs fiasco, had a hand in this decision.

In his book, *The Advanceman*, Bruno described the unusual and bitter fight that he had with Connally over the Texas planner motorcade route. To this day, Bruno has not been able to understand why Governor Connally was so adamant that the death route be taken. According to Bruno, Connally became so insistent that the Texas planned parade route and luncheon site be followed that a strong argument broke out. When the Connally-Bruno dispute reached heated stages, according to Bruno, Connally got on the telephone to the White House and in Bruno's presence (with him hearing only one side of the conversation), it appeared that the White House agreed with his plans since he was in charge of the trip. Bruno then relented and let the proposed motorcade and luncheon site proceed as planned by the Texans. After the assassination Bruno learned that the White House Staff had **not** agreed with Connally at all.[12]

Pay attention to Senator Yarborough's comment, for it will become important in a moment, in the context of other things he said after the assassination. It is clear, however, that Yarborough suspected something, and was clearly implicating Johnson and Connally in it. And it is also clear from Bruno's recounting, that the Texas planners were insistent on the changes to the motorcade route that nullified normal security procedures, a crucial component, it will be recalled, of normal coups d'état.

To make matters worse, Connally flew to Washington on October 4, 1963 in order to make the final arrangements for the trip with Kennedy and Johnson. "According to members of the White House staff, Kennedy had been advised *not* to make the trip and those involved in his administration still insist that it was Johnson and Connally who urged that the trip go on as planned."[13] Later that evening, Johnson and Connally dined together privately. No details of this private dinner meeting have ever been forthcoming, and the Warren Commission ignored all these facts.[14] A mere 12 days after Connally's Washington, D.C. trip, Oswald obtained his job at the School Book Depository, when no job opening had even been posted.[15]

Once again, this constellation of facts would most likely have led any grand jury, had one ever been empanelled, to indict at least Connally if not Johnson, for the crime of conspiracy to murder the President.

---

[12] Zirbel, *The Texas Connection*, p. 163, italicized emphasis added, boldface emphasis in the original.

[13] Ibid, p. 164.

[14] Ibid.

[15] Ibid, p. 165.

b. Four Oddities: Senator Yarborough, Oswald's Initial Request for a Lawyer, Connally's Exclamation, and the Motorcade Press Car

The case for an actual conspiracy to commit the murder becomes very strong when one examines four other oddities: (1) Senator Yarborough's statements after the assassination regarding Vice President Johnson's behavior, (2) Oswald's initial request for legal representation, (3) Connally's exclamation just moments after he had been struck by one of the bullets, and (4) the motorcade's press car.

According to Senator Yarborough (whom it will be recalled was Johnson's political enemy, and whom Johnson wanted to ride in the President's limousine instead of his ally Governor Connally), the Vice President had his ear up to a small walkie-talkie whose volume was turned down quite low, at the very moment of the assassination.[16] Why would Johnson need to be listening to any radio communications at all, since these normally fell within the purview of the Secret Service in any case during motorcades? Why would Johnson, instead of waving to the crowds, be listening to a walkie-talkie?

One of the most telling, and damning, bits of evidence of a conspiracy in play in Dallas on that day was Oswald's initial request for a lawyer, *before he had even been charged with the crime of murdering the President.* On those occasions when he was being hustled back and forth between his jail cell and the interrogation room, Oswald would shout things to the press. On one such occasion, he shouted that he wanted a particular lawyer in New York City to represent him. This lawyer had gained fame in the 1950s for

> representing several criminal defendants in a criminal conspiracy case brought against them by the United States government. (Oswald's) request, made before Oswald was even formally charged with a crime, was *not* an oddball antic as some people originally believed. Rather, journalists and legal scholars have now concluded after research that this was a clue as to what actually may have happened. Oswald *wanted a lawyer 1,500 miles away* who was proficient in representing persons charged with a conspiracy crime against the government. While Oswald was never charged with conspiracy, and while the Warren Commission found no conspiracy to exist, Oswald at the time of his arrest — by his request for a particular lawyer, disclosed to the world

---

[16] Zirbel, *The Texas Connection,* p, 218.

the real criminal charges that he knew should have been issued against him.[17]

Indeed, Oswald's famous shouted statement to the press — "I'm just a patsy!" — reinforces Zirbel's interpretation of this strange request.

The third oddity is Governor Connally's own excited statement just moments after he had been shot. It will be recalled that Johnson argued bitterly with Kennedy the night before the assassination over the placement of his political enemy, Senator Ralph Yarborough, in the presidential limousine. Kennedy won the argument, and Governor Connally, and not Senator Yarborough, rode with the President.

When Connally himself was struck with a bullet, he exclaimed "Oh no, oh my God, *they* are going to kill us all." This is known in law as an "excited utterance" and is accepted as valid evidence in courts of law "because of the spontaneity of such statements following an event. Experience has shown that what a person blurts out in immediate response to a crisis is normally reliable and truthful since there is not time to think or make up a story." So why would Governor Connally blurt out "*they* are going to kill us all"? This statement, plus the fact that Johnson originally wanted *Yarborough* to ride in the place where Connally actually rode suggests that Yarborough himself may have also been a target. Connally's "excited utterance," in other words, is yet more evidence that there was a conspiracy, and that he knew about it.

Finally, but by no means the least important oddity, is the fact that the original planning for the motorcade called for the press car to follow behind the Secret Service bodyguards' car, which followed directly behind the presidential limousine. But, at the last minute, on the day of the motorcade, the press car was moved to the very end of the motorcade, bringing up the rear, an action that deliberately prevented the press from filming and photographing the moment of the crime.[18] To this day, no one knows who ordered the change.

While none of these details in and of themselves are damning of Lyndon Johnson, viewed together they do paint a consistent picture, not only of foreknowledge of a conspiracy on the part of Connally and Oswald, but of detailed planning in its execution, planning that included Johnson. Johnson's actions in wishing to place his political enemy in the presidential limousine, and then listening to a walkie-talkie at the moment of the crime itself, are reasonably viewed as suspicious.

---

[17] Zirbel, *The Texas Connection*, p. 181.
[18] Ibid, p. 172.

Finally, there is one last point to be mentioned. While there are numerous, and in my view, almost insurmountable problems, with her story,[19] Johnson's alleged mistress of 20 years, Madeline Duncan Brown, claimed that the plot to assassinate Kennedy was actually hatched as early as the Democratic National Convention in 1960, between Johnson and Texas oil man H.L. Hunt.[20]

Whether or not her story will ultimately be proven true or not is a matter that only assassination research and time will tell, though for the moment, it does not look good for her claims.

Nonetheless, the planning, as has been seen, deeply involved Lyndon Johnson, and as we saw in chapter two, Johnson is heavily implicated after the crime in the suppression and actual alteration of evidence. Only Johnson was in a position of sufficient authority after the crime to strong arm federal agencies into these activities.

And only Johnson was in a similar position during the planning of the Texas trip to use his power to suppress normal security procedures. These would be enough at least to gain Johnson an indictment for the crime, but perhaps not a conviction had it gone to trial. The question that remains is, do his activities after the assassination implicate him, at the minimum, as an accessory after the fact?

---

[19] See Dave Perry, "Texas in the Morning Imagination," http://davesjfk.com/browns.html.

[20] "Madeleine Duncan Brown," *Wikipedia*, en.wikipedia.org/wiki/Medeleine _Duncan_Brown

9
LBJ AND THE AFTERMATH:
ACCESSORY AFTER THE FACT

*"It is not known that Johnson himself plotted against Kennedy, or needed
to; his backers included men far more experienced in intrigue."*
Peter Dale Scott[1]

O ne of the surest indicators that there was a conspiracy to
assassinate President Kennedy and to install a new government
friendly to the interests of the coalescing groups involved in the
crime is the fact that the Warren Report's "lone nut" theory of Oswald
was actually proposing a "solution" to the crime where the principal
perpetrator had no other known or plausible motive for committing it,
other than just plain old kookiness, whereas the principal suspects
surveyed in the previous pages, including Johnson himself, did have
ample motives to do so.[2] The Warren Commission had, in other words,
done something completely unique and unprecedented in the history of
criminal investigations: it had abandoned motive as a clue to the solution
of the crime and as a means of determining its probable perpetrators.[3]

[handwritten margin note: Commission abandoned motive.]

The Warren Commissioners were themselves, of course, all carefully
selected and appointed by President Lyndon Johnson (after careful and
close consultation with FBI director J. Edgar Hoover), and this fact, plus
Johnson's own role in the alteration and suppression of evidence, should
be viewed as part of a case implicating him as an accessory to the crime
after the fact, if indeed he was not an actual conspirator.

There can be no doubt that not only was Johnson in a *position* to
order the alteration and suppression of evidence, but that he actually *did*
so. In chapter two we examined the case that *implicated* Johnson in the
suppression and alteration of crucial forensic evidence stemming from
the autopsy of President Kennedy. We now add to this building case the
final component of his actual and explicit involvement in the deliberate
tampering with the evidence of a crime. It is this tampering with the
evidence, and the establishment of the Warren Commission itself with its
carefully pre-arranged conclusion of Oswald acting alone, that
establishes Johnson, at the minimum, as an accessory after the fact.

---

[1] Peter Dale Scott, *Deep Politics and the Death of JFK*, p. 227.
[2] Zirbel, *The Texas Connection*, p. 23.
[3] Ibid, p. 112.

A. Johnson's Tampering with the Evidence of the Limousine, and Other Post-Assassination Evidence And Investigation Tampering

John Fitzgerald Kennedy was not even buried when President Lyndon Johnson began the process of tampering with the evidence. The first on his list of things to be taken care of was Kennedy's limousine itself, which Johnson ordered to Detroit to be stripped and completely refurbished. The entire interior of the car, including the windows and the all important windshield that showed clear evidence of being struck by bullets in the films of the assassination, were stripped and destroyed, and the blood stains and other tissues were removed. This, notes researcher Craig Zirbel, is legally in and of itself a crime. [4]

Additionally, Johnson's close aide and assistant, Cliff Carter, ordered Secret Service agents to retrieve Governor Connally's clothing, which was then laundered, thus destroying key forensic evidence that might have indicated more than one shooting team. [5] As if that were not enough, Johnson himself ordered Carter to call three people:

> ...(The) first call was to Dallas District Attorney Henry Wade *ordering him not* to allege a conspiracy — whether "he could prove it or not" and to "just charge Oswald with plain murder." Wade charged Oswald alone with the murder. The second and third calls were to Dallas Police Chief Curry and Captain Fritz. Each man received similar calls from Carter insisting that all local evidence be immediately turned over to the FBI in Washington (who had no jurisdiction in the case)[6] ...when people refused to obey Cliff Carter's orders, a follow up demand actually came via a personal telephone call from President Lyndon B. Johnson. The persuasion obviously worked because within less than 12 hours after Kennedy's murder all evidence collected in the case to that point was sent to Washington, D.C., including Oswald's gun and the "miracle bullet."[7]

This should raise one's "suspicion meters" to the danger zone, because the crime for which Oswald was charged, murder, was a charge not involving conspiracy, and therefore, no federal jurisdiction could occur. The trial of Oswald would have taken place in Texas.

---

[4] Zirbel, *The Texas Connection*, p. 218.

[5] Ibid, p. 15.

[6] Ed. note: at that time there was no federal law in place giving the federal government jurisdiction in the case of a murdered president outside of the District of Columbia. Q.v. Zirbel, p. 18.

[7] Ibid, p. 18.

280

So why send all the evidence for a looming Texas trial to Washington, D.C.? "One suggested answer," says Zirbel, "is that it was never part of the plan to let Oswald live long enough to be tried — at least that is what happened and the shipping of the evidence out Friday night at Lyndon Johnson's request is consistent with such a plan."[8] Indeed, there was evidence that such was the plan, evidence we shall encounter in the next section.

Other evidence tampering occurred that does not show the direct intervention of Lyndon Johnson, but that nevertheless indicates a wider involvement of other people in evidence tampering. One of the most famous examples of this is the Stemmons Freeway sign on Elm street, which shows up clearly in some of the Zapruder film versions. In some photographs, this sign apparently had been struck by a bullet. If so, then this would have been evidence of four shots, and since the official version of Oswald the "lone nut" firing off three shots from an inaccurate Mannlicher-Carcano at a moving retreating target was already becoming the standard spin, such evidence had to be suppressed since it represented testimony to more than one shooter, and therefore ipso facto, to a conspiracy. The sign was removed and disappeared shortly after the assassination, but no one knows to this day who ordered it done, nor where the sign went.[9] Two candidates, however, immediately suggest themselves: Dallas mayor Earl Cabell, and Texas Governor John Connally.

One final and crucial bit of evidence tampering that once again clearly implicates Johnson are the tapes of the press conference held by the Dallas Parkland hospital doctors after the President had been pronounced dead. The press conference was barely over when "the Secret Service, under orders from someone, seized all tapes of the press conference and refused to release them."[10] Johnson was, of course, at that point of time still in Dallas and already the *de facto* President of the United States, and thus had authority over the Secret Service.

It is also crucial to point out that Johnson moved very deliberately after the assassination in conformity with the operational requirements of coups d'état by neutralizing potential opposition, and he did so in two significant ways. At the time that Johnson was acting to forestall a Texas investigation of the crime via a trial of Oswald, by having all the evidence ordered to Washington, D.C., there was another problem:

---

[8] Zirbel, *The Texas Connection,* p. 16.
[9] Ibid, p. 13.
[10] Ibid, p. 14.

Attorney General Robert Kennedy, J. Edgar Hoover's boss, and the head of the Justice Department. If for any reason the investigation became federal, then Robert Kennedy would be the one conducting it. He thus formed a nucleus of power around which a potential threat could grow. Additionally, Robert Kennedy and Lyndon Johnson "hated each other."[11]

The second potential threat that Johnson had to neutralize was the growing public suspicion and outcry in the wake of Ruby's nationally-televised murder of Oswald. On the Monday following this second "media murder" the outcry had grown so strong that Johnson moved to quell it, by proposing a special Texas commission "to investigate the crime composed of distinguished Texans whom he personally would select. The public hostility to this proposal was even stronger."[12] By Monday morning, November 25, 1963, in other words, President Johnson was faced with a snowballing popular suspicion regarding the tragic events of the previous weekend on the one hand, and on the other hand was faced with Robert Kennedy's Department of Justice.

Johnson neutralized both potential oppositions by his Executive Order #11130 that created the Warren Commission, effectively doing an end run around any potential Texas state, or Federal Congressional or Department of Justice investigations.[13]

Succinctly stated, Johnson followed *exactly* the operational requirements of classic coups d'état in the immediate aftermath of the coup by neutralizing the potential opposition.

B. Ruby's Statements, LBJ's Actions, and the Johnson-Ruby Connection

There are other little incriminating clues scattered throughout Johnson's post-assassination behavior, and it is worth mentioning three of them in order to set the context for what may be the most damning evidence of all. First, Johnson ordered all of President Kennedy's belongings removed from the Oval Office, with the sole exception of a blood red presidential rug.[14] Secondly, he immediately, upon his return to Washington and occupancy of the White House, fired President Kennedy's secretary. Thirdly, and finally, in what may only be called an act of unjustifiable callousness and harshness, he ordered Mrs. Jackie

---

[11] Zirbel, *The Texas Connection*, p. 20.

[12] Ibid, p. 19.

[13] Ibid, p. 20.

[14] For the significance of this fact it is best to let my friend Richard Hoagland speak!

Kennedy to be moved out of the White House by Monday morning, the day of her dead husband's state funeral![15]

It was almost as if — with the sole exception of the red presidential rug — Johnson did not want anything around to remind him of the assassination.

Lyndon Johnson and Jack Ruby, Oswald's murderer, ran in similar circles and could both boast connections to the Texas oil barons. Ruby, after his first trial and conviction, wrote several letters in which he attempted to tell as much as he dared. In one such letter, Ruby minced no words: "They alone planned the killing, by they I mean Johnson and others... you may learn quite a bit about Johnson and how he has fooled everyone..."[16] But that was not all.

Ruby, as is known, was tried, convicted, and sentenced to death for the murder of Oswald. The conviction was, however, overturned on appeal because the trial judge not only set aside Ruby's lawyers' hundreds of affidavits stating that Ruby could not receive a fair trial in Dallas, but he also would not excuse potential jurors who had watched Ruby execute Oswald on national television. Such egregious errors of jurisprudence guaranteed that any conviction would be overturned and that Ruby would have to be re-tried.

This is, of course, exactly what happened.

After the Appellate Court had thrown out Ruby's conviction, the Dallas District Attorney who had prosecuted the case, Henry Wade,. began to negotiate a plea bargain with Ruby's lawyers, which included a plea of guilty to a lesser charge and an offer to allow Ruby *to go completely free if he did so!*[17] Ruby, of course, died of "convenient cancer" before the negotiations could be concluded, adamantly insisting to family and friends that he was being slowly murdered by the injection of cancerous cells![18]

Shades of Dr. Mary Sherman and Dr. Alton Ochsner!

In 1964, as Ruby was waiting the results of his appeal, he composed a sixteen page letter to a fellow inmate who was leaving the jail. According to assassination researcher Jim Marrs, "Ruby asked the prisoner to memorize the names and facts in the letter, then destroy it."[19] The prisoner, however, decided to keep it and sell it, and it eventually

---

[15] Zirbel, *The Texas Connection*, p. 116.
[16] Ibid, p. 207.
[17] Ibid, p. 210.
[18] Ibid, pp. 210-211.
[19] Marrs, *Crossfire: the Plot That Killed Kennedy*, p. 430.

wound up in the possession of Penn Jones, who had purchased it from a New York autograph collector named Charles Hamilton, who had had the handwriting in the letter appraised. That appraisal concluded that the letter was authentic.[20]

Given all that we have now discovered about the coalescing groups in the assassination — Mafia, rogue elements within American intelligence, Cubans, Nazis, Texas oil barons, FBI, Secret Service, and so on — the letter makes extremely interesting reading, despite its rambling character:

> First, you must realize that the people here want everyone to think I am crazy, so if what I know is actually (sic), and then no one will believe me, because of my supposed insanity. Now, I know that my time is running out... they plan on doing away with (me)... As soon as you get out you must read Texan looks at Lyndon (*A Texan Looks at Lyndon: A Study in Illegitimate Power*, by J. Evetts Haley; Palo Duro Press, 1964) and it might open your eyes to a lot of things. *This man (Johnson) is a Nazi in the worst order.* For over a year now they have been doing away with my people... don't believe the Warren report, that was only put out to make me look innocent in that it would throw the Americans and all the European country's (sic) off guard... There are so many things that have been played with success that it would take all night to write them out... There wouldn't be any purpose of my writing you all of this unless you were convinced of how much I loved my country... *I am going to die a horrible death anyway,* so what would I have to gain by writing all this. So you must believe me... *Johnson is going to try to have an all-out war with Russia* and when that happens, Johnson and his cohorts will be on the side-lines where they won't get hurt, while the Americans may get wiped out. *The only way this can be avoided is that if Russia would be informed as to (who) the real enemies are,* and in that way they won't be tricked into starting a war with the U.S...[21]

Marrs' own comments regarding this unique letter are also worth noting:

> These comments will always intrigue researchers. Was Ruby merely speculating or were his messages born of secret knowledge? Did he know that Johnson and the people behind him wanted war — only mistaking Russia for Asia? And were his warnings of Nazis taking over

---

[20] Marrs, *Crossfire: The Plot That Killed Kennedy*, p. 430.
[21] Cited in Jim Marrs, *Crossfire: The Plot That Killed Kennedy*, p. 430, emphasis added.

rooted somewhere in a knowledge of the mentality of the people he knew were behind the assassination?[22]

But given the fact that Ruby *did* die a horrible death, given the fact that he was acquainted with the Hunts and attended the same gambling clubs as they, and given the fact that they in turn had deep connections to rogue elements both within the CIA and with the much more sinister connections with the German *Bundesnachrichtendienst* of Nazi General Reinhard Gehlen, not to mention that Johnson *did* commit to an "almost all out" war in Vietnam with Russian client state North Vietnam, and given the fact that Jack Ruby was Jewish, one must entertain the possibility that Ruby *knew exactly what he was talking about.*

For researcher Craig Zirbel, when Ruby's statements are viewed together with Johnson's actions "it becomes crystal clear that Johnson was aware that Kennedy was going to be murdered."[23] Even if that is *not* the case, it is certainly clear that Johnson, by his policies and behaviors after the assassination, acted as if he knew who was ultimately behind the murder, for at every turn, he acted in their interests as well as his own, in suppressing any evidence tending to incriminate him, or them. Nowhere more did he do this more clearly than in his selection of the members of the Warren Commission itself.

---

[22] Marrs, *Crossfire: The Plot That Killed Kennedy*, p. 431.
[23] Zirbel, *The Texas Connection*, p. 223.

10
THE ARCHITECTURE OF THE CONSPIRACY

*"...(The) trouble the researchers have met in grappling with the
conspiracy to kill the President was that it was simply overwhelming in
its proportions and in its complexity. It was a monstrous conundrum, the
likes of which, in al the annals of crime, had never before been
encountered... (There) were too many possibilities, too many questions,
too many possible motives and too many suspects... (the) basic problem
with examining the assassination data was that the conspiracy to kill the
President was perceived as one enormous plot and that perception of it
was calculated to make it appear overwhelming."*
Matthew Smith[1]

It has been called a conspiracy, and a coup d'état, and there are clearly
elements of both present in the assassination of President Kennedy.
But as has by now been made abundantly clear, to call it a coup d'état
or a conspiracy in any classic sense is to ignore the sheer size and scope
of the coalescing interests represented in it. Assassination literature
abounds with books arguing that this or that group surveyed in the
previous pages was *the* group that planned and executed the crime. The
trouble is, arguable and plausible cases can be advanced for all of them.

We are not therefore dealing with a conspiracy nor a coup d'état in
the standard senses of the terms, for all the groups represented would, in
some fashion, have at least *learned* of a plot to kill the President, and
acquiesced in them for the protection of their own interests, interests that
were threatened by Kennedy. The real question is, who *are* the *deepest*
players and therefore the most likely planners? We need not think of a
vast circle or "committee" of people. Given the connections of all of
these groups, no more than one representative from each would have
been needed in the "planning committee," if even that many; in other
words, no more than, say, ten people might have been involved at the
very nucleus at the maximum, and possibly no more than three or four,
as will be seen in a moment.

So how does one speculate and rationalize the putative architecture
of this conspiracy?

This book has argued that there are three significant clues that have
been suggested by various researchers, but that have never been

---

[1] Matthew Smith, *JFK: The Second Plot* (Edinburgh and London:
Mainstream Publishing, 2008), p. 265.

adequately assembled into one coherent picture. These three things I believe to be the salient clues to its overall architecture and these three have formed the methodology followed throughout this book:

1) The Torbitt Document, with its allegations of FBI, NASA, and rogue intelligence involvement, inclusive of rogue CIA groups and a shadowy "Fascist" or "Nazi International". Indeed, as this book has attempted to demonstrate as a part of its underlying methodology, the specific claims of the Torbitt Document have rarely — if ever — been adequately investigated and hence, few if any have attempted to rationalize its claims of the groups involved at the highest echelons of its planning and execution; yet, as we have thus far seen, plausible rationalizations abound even for its more sensational allegations;

2) Lyndon Johnson's role, statements, and particularly, his activities in the aftermath of the crime in forestalling any actual competent criminal investigation of it, activities that included the active and direct suppression and tampering with evidence by Johnson or his personal staff;

3) Johnson's selection of the Warren Commissioners, which, upon close examination, reveals one significant thing: whether or not Johnson was involved in the actual planning of the crime, it is clear that if he was not, he nevertheless accurately read and very clearly assessed the interests of the groups that *may* have been involved with it very clearly, and was careful to select commissioners who would represent and protect those interests.

On this view, these three components become vital clues into unraveling the actual architecture of the conspiracy, with the Warren Commission members functioning as a kind of Rosetta stone or template to unravel those interests. The last version of our template of the three levels of the crime — its execution itself, the running and positioning of Oswald and his doubles, and the post-crime cover-up — looked like this:

The Murder Itself	Anti-Castro Cubans The Mafia FBI (Hoover) CIA Big Oil The Military Bankers (Federal Reserve) Nazis	Anti-Castro Cubans The Mafia FBI (Hoover) CIA Big Oil The Military Bankers (Federal Reserve) Nazis Masons (details of the crime, motive of transformation of social consciousness)	Anti-Castro Cubans The Mafia FBI (Hoover) CIA Big Oil The Military Bankers (Federal Reserve) Nazis Masons (details of the crime, motive of transformation of social consciousness)
The Framing of Oswald (via doubles, planted evidence, etc)	FBI (Hoover) CIA The Secret Service The Military Nazis (De Mohrenschildt) Texas Big Oil (De Morhenschildt)	FBI (Hoover) CIA The Secret Service The Military Nazis (De Mohrenschildt) Texas Big Oil (De Mohrenschildt)	FBI (Hoover) CIA The Secret Service The Military Nazis (De Mohrenschildt) Texas Big Oil (De Mohrenschildt)
The Long-term Cover-up	FBI (Hoover) CIA (Dulles) Bankers (McCloy) Nazis (McCloy) Masons (Hoover and Warren) *Secondary Level:* Mafia (Boggs) Nazis Texas Big Oil (De Mohrenschildt)	FBI (Hoover) CIA (Dulles) Bankers (McCloy) Nazis (McCloy Masons (Hoover and Warren) *Secondary Level:* Mafia (Boggs) Nazis Texas Big Oil (De Mohrenschildt)	FBI (Hoover) CIA (Dulles) Bankers (McCloy) Nazis (McCloy) Masons (Hoover and Waren) *Secondary Level:* Mafia (Boggs) Nazis Texas Big Oil (De Mohrenschildt)

Let us look closer at the four Warren Commissioners represented in the last stage of the chart, for their presence indicates that the deep interests that they represent had the means, the motive, and the opportunity to perpetuate a cover-up. These are as follows:

1) *Congressman Hale Boggs of Louisiana:* As was noted in previous pages, Boggs was heavily tied to the Mafia machine of New Orleans mobster Carlos Marcello, whom the Kennedy administration had unceremoniously deported from the United States. Upon his return, Marcello vowed to get Kennedy, and also indicated that a patsy would be selected and positioned to take the fall for the crime. In retrospect, Marcello's statements were unerringly accurate, and this suggests a strong possibility that the Mafia was indeed represented in aspects of the planning and cover-up.

2) *Wall Street Attorney John J. McCloy:* McCloy is perhaps the most crucial key to the deep architecture, for McCloy represents a veritable cluster of the coalescing bureaucratic, corporate, and intelligence interests:

    a) Prior to World War Two, McCloy was the American attorney for the notorious, and notoriously powerful, German chemicals cartel I.G. Farben. As such, he was invited to sit in Adolf Hitler's box at the 1936 Berlin Olympics;

    b) After World War Two, McCloy was the High Commissioner for Germany, and in that role, pardoned thousands of Nazis to expedite their transfer to the United States under Operation Paperclip. It could indeed be said that McCloy played the pivotal role in the transfer not only of Nazi scientists and technology to American shores, but through them, the transfer of Nazi ideology as well;

    c) McCloy was also an attendee of early Bilderberger meetings as well, along with fellow Warren Commissioner Allen Dulles.[2] I have noted elsewhere that one of the early purposes of the Bilderberger Group was to coordinate financial and political policy between the surviving post-war Nazi International, literally awash in liquid assets, on the one hand, and the Anglo-American corporate world on the other.[3] McCloy, given his vast corporate connections as a Wall Street lawyer, as the former American attorney for the notorious I.G. Farben Cartel, and as a former Allied High Commissioner for Germany, was a perfect candidate for such meetings, and therefore we are justified in viewing him

---

[2] Daniel Estulin, *The True Story of the Bilderberger Group* (Walterville, Oregon: TrineDay LLC, 2007), p. 28.
[3] See my *Babylon's Banksters*, pp. 64-75.

290

as a key liaison between those two elites, and a key representative of their interests on the Warren Commission. As such, McCloy also parallels the role alleged for the lawyer Bloomfield in the Torbitt Document, for Bloomfield, in forming Permindex, is another symbol of the deep understanding and coalescence of interests of the Anglo-American and post-war Fascist elites;

d) More generally speaking, in these positions, and in his position as a member of a powerful Wall Street legal firm, McCloy was more than familiar with the niceties of international finance and corporate power, and thus was the perfect choice to represent and protect those interests on the Commission as well. So while Texas petroleum interests are *not directly* represented on the commission, McCloy, via his experience with I.G. Farben and all its pre-war deals with American firms such as Standard Oil and DuPont, was more than able to represent their interests. In fact, his selection for membership I believe was made precisely in order to have someone represent those interests who could not be directly tied to the Texas oilmen but who nonetheless fully appreciated the deep extent of their connections.

3) *Former CIA Director Allen Dulles:* Allied to McCloy is Allen Dulles, whose selection is clearly made in order to protect the interests of the CIA and other American intelligence agencies that are clearly implicated in the planning, if for no other reason than the CIA's previous experience in running successful foreign coups. But there is one more crucial thing to note:

a) It was Allen Dulles who as the OSS station chief in Zurich, Switzerland during World War Two negotiated the deal with Nazi General Reinhard Gehlen to maintain Gehlen's military intelligence organization entirely intact after the war, and to run it as an espionage ring inside the Soviet bloc. Thus it was Dulles who also participated to a great degree, along with McCloy, in ensuring the post-war survival of *structured organizations* of Nazi power. It was this element, I believe, that Premier Khrushchev alluded to in his statements to Eisenhower that certain rogue groups within American intelligence were possibly formulating policy without the oversight of the executive branch. It was this group that I also believe was intended to be the target of Eisenhower's famous "military-industrial complex" speech upon leaving

office. This group, in conjunction with its now known
connections to organized crime's money laundering schemes,
via Permindex and other CIA fronts, that had deep
connections to the other groups of coalescing interests;

4) *Chief Justice Earl Warren:* Finally, we have noted the curious and
deeply occult and Masonic aspects of the assassination itself.
Chief Justice Warren, as a high ranking Mason, founded the
research and intelligence lodge of American masonry, the *Ars
Quattuor Coronati* lodge, and hence, was in a perfect position to
represent those interests. He, with his and Dulles' close contact
with 33rd degree Freemason and FBI director J. Edgar Hoover,
had close control over steering the Warren Commission's *Report*
in the sole direction of Lee Harvey Oswald acting alone.

These commissioners are thus suggestive of three groups at the
deepest levels of the conspiracy whose long-term interests had to be
represented and protected: (1) Rogue elements within the CIA and
American intelligence, allied with the high corporate Anglo-American
elite, (2) the Nazis or Fascists, deeply embedded within the fabric of the
American military-industrial complex and within NASA, and represented
also in independent agencies such as the German BND, Permindex, and
other Nazi "corporate fronts," and (3) a group or interest that we may call
"deeply occulted elements" or "deep Masonry," an institution also deeply
embedded in American "parapolitical" power structures.

It is important to note that while two of these groups — the Masons
and the Nazis — would seem the most improbable players in the
conspiracy, that they nonetheless are heavily represented on the
Commission, and that they *alone* would have had the detailed knowledge
to plan the occult and ritual aspects of the crime. Moreover, the presence
of McCloy, with all his murky pre- and post-war connections to the
Nazis, weirdly corroborates Jack Ruby's "wilder" statements that Nazis
were somehow involved in the assassination. It also corroborates similar
statements made in the Torbitt Document itself. It should also be noted
that the sheer size and scope of the groups represented by these four
commissioners — the Mafia, American Intelligence, the corporate
community, the Nazis, and the "Deep Masonry" — also corroborates
other well-known statements of Ruby, namely, that the structure of the
plot was very large.

It is in this context that Lyndon Johnson's selection of these
members, in close consultation with Hoover, should be viewed and
understood, for *at the minimum*, their selection by Johnson indicates that

if he was *not* involved in the actual crime, then he was politically astute enough to know who *was*, and *acted to protect their interests* in the formation of the cover-up itself. In short, he was an accessory after the fact.

Assembling all the clues presented and argued in this book, we come up with the following basic architecture:

1) *Texas Petroleum Interests* were clearly involved and implicated, and given its connections via the Hunts to the German BND and General Gehlen's organization (which probably was operationally responsible for running Oswald into the Soviet Union and maintaining surveillance and contact with him there), the Texas oil barons, contrary to popular opinion, *would* have had the ability to create doubles (a standard Nazi security and intelligence practice) and position Oswald as a patsy at the Book Depository. Moreover, they would have had the intelligence and Mafia connections to select, coordinate, and position the actual shooting teams as well. In this respect, De Mohrenschildt's role as Oswald's "handler" in Dallas is crucial, for he had connections to both groups. This running of Oswald by the German BND would have been initially done under CIA auspices, thus implicating the agency whether or not that relationship continued after Oswald's return to the United States.

2) *The Mafia, "Deep Masonry," and the Nazi organizations* would very likely have provided the actual "soldiers" on the ground to do the shooting. Ruby's involvement in the murder of Oswald, doubtless under some sort of duress and pressure, is testament enough to Mafia involvement at an operational level. In this respect it is also important to understand the symbolism suggested by the two different rifles that were fastened to the crime, the initially-reported German Mauser, and the Italian Mannlicher-Carcano. These, like the Masonic symbolism of the "Three Tramps," is part and parcel of occult procedure, for it is a doctrine in the performance of ritual magical acts, that the intended targets be informed at some level and in some way as to who is committing and performing the act. The latter connection would have also had the means and motive, along with the deeply occulted structures of power within NASA, to prevent Kennedy's sharing of space secrets with the Russians, secrets that were a potential goldmine of ancient information and technologies. This, perhaps, was the deepest and most hidden

motivation for the assassination, for those two deep parapolitical powers — the Masons and the Nazis — both had esoteric doctrines concerning humanity's ancient off-planet origins, and the technological sophistication of a long-vanished civilization that once existed. Whatever might be recovered from any Moon missions had, therefore, to be kept out of Soviet hands and monopolized by those groups.[4] The very involvement of these two groups would have implicated allied rogue elements within the FBI and CIA as well, and these two agendas were heavily implicated and were doubtless involved in aspects of the planning of the coup, as has been seen in previous pages.

But in the final analysis, it is these two groups — the Texas oil barons, and the Mafia-Nazi nexus — that form the deep core, for they tie together Ruby's statements and actions, and they are connected to all the other groups. Notably, Lyndon Johnson is tied to *all* of them, and *only* Johnson would have had the authority both before and after the assassination to order the Secret Service and other Federal agencies to lift normal security protocols and to tamper with the evidence, as he clearly did. This raises dramatically the possibility that Johnson was indeed involved at a high level, and as an actual conspirator, as Torbitt originally maintained, and as Ruby also indicated.

Succinctly put, from the examination surveyed in this book, there is abundant evidence that the original allegations of the Torbitt Document, and the statements of Jack Ruby, concerning a deep and widely extended conspiracy, are true, even in their more fantastic elements.

Regardless if one accepts this analysis of the deep core of the conspiracy, the assassination discloses disturbing features of the parapolitical structures of power in America, the structures that were there *before* the assassination, and that stepped boldly and brazenly onto the stage, planned and executed a treasonous crime, and overthrew the government that threatened their varied interests. The perpetrators are

---

[4] In this respect it is worth noting two things that I mentioned in my book *Roswell and the Reich*, namely, that (1) the NASA Nazis had successfully, and ominously, duplicated within NASA the exact command structure that they occupied in Hitler's rocket program in Nazi Germany, and (2) that American counter-intelligence, in the wake of the Roswell incident, had concluded that many of the Nazi Paperclip scientists were maintaining some sort of contact with Latin America and were receiving funds from undisclosed, non-American, sources. (See *Roswell and the Reich*, pp. 352-357)

now long dead, as are all of the Warren Commissioners. Hoover and Johnson are dead.

But the interests that they represented — government by gunshot, conspiracy, cabal, occult magic — have not disappeared. America has been governed since then as a banana republic, with a succession of sock puppet "leaders" responsive only to those interests and not to the public good. We have been rocked by scandal and crisis after scandal and crisis.

The real question is, what lessons are we to learn from it? What can we *do* about it?

What lesson or lessons emerge from it all?

There is one over-riding answer, deeply embedded within the history of western culture and thought, which made corporate power, the covert power of bureaucracies and intelligence agencies, possible. There is one answer that lies at the root of their genocidal policies, one answer that lies at the core of all magical working, and that answer is that *person and soul are identical, equivalent entities in the ritual ontologies of power.* It is, indeed, an old theological error of the western churches, Rome leading the pack. This is neither the time nor the place to discuss in detail that error nor how it arose.

But consider its effects in history and law and the rise of corporate power and the modern abuses thereof. Our ordinary language usage teaches the distinction of these two things; we say "I *have* a soul" but "I *am* a person," identifying the former with the functions common to human nature, but individuating them absolutely uniquely in the person which is never reducible to them. To equate and identify the functions of the soul with the uniqueness of the person is therefore an egregious error. America may have a corporate "soul" but no one speaks of "the person of America," though vested interests are bending every effort to transform America, and other countries, into nothing but corporations, and to say precisely that.

It enshrines itself in western law in the form of the "corporate person," a special charter, deeply embedded in feudalism, of a collection of individual persons engaged in the performance of common tasks for a specialized interest, thus enabling the criminal and conspirator to cloak their activities behind an enormous power in the sanction of law, for how does one *punish* such a corporate person? How does one arrest the galloping power of corporations bent on "whole person management," of calling people in to work for useless meetings on their days off, and intruding themselves into all aspects of private human life? How does one arrest the ever-growing tendency to speak in the tyrannical language of "the team player" and restore the individual person and his or her creativity?

It is a doctrine that readily lends itself to occult manipulations such as have been described here, for one individual, acting in the capacity of the corporate person and at the pinnacles of corporate power, can damn the whole. We know the doctrine well, for it is the doctrine at the core of western Christendom: original sin, and Adam is in that doctrine the original corporate person.[5] It was the doctrine that made God himself the heavenly banker intent upon collecting an infinite debt, and mankind the debtor forever working it off but incapable of doing so.

Until we understand that this doctrine, deeply embedded within the western consciousness, allows for, indeed, demands the moral transference of guilt and debt via the mechanism of association with the corporate person, we will not understand that it is the sole basis for all occult operations of magic, of the transference of power, guilt, and mentality from one person to another.

It is this doctrine that is the basis of all occult and magical working of the ritual sacrifice in general, and in particular the alchemical transformation of the American consciousness that played itself out that day in Dealey Plaza, involving all in America's "original sin" by the act of consent. Such power cannot be had nor exercised without the presupposition of the corporate person who stands, as one, for all.

If the deep parapolitical powers that planned and executed the Kennedy assassination and that have thereby maintained themselves to this day are ever to be successfully rooted out and their power broken, this special status in law, this egregious error, must sooner or later, be addressed, and overturned, and the sovereignty of the real human person, and not the corporate person, restored. Mere regulation — though a step in the right direction — will not do it alone. The doctrine itself must eventually be challenged, and that equation, which has taken such deep hold on the western mind and through it, the world, must be jettisoned.

The tide has already turned, for in the time of John Kennedy — this author remembers it well — it was somewhat of a political axiom that "what is good for Detroit is good for America." We have heard echoes of this in recent times with the 21st century variation on that theme: "too big to fail." But the events of the past three to four decades, as corporations

---

[5] It should be noted that this doctrine, in its classical Western form, is common both to Roman Catholicism and to all Protestant and evangelical churches in one form or another. It is *not*, however, the doctrine of the eastern churches.

have shipped wholesale America's once mighty manufacturing base overseas, as they have recklessly expanded and then ruthlessly and with draconian precision contracted credit, the old adage does not have the currency and cachet with the American people that it once had. Many have woken up to the abuses of corporate power in this country and abroad, but without understanding the nature and root of that abuse: the doctrine of the corporate person itself. Kennedy was both the victim of and sacrifice to that god, for he did not threaten the public good, but merely a group of coalescing corporate and bureaucratic interests, and the doctrine of the corporate person at the root of their power.

BIBLIOGRAPHY:
WORKS CITED OR CONSULTED:

Bellant, Russ. *Old Nazis, The New Right, and the Republican Party.* Boston. South End Press. 1991. ISBN 0-89608-418-3.

Collins, Philip Darrell, and Collins, Paul David. *The Ascendancy of the Scientific Dictatorship: An Examination of the Epistemic Autocracy, from the 19th to the 21st Century.* BookSurge LLC. 2006. ISBN 1-4196-3932-3.

Crenshaw, Charles A., M.D. *JFK: Conspiracy of Silence.* New York. Signet-Penguin. 1992. ISBN 0-451-40346-0.

Epstein, Edward Jay. *Legend: the Secret World of Lee Harvey Oswald.* New York. Reader's Digest Press, McGraw-Hill Book Company. 1978. No ISBN.

Estulin, Daniel. *The True Story of the Bilderberg Group.* Walterville, Oregon: TrineDay. 2007. ISBN 978-09777953-4-5.

Farrell, Joseph P. *Babylon's Banksters: The Alchemy of Deep Physics, High Finance, and Ancient Religion.* Port Townsend, Washington: Feral House. 2010. ISBN 978-1-932595-6.

Farrell, Joseph P. *Roswell and The Reich: The Nazi Connection.* Kempton, Illinois: Adventures Unlimited Press. 2010. ISBN 978-1-1935487-05-0.

Farrell, Joseph P. *The SS Brotherhood of the Bell: NASA's Nazis, JFK, and Majic-12.* Kempton, Illinois: Adventures Unlimited Press. 2006. ISBN 1-931882-61-4.

Fensterwald, Bernard, Jr., and Ewing, Michael. *Coincidence or Conspiracy?* New York. Zebra Books (Kensington Publishing Corp.) 1977. No ISBN.

Fetzer, James H., Ph.D., ed. *The Great Zapruder Film Hoax: Deceit and Deception in the Death of JFK.* Chicago: Catfeet Press. 2003. ISBN 0-8126-9547-X.

Bibliography

Flammonde, Paris. *The Kennedy Conspiracy: An Uncommissioned Report on the Jim Garrison Investigation.* New York. Meredith Press. 1969. No ISBN.

 Garrison, Jim. *On the Trail of the Assassins.* New York. Time-Warner. 1988. ISBN 0-446-36277-8.

Haslam, Edward T. *Dr. Mary's Monkey: How the Unsolved Murder of a Doctor, a Secret Laboratory in New Orleans and Cancer-Causing Monkey Viruses are Linked to Lee Harvey Oswald, the JFK Assassination, and Emerging Global Epidemics.* Walterville, Oregon: TrineDay. 2007. ISBN 978-9777953-0-6.

Hepburn, James. *Farewell America: The Plot to Kill JFK.* Penmarin Books. 2002. ISBN 1-883955-32-7.

Hidell, Al, and D'Arc, Joan. *The Complete Conspiarcy Reader: From the Deaths of JFK and John Lennon to Government-Sponsored Alien Cover-ups.* New York. MJF Books. 1998. ISBN1-56731-557-7.

Hoagland, Richard C., and Bara, Mike. *Dark Mission: the Secret History of NASA.* (Revised edition) Port Townsend, Washington. Feral House. 2009. ISBN 978-932595-48-2.

Hoffman, Michael A. II. *Secret Societies and Psychological Warfare.* Coeur d'Alene, Idaho. Independent History and Research. 2001. ISBN 978-0-9703784-1-5.

Kieth, Jim, ed. *The Gemstone File.* Atlanta, GA. Illuminet Press. 1992. ISBN 0-9626534-5-4.

Krüger, Henrik. *The Great Heroin Coup: Drugs, Intelligence, and International Fascism.* Boston. South End Press. 1980. ISBN 0-89608-031-5.

Lane, Mark. *A Citizen's Dissent: Mark Lane Replies.* New York. Fawcett Crest. 1968. No ISBN.

Lane, Mark. *Plausible Denial: Was the CIA Involved in the Assassination of JFK?* New York. Thunder's Mouth Press. 1991. ISBN1-56025-000-3.

Bibliography

Lawrence, Lincoln, and Thomas, Kenn. *Mind Control, Oswald, and JFK: Were We Controlled?* Kempton, Illinois: Adventures Unlimited Press. 1997. ISBN 0-932813-46-1.

Lebedev, Mikhail, *Treason – for My Daily Bread.* Trans. from the German by W.G. Stanton. Guernsey, Vallancey Press. 1977. ISBN 0-905589009.

Leek, Sybil, and Sugar, Bert R. *The Assassination Chain.* New York. Corwin Books. 1976. No ISBN

Levenda, Peter. *Sinister Forces: A Grimoire of American Political Witchcraft: Book One: The Nine.* Walterville, Oregon: TrineDay. 2005. ISBN 0-9752906-2-2.

Lifton, David S. *Best Evidence: Disguise and Deception in the Assassination of John F. Kennedy.* New York: Carroll and Graf Publisher, Inc. 1988. ISBN 0-88184-438-1.

Livingston, Harrison Edward. *Killing Kennedy: and the Hoax of the Century.* New York: Carroll and Graf. 1995. ISBN0-7867-0195-1.

Luttwalk, Edward. *Coup d'État: A Practical Handbook.* Cambridge, Massachusetts. Harvard University Press. 1968. ISBN 0-674-17547-6.

Marrs, Jim. *Crossfire: The Plot that Killed Kennedy.* New York: Carroll and Graf. 1989. ISBN 0-88184-648-1.

Newman, John. *Oswald and the CIA.* New York. Carroll and Graf. 1995. ISBN0-7867-0131-5.

Opotwsky, Stan. *The Kennedy Government.* New York: Popular Library. 1961.

Prouty, L. Fletcher. *JFK: The CIA, Vietnam, and the Plot to Assassinate John F. Kennedy.* Seacaucus, NJ. Carol Publishing Group.1992. ISBN1-55972-130-8.

301

Bibliography

Prouty, L. Fletcher. *The Secret Team: The CIA and its Allies in Control of the United States and the World.* New York. Skyhorse Publishing. 2008. ISBN 978-1-60239-229-8.

 Roberts, Craig, and Armstrong, John. *JFK: The Dead Witnesses.* Consolidated Press International. 1995. ISBN 0-9639062-3-2.

 Roberts, Craig. *The Kill Zone: A Sniper Looks at Dealey Plaza.* Consolidated Press International. 1994. ISBN 0-9639062-0-8.

Scheim, David E. *Contract on America: the Mafia Murder of President John F. Kennedy.* New York. Zebra Books (Kensington Publishing Corp.). 1988. ISBN 0-8217-2615-3.

Smith, Matthew. *JFK: The Second Plot.* Edinburgh and London: Mainstream Publishing. 2008. ISBN 9781840185010.

Thomas, Kenn, and Childress, David Hatcher. *Inside the Genstone File: Howard Hughes, Onassis and JFK.* Kempton, Illinois. Adventures Unlimited Press. 2001. ISBN 0-932813-66-6.

Thomas, Kenn, ed. *NASA, Nazis, and JFK: The Torbitt Document and the JFK Assassination.* Kempton, Illinois. Adventures Unlimited Press. 1996. 0-932813-39-9.

 Weiner, Tim. *Blank Check: The Pentagon's Black Budget.* New York. Time-Warner. 1991. ISBN 978-0-446-39275-4.

Weisberg, Harold. *Whitewash II: The FBI-Secret Service Cover-up.* New York. Dell. 1967. No ISBN.

Weisberg, Harold. *Whitewash: the Report on the Warren Report.* New York. Dell. 1965. No ISBN.

 Zirbel, Craig I. *The Texas Connection.* New York. Time-Warner. 1991. 0-446-36433-9.

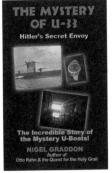

REICH OF THE BLACK SUN
Nazi Secret Weapons & the Cold War Allied Legend
by Joseph P. Farrell

Why were the Allies worried about an atom bomb attack by the Germans in 1944? Why did the Soviets threaten to use poison gas against the Germans? Why did Hitler in 1945 insist that holding Prague could win the war for the Third Reich? Why did US General George Patton's Third Army race for the Skoda works at Pilsen in Czechoslovakia instead of Berlin? Why did the US Army not test the uranium atom bomb it dropped on Hiroshima? Why did the Luftwaffe fly a non-stop round trip mission to within twenty miles of New York City in 1944? *Reich of the Black Sun* takes the reader on a scientific-historical journey in order to answer these questions. Arguing that Nazi Germany actually won the race for the atom bomb in late 1944,

352 PAGES. 6x9 PAPERBACK. ILLUSTRATED. BIBLIOGRAPHY. $16.95.
CODE: ROBS

THE GIZA DEATH STAR
The Paleophysics of the Great Pyramid & the Military Complex at Giza
by Joseph P. Farrell

Was the Giza complex part of a military installation over 10,000 years ago? Chapters include: An Archaeology of Mass Destruction, Thoth and Theories; The Machine Hypothesis; Pythagoras, Plato, Planck, and the Pyramid; The Weapon Hypothesis; Encoded Harmonics of the Planck Units in the Great Pyramid; High Freqquency Direct Current "Impulse" Technology; The Grand Gallery and its Crystals: Gravito-acoustic Resonators; The Other Two Large Pyramids; the "Causeways," and the "Temples"; A Phase Conjugate Howitzer; Evidence of the Use of Weapons of Mass Destruction in Ancient Times; more.

290 PAGES. 6x9 PAPERBACK. ILLUSTRATED. $16.95. CODE: GDS

THE GIZA DEATH STAR DEPLOYED
The Physics & Engineering of the Great Pyramid
by Joseph P. Farrell

Farrell expands on his thesis that the Great Pyramid was a maser, designed as a weapon and eventually deployed—with disastrous results to the solar system. Includes: Exploding Planets: A Brief History of the Exoteric and Esoteric Investigations of the Great Pyramid; No Machines, Please!; The Stargate Conspiracy; The Scalar Weapons; Message or Machine?; A Tesla Analysis of the Putative Physics and Engineering of the Giza Death Star; Cohering the Zero Point, Vacuum Energy, Flux: Feedback Loops and Tetrahedral Physics; and more.

290 PAGES. 6x9 PAPERBACK. ILLUSTRATED. $16.95. CODE: GDSD

THE GIZA DEATH STAR DESTROYED
The Ancient War For Future Science
by Joseph P. Farrell

Farrell moves on to events of the final days of the Giza Death Star and its awesome power. These final events, eventually leading up to the destruction of this giant machine, are dissected one by one, leading us to the eventual abandonment of the Giza Military Complex—an event that hurled civilization back into the Stone Age. Chapters include: The Mars-Earth Connection; The Lost "Root Races" and the Moral Reasons for the Flood; The Destruction of Krypton: The Electrodynamic Solar System, Exploding Planets and Ancient Wars; Turning the Stream of the Flood: the Origin of Secret Societies and Esoteric Traditions; The Quest to Recover Ancient Mega-Technology; Non-Equilibrium Paleophysics; Monatomic Paleophysics; Frequencies, Vortices and Mass Particles; "Acoustic" Intensity of Fields; The Pyramid of Crystals; tons more.

292 pages. 6x9 paperback. Illustrated. $16.95. Code: GDES

SECRETS OF THE UNIFIED FIELD
The Philadelphia Experiment, the Nazi Bell, and the Discarded Theory
by Joseph P. Farrell

Farrell examines the now discarded Unified Field Theory. American and German wartime scientists and engineers determined that, while the theory was incomplete, it could nevertheless be engineered. Chapters include: The Meanings of "Torsion"; Wringing an Aluminum Can; The Mistake in Unified Field Theories and Their Discarding by Contemporary Physics; Three Routes to the Doomsday Weapon: Quantum Potential, Torsion, and Vortices; Tesla's Meeting with FDR; Arnold Sommerfeld and Electromagnetic Radar Stealth; Electromagnetic Phase Conjugations, Phase Conjugate Mirrors, and Templates; The Unified Field Theory, the Torsion Tensor, and Igor Witkowski's Idea of the Plasma Focus; tons more.

340 pages. 6x9 Paperback. Illustrated. Bibliography. Index. $18.95. Code: SOUF

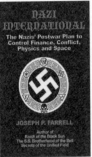

NAZI INTERNATIONAL
The Nazi's Postwar Plan to Control Finance, Conflict, Physics and Space
by Joseph P. Farrell

Beginning with prewar corporate partnerships in the USA, including some with the Bush family, he moves on to the surrender of Nazi Germany, and evacuation plans of the Germans. He then covers the vast, and still-little-known recreation of Nazi Germany in South America with help of Juan Peron, I.G. Farben and Martin Bormann. Farrell then coversNazi Germany's penetration of the Muslim world including Wilhelm Voss and Otto Skorzeny in Gamel Abdul Nasser's Egypt before moving on to the development and control of new energy technologies including the Bariloche Fusion Project, Dr. Philo Farnsworth's Plasmator, and the work of Dr. Nikolai Kozyrev. Finally, Farrell discusses the Nazi desire to control space, and examines their connection with NASA, the esoteric meaning of NASA Mission Patches.

412 pages. 6x9 Paperback. Illustrated. References. $19.95. Code: NZIN

ARKTOS
The Polar Myth in Science, Symbolism & Nazi Survival
by Joscelyn Godwin

Explored are the many tales of an ancient race said to have lived in the Arctic regions, such as Thule and Hyperborea. Progressing onward, he looks at modern polar legends: including the survival of Hitler, German bases in Antarctica, UFOs, the hollow earth, and the hidden kingdoms of Agartha and Shambala. Chapters include: Prologue in Hyperborea; The Golden Age; The Northern Lights; The Arctic Homeland; The Aryan Myth; The Thule Society; The Black Order; The Hidden Lands; Agartha and the Polaires; Shambhala; The Hole at the Pole; Antarctica; more.

220 Pages. 6x9 Paperback. Illustrated. Bib. Index. $16.95. Code: ARK

PARAPOLITICS!
Conspiracy in Contemporary America
by Kenn Thomas

From the Kennedy assassination to 9/11, Thomas examines the underlying parapolitics that animate the secret elites and the war-ravaged planet they manipulate. Contents include: Octopus Redux; Previously unpublished interview with the girlfriend of Octopus investigator Danny Casolaro; Orgone; Wilhelm Reich: Eisenhower's secret ally against the aliens; Clinton era conspiracies; You Too Can Be a Researcher: How to use the Freedom of Information Act; Anthrax Terrorists; Media Mindwash; 9/11 Commission Omission, and much, much more.

340 Pages. 6x9 Paperback. Illustrated. $20.00. Code: PPOL

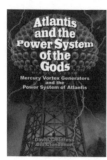

ATLANTIS & THE POWER SYSTEM OF THE GODS
by David Hatcher Childress and Bill Clendenon

Childress' fascinating analysis of Nikola Tesla's broadcast system in light of Edgar Cayce's "Terrible Crystal" and the obelisks of ancient Egypt and Ethiopia. Includes: Atlantis and its crystal power towers that broadcast energy; how these incredible power stations may still exist today; inventor Nikola Tesla's nearly identical system of power transmission; Mercury Proton Gyros and mercury vortex propulsion; more. Richly illustrated, and packed with evidence that Atlantis not only existed—it had a world-wide energy system more sophisticated than ours today.

246 PAGES. 6x9 PAPERBACK. ILLUSTRATED. $15.95. CODE: APSG

THE ANTI-GRAVITY HANDBOOK
edited by David Hatcher Childress

The new expanded compilation of material on Anti-Gravity, Free Energy, Flying Saucer Propulsion, UFOs, Suppressed Technology, NASA Cover-ups and more. Highly illustrated with patents, technical illustrations and photos. This revised and expanded edition has more material, including photos of Area 51, Nevada, the government's secret testing facility. This classic on weird science is back in a new format!

230 PAGES. 7x10 PAPERBACK. ILLUSTRATED. $16.95. CODE: AGH

ANTI–GRAVITY & THE WORLD GRID

Is the earth surrounded by an intricate electromagnetic grid network offering free energy? This compilation of material on ley lines and world power points contains chapters on the geography, mathematics, and light harmonics of the earth grid. Learn the purpose of ley lines and ancient megalithic structures located on the grid. Discover how the grid made the Philadelphia Experiment possible. Explore the Coral Castle and many other mysteries, including acoustic levitation, Tesla Shields and scalar wave weaponry. Browse through the section on anti-gravity patents, and research resources.

274 PAGES. 7x10 PAPERBACK. ILLUSTRATED. $14.95. CODE: AGW

ANTI–GRAVITY & THE UNIFIED FIELD
edited by David Hatcher Childress

Is Einstein's Unified Field Theory the answer to all of our energy problems? Explored in this compilation of material is how gravity, electricity and magnetism manifest from a unified field around us. Why artificial gravity is possible; secrets of UFO propulsion; free energy; Nikola Tesla and anti-gravity airships of the 20s and 30s; flying saucers as superconducting whirls of plasma; anti-mass generators; vortex propulsion; suppressed technology; government cover-ups; gravitational pulse drive; spacecraft & more.

240 PAGES. 7x10 PAPERBACK. ILLUSTRATED. $14.95. CODE: AGU

PRODIGAL GENIUS: The Life of Nikola Tesla
by John J. O'Neill

This special edition of O'Neill's book has many rare photographs of Tesla and his most advanced inventions. Tesla's eccentric personality gives his life story a strange romantic quality. He made his first million before he was forty, yet gave up his royalties in a gesture of friendship, and died almost in poverty. Tesla could see an invention in 3-D, from every angle, within his mind, before it was built; how he refused to accept the Nobel Prize; his friendships with Mark Twain, George Westinghouse and competition with Thomas Edison. Tesla is revealed as a figure of genius whose influence on the world reaches into the far future. Deluxe, illustrated edition.

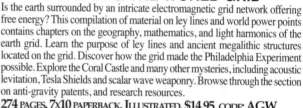

408 pages. 6x9 Paperback. Illustrated. $18.95. Code: PRG

GRAVITATIONAL MANIPULATION OF DOMED CRAFT
UFO Propulsion Dynamics
by Paul E. Potter

Potter's precise and lavish illustrations allow the reader to enter directly into the realm of the advanced technological engineer and to understand, quite straightforwardly, the aliens' methods of energy manipulation: their methods of electrical power generation; how they purposely designed their craft to employ the kinds of energy dynamics that are exclusive to space (discoverable in our astrophysics) in order that their craft may generate both attractive and repulsive gravitational forces; their control over the mass-density matrix surrounding their craft enabling them to alter their physical dimensions and even manufacture their own frame of reference in respect to time. Includes a 16-page color insert.
624 pages. 7x10 Paperback. Illustrated. References. $24.00. Code: GMDC

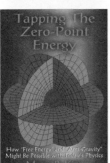

TAPPING THE ZERO POINT ENERGY
Free Energy & Anti-Gravity in Today's Physics
by Moray B. King

King explains how free energy and anti-gravity are possible. The theories of the zero point energy maintain there are tremendous fluctuations of electrical field energy imbedded within the fabric of space. This book tells how, in the 1930s, inventor T. Henry Moray could produce a fifty kilowatt "free energy" machine; how an electrified plasma vortex creates anti-gravity; how the Pons/Fleischmann "cold fusion" experiment could produce tremendous heat without fusion; and how certain experiments might produce a gravitational anomaly.
180 PAGES. 5x8 PAPERBACK. ILLUSTRATED. $12.95. CODE: TAP

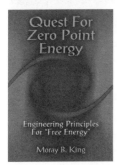

QUEST FOR ZERO-POINT ENERGY
Engineering Principles for "Free Energy"
by Moray B. King

King expands, with diagrams, on how free energy and anti-gravity are possible. The theories of zero point energy maintain there are tremendous fluctuations of electrical field energy embedded within the fabric of space. King explains the following topics: TFundamentals of a Zero-Point Energy Technology; Vacuum Energy Vortices; The Super Tube; Charge Clusters: The Basis of Zero-Point Energy Inventions; Vortex Filaments, Torsion Fields and the Zero-Point Energy; Transforming the Planet with a Zero-Point Energy Experiment; Dual Vortex Forms: The Key to a Large Zero-Point Energy Coherence. Packed with diagrams, patents and photos.
224 PAGES. 6x9 PAPERBACK. ILLUSTRATED. $14.95. CODE: QZPE

DARK MOON
Apollo and the Whistleblowers
by Mary Bennett and David Percy

Did you know a second craft was going to the Moon at the same time as Apollo 11? Do you know that potentially lethal radiation is prevalent throughout deep space? Do you know there are serious discrepancies in the account of the Apollo 13 'accident'? Did you know that 'live' color TV from the Moon was not actually live at all? Did you know that the Lunar Surface Camera had no viewfinder? Do you know that lighting was used in the Apollo photographs—yet no lighting equipment was taken to the Moon? All these questions, and more, are discussed in great detail by British researchers Bennett and Percy in *Dark Moon*, the definitive book (nearly 600 pages) on the possible faking of the Apollo Moon missions. Tons of NASA photos analyzed for possible deceptions.
568 PAGES. 6x9 PAPERBACK. ILLUSTRATED. BIBLIOGRAPHY. INDEX. $32.00. CODE: DMO

LOST CITIES & ANCIENT MYSTERIES OF THE SOUTHWEST
By David Hatcher Childress

Join David as he starts in northern Mexico and searches for the lost mines of the Aztecs. He continues north to west Texas, delving into the mysteries of Big Bend, including mysterious Phoenician tablets discovered there and the strange lights of Marfa. Then into New Mexico where he stumbles upon a hollow mountain with a billion dollars of gold bars hidden deep inside it! In Arizona he investigates tales of Egyptian catacombs in the Grand Canyon, cruises along the Devil's Highway, and tackles the century-old mystery of the Lost Dutchman mine. In Nevada and California Childress checks out the rumors of mummified giants and weird tunnels in Death Valley, plus he searches the Mohave Desert for the mysterious remains of ancient dwellers alongside lakes that dried up tens of thousands of years ago. It's a full-tilt blast down the back roads of the Southwest in search of the weird and wondrous mysteries of the past!

486 Pages. 6x9 Paperback. Illustrated. Bibliography. $19.95. Code: LCSW

TECHNOLOGY OF THE GODS
The Incredible Sciences of the Ancients
by David Hatcher Childress

Childress looks at the technology that was allegedly used in Atlantis and the theory that the Great Pyramid of Egypt was originally a gigantic power station. He examines tales of ancient flight and the technology that it involved; how the ancients used electricity; megalithic building techniques; the use of crystal lenses and the fire from the gods; evidence of various high tech weapons in the past, including atomic weapons; ancient metallurgy and heavy machinery; the role of modern inventors such as Nikola Tesla in bringing ancient technology back into modern use; impossible artifacts; and more.

356 PAGES. 6x9 PAPERBACK. ILLUSTRATED. BIBLIOGRAPHY. $16.95. CODE: TGOD

VIMANA AIRCRAFT OF ANCIENT INDIA & ATLANTIS
by David Hatcher Childress, introduction by Ivan T. Sanderson

In this incredible volume on ancient India, authentic Indian texts such as the *Ramayana* and the *Mahabharata* are used to prove that ancient aircraft were in use more than four thousand years ago. Included in this book is the entire Fourth Century BC manuscript *Vimaanika Shastra* by the ancient author Maharishi Bharadwaaja. Also included are chapters on Atlantean technology, the incredible Rama Empire of India and the devastating wars that destroyed it.

334 PAGES. 6x9 PAPERBACK. ILLUSTRATED. $15.95. CODE: VAA

LIQUID CONSPIRACY
JFK, LSD, the CIA, Area 51 & UFOs
by George Piccard

Underground author George Piccard on the politics of LSD, mind control, and Kennedy's involvement with Area 51 and UFOs. Reveals JFK's LSD experiences with Mary Pinchot-Meyer. The plot thickens with an ever expanding web of CIA involvement, from underground bases with UFOs seen by JFK and Marilyn Monroe (among others) to a vaster conspiracy that affects every government agency from NASA to the Justice Department. This may have been the reason that Marilyn Monroe and actress-columnist Dorothy Kilgallen were both murdered. Focusing on the bizarre side of history, *Liquid Conspiracy* takes the reader on a psychedelic tour de force. This is your government on drugs!

264 Pages. 6x9 Paperback. Illustrated. $14.95. Code: LIQC

THE TESLA PAPERS
Nikola Tesla on Free Energy & Wireless Transmission of Power
by Nikola Tesla, edited by David Hatcher Childress

David Hatcher Childress takes us into the incredible world of Nikola Tesla and his amazing inventions. Tesla's fantastic vision of the future, including wireless power, anti-gravity, free energy and highly advanced solar power. Also included are some of the papers, patents and material collected on Tesla at the Colorado Springs Tesla Symposiums, including papers on: •The Secret History of Wireless Transmission •Tesla and the Magnifying Transmitter •Design and Construction of a Half-Wave Tesla Coil •Electrostatics: A Key to Free Energy •Progress in Zero-Point Energy Research •Electromagnetic Energy from Antennas to Atoms •Tesla's Particle Beam Technology •Fundamental Excitatory Modes of the Earth-Ionosphere Cavity

325 PAGES. 8x10 PAPERBACK. ILLUSTRATED. $16.95. CODE: TTP

UFOS AND ANTI-GRAVITY
Piece For A Jig-Saw
by Leonard G. Cramp

Leonard G. Cramp's 1966 classic book on flying saucer propulsion and suppressed technology is a highly technical look at the UFO phenomena by a trained scientist. Cramp first introduces the idea of 'anti-gravity' and introduces us to the various theories of gravitation. He then examines the technology necessary to build a flying saucer and examines in great detail the technical aspects of such a craft. Cramp's book is a wealth of material and diagrams on flying saucers, anti-gravity, suppressed technology, G-fields and UFOs. Chapters include Crossroads of Aerodymanics, Aerodynamic Saucers, Limitations of Rocketry, Gravitation and the Ether, Gravitational Spaceships, G-Field Lift Effects, The Bi-Field Theory, VTOL and Hovercraft, Analysis of UFO photos, more.

388 PAGES. 6x9 PAPERBACK. ILLUSTRATED. $16.95. CODE: UAG

THE COSMIC MATRIX
Piece for a Jig-Saw, Part Two
by Leonard G. Cramp

Cramp examines anti-gravity effects and theorizes that this super-science used by the craft—described in detail in the book—can lift mankind into a new level of technology, transportation and understanding of the universe. The book takes a close look at gravity control, time travel, and the interlocking web of energy between all planets in our solar system with Leonard's unique technical diagrams. A fantastic voyage into the present and future!

364 PAGES. 6x9 PAPERBACK. ILLUSTRATED. BIBLIOGRAPHY. $16.00. CODE: CMX

THE A.T. FACTOR
A Scientists Encounter with UFOs
by Leonard Cramp

British aerospace engineer Cramp began much of the scientific anti-gravity and UFO propulsion analysis back in 1955 with his landmark book *Space, Gravity & the Flying Saucer* (out-of-print and rare). In this final book, Cramp brings to a close his detailed and controversial study of UFOs and Anti-Gravity.

324 PAGES. 6x9 PAPERBACK. ILLUSTRATED. BIBLIOGRAPHY. INDEX. $16.95. CODE: ATF

ORDER FORM

10% Discount When You Order 3 or More Items!

One Adventure Place
P.O. Box 74
Kempton, Illinois 60946
United States of America
Tel.: 815-253-6390 • Fax: 815-253-6300
Email: auphq@frontiernet.net
http://www.adventuresunlimitedpress.com

Please check: ☑

☐ This is my first order   ☐ I have ordered before

Name	
Address	
City	
State/Province	Postal Code
Country	
Phone day	Evening
Fax	Email

Item Code	Item Description	Qty	Total

Please check: ☑

	Subtotal ▶	
	Less Discount-10% for 3 or more items ▶	
☐ Postal-Surface	Balance ▶	
☐ Postal-Air Mail (Priority in USA)	Illinois Residents 6.25% Sales Tax ▶	
	Previous Credit ▶	
☐ UPS (Mainland USA only)	Shipping ▶	
	Total (check/MO in USD$ only) ▶	

☐ Visa/MasterCard/Discover/American Express

Card Number

Expiration Date

10% Discount When You Order 3 or More Items!